D1288172

Wreckage

My Father's Legacy of Art & Junk

Sascha Feinstein

Lewisburg
BUCKNELL UNIVERSITY PRESS

Published by Bucknell University Press
Copublished by The Rowman & Littlefield Publishing Group, Inc.
4501 Forbes Boulevard, Suite 200, Lanham, Maryland 20706
www.rowman.com

Unit A, Whitacre Mews, 26-34 Stannary Street, London SE11 4AB

British Library Cataloguing in Publication Information Available

Library of Congress Cataloging-in-Publication Data

ISBN: 978-1-61148-785-5 (cloth : alk. paper)
ISBN: 978-1-61148-786-2 (electronic)

♾™ The paper used in this publication meets the minimum requirements of
American National Standard for Information Sciences—Permanence of Paper
for Printed Library Materials, ANSI/NISO Z39.48-1992.

Printed in the United States of America

for my children
Kiran & Divia

The room was packed to within two feet of the ceiling, and workmen could only crawl in the narrow space. They began emptying the room by throwing things out the window into the rear courtyard. A gas chandelier, the top from a horse drawn carriage, and a rusted bicycle were among the first things to come crashing down, along with an old set of bedsprings and sawhorse. The crowds swelled to witness the spectacle and to see if the rumors of a house filled with treasures were true. In the first two days, workers removed nineteen tons of debris.

Randy O. Frost and Gail Steketee, Stuff

By what rational or formal means, we ask ourselves, do we *measure* the difference between the rhythms of a Volkswagen engine and the rhythms of the Macumba drummers of Brazil; between a photograph of Van Gogh's chair and his painting of that chair? Are not these qualitative distinctions the stuff of life—while yet immeasurable in purely rational terms?

Lawrence Blair, Rhythms of Vision

Projected form . . . is what we feel we're seeing. It expresses the inner life, the release of energy from its invisible drive toward visible shape. Created by organic urgency, by the inexorable press of life toward fullness, projected form masses energies that seem to burgeon out of some generative core into forms vibrant beyond their defined contour, as if the contour itself were an alert, elastic swell. It rules out a fixed outline as an expression of nature's pulse, because nature's pulse is mobile and elastic.

Sam Feinstein, "How Does Cézanne Do It?"

~

Contents

CHAPTER ONE

~

Wisteria

He who buries a treasure buries himself with it.

—Gaston Bachelard

I knew the nine-foot stone table probably remained within the visually impenetrable bramble and vines. My father had built the structure from monstrous rocks, each roughly two and a half feet in width. Onto the top, he cemented several stoneware plates—discards from his oldest friend, the potter Harry Holl—and crucibles for slag that he'd recovered from a local foundry, as well as a candelabra that he had bent and soldered with the dance-like joy of Kandinsky. Now, two years after his death in 2003, having inherited our summer home on Cape Cod, I began to slash at thick growth. He had built the table thirty-five feet from the back of the house, and a mere fifteen feet away from a path alongside the barn. It was not, in other words, remotely located. And yet, my wife, Marleni, who had been visiting the residence since 1987, never knew the table existed until I excavated the ruin.

By that time, most of the property had been overwhelmed by wilderness. In fact, almost nothing of value seemed to be growing in that landscape behind the house. Much of the ground had been consumed by bamboo, which my father had planted on the advice of Harry Holl, and those roots extended across the lawn, foresting around the house and outmuscling even the tenacious poison ivy and wisteria. One could hardly walk around the property, but after my father's death, I felt driven to clear the land. I wanted it to

1

breathe again. Still more practically and passionately, I wanted my family—my wife and our children, Kiran and Divia—to enjoy themselves without the constant fear of ticks and Lyme disease. Obviously, too, my desire for a literal clearing reflected a psychic cleansing. And I wanted to begin by unearthing that stone table, a kind of Maya artifact by that point. I approached the challenge like a spirited though inexperienced archeologist.

While vine, brush, and tree growth had dismantled a few of the rocks, the table had fared quite well over the decades. More surprising, though, was a large rhododendron—one I suddenly recalled from childhood—located a few feet away from the table, a woodland native that had miraculously survived the onslaught of foliage. Rich and healthy amid dead branches and encroaching bamboo, the impressive bush emerged with dignity.

I cut around it, cautiously removing poison ivy and extricating bamboo from the perimeter. I chain sawed overhanging oak branches for sunlight and, for a radius of about three feet, raked away thick layers of brittle sticks and decay. In just one afternoon of focused work on the surrounding grounds, the change was extraordinarily visible. The rhododendron blossomed without blooming.

The bush had done remarkably well. Still, I wondered why, after so many years, it hadn't grown even more. The cause—as was so often the case—involved my father's hoarding.

Inside the large rhododendron I uncovered a heavy television tube, roughly thirty inches wide, cracked but still intact. Beside it, I found five car wheel rims, each rusted a rugged brown, as well as scraps of iron and steel from unknown sources. I unearthed a sink basin. When everything had been removed, I tried to plunge the tines of my metal rake into the soil but hit what I assumed to be rock until the rake shrieked from metal grinding metal. Eventually, with a crowbar, I pried up a buried cast-iron stove top. Beneath that, I extracted another cast-iron piece, this one fairly level and therefore more compliant as a bottom layer. With each excavation, I wanted to believe that the bush became more and more alive.

That goal became my singular focus and thought; because I'd been raised in a world of junk, the artifacts within the rhododendron impressed me with their size and weight, but I wasn't bewildered or even terribly surprised. These would have been remnants of a forthcoming project. The cast iron and wheel rims would create foundational bulk; the TV tube might have become a window of some sort. We'll never know—but I do know that he had plans, and that he probably used the density of that bush to camouflage his materials until the years of growth camouflaged his ambition.

I nourished the earth with fertilizer and fresh topsoil and returned the following year, expecting to see more growth. The rhododendron had, in fact, inched skyward, but I had anticipated many more young sprouts from its center. Perhaps, I thought, I only needed to upturn the soil a bit more, so I dug more aggressively with the metal rake. This time, its teeth met rock, not metal. Two feet to the right: the same sound. To the left as well. With a shovel, I began to pry out of the ground massive chunks of cement that had almost completely ringed the rhododendron, each slab about two-and-a-half inches thick and some weighing forty or fifty pounds. In five wheelbarrow loads, each requiring me to lean forward with all my weight and strain my quads to coax the stressed wheel forward, I moved the cement across the property and stacked the blocks beside another unfinished project: two cement pillars he created shortly after he bought the house, the remains of an abandoned barbeque pit.

At that point, the sheer magnitude of this inorganic material did indeed astonish me. Who could imagine a single bush concealing that much rubble and trash? Yet this evidence of coveted artifacts typified everything else in my father's life. If you could get something for free, keep it; you may be able to use it at some point.

For several years, I assumed the primary part of that philosophy had to do with immigrants from a certain generation. Born in 1915, my father left the Ukraine in 1919 with his entire family. Their hometown, Voronovitza, located between Odessa and Kiev, had been savaged both by their countrymen and, later, the Nazis. As far as I know, not a single member of my father's family returned to that location; I suppose part of the immigrant's creed must be to let go and move on. Their journey to the United States took two years, during which time the Russian currency changed, literally bankrupting my already compromised relatives. My father and his parents eventually settled in Philadelphia, where my grandfather miraculously expanded a simple fruit stand into a lucrative business. During the Great Depression, my grandparents again lost almost all their money when the banks collapsed. And, again, they rebuilt their lives.

I have read the works of scholars who insist that there's no direct connection between immigrants from this time and compulsive hoarders, but I have my doubts. If your childhood is saturated with loss and recovery, with financial tragedy and constant regrowth, how can one not covet free discarded artifacts? We carry with us the imprinted DNA of childhood experience, and one might say the circumstances that impoverished my family members simultaneously invigorated their ambition not merely to survive but to thrive.

That said, I cannot draw any direct lines between my father's uncompromising artistic desires and his business-driven family. The eldest son of three (the middle son became a successful restaurateur, the youngest a world-renowned figure in the medical world), he eschewed commercialism from an early age, spending more time, as my grandmother once told me, rendering sketches of customers than helping run the fruit business. And his natural leaning toward abstract expressionism also seems to have been formed independently of any societal (much less familial) influence. Later, in 1949, he actively sought out Hans Hofmann, the master teacher and pioneering painter in the field of abstract expressionism, but his impulse to work abstractly—his urgent, personal drive to transform ambiguity into something lasting and organic—began before his influential experiences with Hofmann.

Eight years after my father's death, I returned to our summer house on Cape Cod for a week in May to contemplate the strange connections between hoarding and artistic creativity, but also to survey the property where two large oaks had fallen in the winter nor'easter. Although the sight of massive trees reduced to horizontal corpses shocked me, the carnage didn't entirely surprise me because the oaks had been strangled by wisteria vines, some thicker than my thighs. Such vines had killed and uprooted many smaller trees, twisting around bark until they snapped from fatigue and rot. Many hung like strange fruit from muscular limbs of nearby trees. I've never been able to hear the "sucking and sobbing cells" described in Theodore Roethke's root cellar poems, but the drama of decades-old wisteria makes even a city boy consider the daunting exuberance of the natural world, including our own vulnerable existence. Like a cancer, a driven string of growth no wider than a swizzle stick projected itself skyward, found bark, gripped, investigated, and slowly thickened as the host withstood strangulation for as long as it could, retaining a sculptural beauty until the entire structure collapsed into a shattered mess, valuable to no one except carpenter ants and woodland scavengers.

It is in the nature of wisteria to consume. When these vines adorn the dead, they revitalize the Cape landscape with lavender glory. And during its inexorable growth—to reach the heights that cause the hanging blooms to swell in the air like frilly baubles—wisteria gradually kills what allows it to ascend.

Now on the ground along with the oaks, the vines challenged me more than the hardwood. The previous summer, when I'd viewed them from thirty feet below, they seemed merely nebulous; spread across the soil, they posed a significant challenge for someone not used to such an aftermath. Smashed, heaped, and sprawling, the tangled vines resisted the chain saw, giving way just enough to stifle most cuts, yet they shrouded the expanse of branches, suffocating my resolve the way they had overwhelmed their hosts.

And as I struggled with the chain saw and various loppers, and with my own body wet with fatigue, my mind traveled not merely to the parasitic qualities of nature but, curiously enough, to the nature of hoarding, and how the cycles of growth and decay can mimic one another with remarkable absoluteness. Just shy of two acres, the Cape property, which had passed to me, an only child, included three buildings: a modest house and barn, and a small studio toward the back. And if, metaphorically, those structures were hardwood trees, my father was the wisteria. Like those blooming vines in their most astonishing presence, their passionate blooms more gorgeous than anything offered by oaks or maples, he transformed these Puritan buildings into locations that flourished with his relentlessly creative nature. In the studio, which had probably been erected as a shed when the land had been farmed for asparagus, he painted large canvases with as much symphonic energy as the natural world itself. Twice a week during the summer, he taught art in the barn, and he artistically modified the house, not so much to exhibit his art but to *be* a kind of sculpture. Puritan conservatism relinquished itself to bold abstract expressionism.

But in the process, largely because he amassed ongoing collections of junk, the structures began to mulch into the ground. For him, buildings were merely shells to be used in order to make art and store the planet's refuse. Everything else about a home, including foundational security, became secondary, if not expendable. Loath to pay professionals, he'd "repair" interior and exterior problems superficially, not heeding warning signs of calamitous decay. When he died in the Cape house at the age of eighty-eight, the residence had a fully rotten foundation, collapsing ceilings, no working septic system, and enough mice skeletons to line a small crypt. The electrical wiring had become so bizarrely tangled that in order to turn on the dining room light one had to first turn on the kitchen's electric stove.

While the barn and studio had never been renovated for electricity or running water, they had been equally savaged by neglect and had rotted from the inside out. All three buildings had been forced to accommodate ton after ton of refuse, including objects of monumental weight. My father had not intended to create ruins, but he never concerned himself with the catastrophic problems facing his survivors.

And this was but one of three properties that he owned. He had purchased the Cape house in 1960, three years before my birth. (Shortly thereafter, the United States elected Kennedy as president and real estate prices on Cape Cod soared. My father looked like a real estate genius.) Then, in 1965, he bought what would become his primary residence: a brownstone on the Upper West Side of Manhattan. But he also owned a carriage house in Philadelphia, one that he acquired in 1953 during a previous marriage. All three properties shared at least three things: They had been purchased for ridiculously low sums; they were later worth a great deal of money because of their locations; and they were all in disastrous shape. When a student of his witnessed the interior of the Cape house the summer of his death, she asked while tearing, "How could a parent do this to a child?"

But I knew, too, that I had shown her the decrepit structure because I desired empathy. I admit it. I wanted others to know what had been left behind, what I faced. (Did Hercules desire others to witness the Augean stables before he washed them out? Probably not, but unlike that mythic hero, I'm all mortal.) I felt grateful for her tears, which seemed to vindicate my anger and bewilderment.

My father collected only uncollectibles, which is to say, rejected objects that required his vision in order to give them vitality. Anything cracked or shattered. Rotted. Broken pottery, not exquisitely crafted work. Hardened cement. He loved and coveted what had been abandoned and what therefore needed him. Similarly, his most satisfying human exchanges took place among people who sought his artistic vision and viewed him as a guide, often to the point of worship.

I think my father's interest in me waned significantly after I graduated college and became independent. Some of this also had to do with age: He was forty-eight at my birth and just shy of seventy when I graduated college. By then, too, he had begun a fourth, final marriage to a decades-younger student who, as he repeatedly said, required constant validation; their marriage flourished in part because he viewed her as an abandoned object that required his support. For his last eighteen years, he became increasingly insular, bolstering his wife and students while his homes became squirrel-like nests.

So I had returned that May for practical reasons—to clear the collapsed oaks behind the barn—but also to write for a week of solitude before the Cape tourists infiltrated the shorelines, to scratch my way into the strange duality of my father's nature. Although I had resented all the physical wreckage, and emotional wreckage, too, I had no intention of savaging his legacy. Yes, I understood that withholding stories about egocentric behavior and feelings of betrayal can make them fester until you're lost, until they become your mind's Sargasso Sea. And I knew that releasing them too frequently diminishes the artistic urgency for expression. But I also understood the self-suffocating nature of resentment. The teller becomes Lady Anne running out of stamina, even ire, because she can't loathe Richard III more than she's already expressed; sometimes we become the fire that extinguishes our vitriolic flames. Most of all, I feared bitterness. As Melville writes in *Moby-Dick*, "There is a wisdom that is woe; but there is a woe that is madness." Who wants to become the man who laughs at birds that crash into windows?

The world certainly didn't need yet another book of unqualified rage, nor were my feelings unqualified. While my father may have left behind wreckage in all forms, his sensibilities as an artist, and the radiance of the art itself, continue to guide me. To this day, I've never encountered an artist in any field who realized his philosophical vision about creativity more completely in his teaching and own art. As a teacher of writing, I often hear myself talking about the craft as though marginally translating my father's discussions on the visual arts. Like innumerable students, I remain forever grateful for his inspiring artistic clarity.

As for the Herculean challenges of cleaning out the properties, I can also accept, to some degree, his curious denial of practicality, and, again, part of my understanding derives from metaphor: I do not believe wisteria has a malevolent consciousness; it has, as Yeats says of the sea, a "murderous innocence." I believe its natural instinct is to control, and it does that very, very well. But wanting to control your environment and meaning to kill it are very different intents.

Many Cape locals choose to let their trees grapple with the boa-like predators; it's not an easy decision to sacrifice the hanging lavender blossoms. But at an early point in the union between hardwood and wisteria, one can opt to save the tree by killing the vine, and in that same spirit of sacrifice, I was forced to abandon almost thirty tons of my father's possessions in order to save the house and barn.

At the moment, there's a popular TV show called *Hoarders: Buried Alive*. When it debuted, I told my wife and kids that I refused to watch it because I'd been too scarred, a line I meant as both a joke and a fact. But of course I folded, and the episodes are spectacular in terms of collections of garbage. Yet none has spoken to me on a genuinely empathetic level for two important reasons. First, one cannot adequately compare a single home stuffed with stuff to *several* homes—some of which offered space beyond the home itself. (In New York, the brownstone had four floors, a full-length basement, and a courtyard; the Cape property had three structures on almost two acres of land. The two floors of the Philadelphia house felt cavernous.) My father's accumulative nature reached beyond these televised examples if for no other reason than the fact that he had more space to fill, and he filled it.

But the larger separation between his life and the lives of these televised hoarders concerns state of mind: As an artist who worked with much of the junk, he not merely buried himself alive, he also gave life to what should have been buried. The locations for his art classes—the basement in the brownstone, the first floor of the Philly house, and the barn on Cape Cod—became particularly conducive for his hoarding because he created wall-to-wall still lifes, therefore justifying clutter, even as it amassed to the point of an urban jungle, increasingly limiting the central interior like encroaching blindness from glaucoma. Fill a broken bureau to capacity? No problem: Work around it—over it, in front of it. Like modern Larnaka built above ancient Kition in Cyprus, his obsessive collections began to obscure collections from the past.

Nor was there ever any expectation of recovering that past. I never heard my father say, for example, "If I unearth that portion of the still life, I can find X." During my mother's lifetime, the barn and studio had been the primary repositories for the bulk of his prodigious gleaning. The house she controlled to various degrees, often throwing out bagsful of garbage when he went away. In Philadelphia, his previous wife, Barbara, insisted that he could bring in one piece of junk *if* he threw out one piece of junk. (As Frost and Steketee point out in *Stuff*: "Some couples make an uneasy truce in which the non-hoarding spouse controls the living areas of the home, restricting the clutter to the basement, attic, garage, or storage units.") But after my mother's death in 1980, both the Cape and New York properties became, in effect, the crammed Cape barn.

And that barn had largely been turned to ruin. With no hope of ever recovering what had been buried behind those layers, he had opted for burial over excavation. By the time I discovered chests of drawers from decades in the past, mice had transformed the contents into a festering mulch. Anything stuffed had been unstuffed. A city of rodents and insects lived within a world my father unintentionally created. The still life was alive—with millions of creatures that devoured both the structure and its contents: carpenter ants turning the floorboards to lace, powder post beetles pin-holing the rafters to sawdust. Raccoons luxuriating in the barn's unnavigable second story shat buckets of excrement that seeded and molded until the undigested matter turned into something from a B-minus mummy movie. When I encountered fuzz and growth the length of a human torso, I broke into a sweat, froze, and fought an impulse to torch the barn to cinders. Every person has limits; I'd found mine.

What constitutes a collection, and is an obsessive hoarder necessarily a collector? We tend to think of collections as representing our specialized interests, from animal images (turtles, pigs, flamingos) to hobbies (stamps, coins, medals). Sometimes these collections speak to the person's professional life; I have book collections (mainly of poetry, painting, music, and travel) and music collections (mainly jazz). The very wealthy sometimes collect fewer but far pricier objects, such as antique cars. Collections tend to have value, even if there's no intention to sell.

We separate hoarders from collectors by distinguishing random keepsakes from specific items unified by theme. But what if the collector's theme is more universal, with *all* objects relating to one another—where the world's refuse can always be repositioned and therefore revitalized? This was my father's sensibility as an artist, one that governed his life from childhood to death.

In a brilliant essay on Cézanne, my father discusses this sense of connectivity, "plasticity," as it relates to the visual arts:

> Cézanne had referred to his paintings as constructions after nature built out of "plastic equivalents." The word "plastic" originates in the Greek word *plastikos*, which means the power to form or create. (The same source also provides us with "plasma," the forming agent of our blood.) Plasticity is then defined as the state of being plastic, "having the power to form or create." Plasticity, indeed, can be seen as the operative principle, the pulse of life, the universal forming agent. Its process is the creative momentum, the volition that courses through all vitality, through nature, through man, through art. Plasticity, in short, is the unceasing propellant through all phenomenal existence. It is also the rhythmic correlator of Cézanne's pictorial creations.
>
> When does a painting attain plasticity? When all its forms become *one* form, when each color shape, tiny or huge, is seed organically, exactly, in the pictorial field, each a force to further the fullest flowering of oneness. No extra marks, no gaps. Rectangle becomes dance: rhythmic order structured to radiant expression—singular, iconic, unique. Nature's operation furthered.

In his view, plasticity applied to all arts, whether created on canvas, in the air (music), or on stage. But he also saw his houses, and the experiences within them, as a kind of stage for creativity. Random objects—those that had been neglected or discarded—regained identity when repositioned and reconsidered. Conversely, fully independent entities (from functioning appliances to people who declined his continued tutelage) invoked his contempt. He found bright, clear TV images "offensive." Many would rather dismissively label him "eccentric," but, ultimately, his hoarding had much to do with *finding* a center, being centric, working toward what he called "the fullest flowering oneness," despite the destructiveness of that growth.

For obvious reasons, I'm reminded of *Wisteria*, an exceptional album by guitarist Jimmy Raney. The title tune, written by bassist George Mraz, gently climbs with its melody, approximating, perhaps, the movement of the

luscious vine while avoiding its territorial nature. "Out of the blue," writes
Frank van Dixhoorn in the album's liner notes,

> a song is born. Listen to Jimmy Raney's eight bar-solo on *Wisteria*. Did it grow
> silently till the day it was born and recorded? Is it just a matter of coincidence?
> Has it always been there, waiting at his fingertips? That's a secret. The secret of
> this paradoxical, carefully structured and always changing music that we call jazz.

Yes, a type of secret as elemental as the discussions of nature versus nurture.
What forms us, and how does our existing character modify that formation?

On the Cape property, one of our most extraordinary trees happens to
be one of the least "perfect": a mid-sized maple that had been wound tight
with wisteria. When I cut away that mature vine, the trunk remained deeply
scarred from the twisting spiral, a kind of physical struggle that inspires
thoughts of psychic struggle. In New York's American Museum of Natural
History, one of my favorite dioramas has always been the brooding sperm-
whale head partly engulfed by the tentacles of a giant squid—a depiction
of an underwater battle never witnessed by mankind; we only know of this
reality from the suction-cup scars on washed-up whales. And here, in my
own yard, another silent, primordial battle had taken place, albeit of a much
smaller scale and far longer time.

The trunk's image brings to mind the rod of Aesculapius, our medical
symbol of a serpent spiraling up a vertical staff. Given the nature of an icon,
of course, the snake cannot hurt the staff, nor will the rod be damaged from
being entwined; it is the difference, as my father frequently pointed out,
between logo and Logos. Roethke wrote in "The Waking," "Great Nature
has another thing to do / To you and me," and what remains in the case of
this scarred maple is a stunning statement of survival. Arborists who pass by
this tree don't seem to understand why I haven't leveled it, though they nod
respectfully when I say I love its sculptural quality. Where is *my* line dividing
the world's discards and my cherished artifacts?

And how else but through challenge do we ultimately judge our value?
The depth of our humanity depends in part upon the intensity of our battles.
That's certainly true of an artist's endeavor as well. As my father once said
when I taped conversations with him about his years with Hans Hofmann:

> The [Hofmann paintings that] I like the most are the ones he worked on a
> long time and somehow struggled through. The struggle, ultimately when he
> did come through with it, produced not simply a certain surface that would
> be piled up or not piled up, but produced a quality—as all struggle does, as it
> does on a person's face for that matter—that becomes very human and makes
> a one-to-one relationship between itself and the observer.

As he talked about Hans Hofmann, his conversation naturally drifted to other painters, including Albert Pinkham Ryder. Comparing Ryder to Franz Kline, my father said Ryder was "essentially of the sea," adding, "There's a slower, heavier weight in Ryder's paintings that he spent a long time building up. . . . In Ryder's case, although he worked on a relatively small surface, the buildup was in terms of layers of paint to make the form arrive at a dreamlike simplicity." Although Ryder's art looks nothing like my father's, the phrase "layers of paint to make the form arrive at a dreamlike simplicity" applies with startling accuracy to my father's work, especially the large acrylic canvases from his last decades. The new plastic-based paints allowed for dramatically built-up layers—*impasto*—giving many of his canvases an immediate sensory connection to texture. And yet he insisted that texture was not his intent; rather, the *impasto* thickened as he reconsidered and reapplied paint in order to create more cohesive relationships between color and form.

I am also struck, I must add, by certain personal connections with Ryder who, at the end of his relatively short life (1857–1917), became increasingly incapacitated and required more and more assistance from his friends, the Fitzpatricks, in whose house he would eventually die. The book *Albert Pinkham Ryder: Painter of Dreams* by William Innes Homer and Lloyd Goodrich notes a time "when Ryder fell ill with gout and could not move." With help, Louise Fitzpatrick "undertook the heroic job of cleaning out his quarters, much to his distress." The authors then quote Charles Fitzpatrick:

> They cleaned out bags and barrels filled with paper, empty food boxes, ashes, old clothes, especially under garments, and about fifteen white shirts for evening wear, all soiled and in a fearful condition, mice that had decayed in traps, food in pots that had been laid to one side and covered with paper and forgotten. As he laid there helpless, he would accuse them of upsetting his room. When they got one side clean, they would drag him over on the rug to the other.

The landscapes of our homes, like the edges of a canvas, become our boundaries, our locations for creating order but not (one can hope) to the point of sterility. When do we distinguish wilderness from madness? In the rare patches of untouched Cape land, poison ivy, English ivy, wisteria, trumpet vines, honeysuckle, Virginia creeper, and other invasive vines rule. From ground cover to tree top, their tenaciousness is as urgent as the sharks off Chatham's coast, and, my father would argue, as primal as mankind's creative spirit.

CHAPTER TWO

~

New Ventures

To grope down into the bottom of the sea after them; to have one's hands among the unspeakable foundations, ribs, and very pelvis of the world; this is a fearful thing.

—Herman Melville, *Moby-Dick*

At five foot seven-and-a-half, with an expansive chest and bowed legs, my father had a physique that was more in keeping with a wrestler's body than that of a track star, much less a basketball player, and before his heart surgeries he had unnerving physical strength. What he could get his hands on, it seemed, he could move, but sometimes he needed my assistance. I'm only three or four inches taller, but that additional height allowed me to reach farther into Dumpsters loaded with coveted trash. Sometimes, he'd hold my ankles as I'd pivot on my solar plexus to grasp, say, the cracked plastic matting for an office desk, or a two-by-four that may have been part of a door-frame from an apartment down the street. Elastic in my pre- and post-teenage years, I often functioned as his retractable claw.

He advocated junk collecting as an extension of his artistic nature, but also for the sake of being economically savvy. During my childhood, if I asked why he picked up an abandoned washer, nail, or screw on Manhattan's pavement, he'd say, "Would you kick away a dime if you saw it?" Never mind that this was the late '60s, when the tiniest bit of hardware would not have cost anywhere close to ten cents; the logic made sense to me. And it made me admire my father. Here was a man who understood the importance of recycling (even if his actions meant more hoarding than transformation). I felt smug, even, part of a minuscule in-group that appreciated the value of garbage.

Only rarely did this humiliate me. Once, as I balanced a cast-iron radiator on a dolly while my father pulled it through the streets on the Upper West Side, kids in the neighborhood asked what my "grandfather" wanted to do with it. How to respond? That my father was forty-eight when I was born and, therefore, much older than most dads? That he was an artist, someone who desired abandoned objects because he imagined possibility in everything? Where to begin, given the consciousness of middle-class America? I just kept silent.

On the Cape, one didn't need to seek out Dumpsters because the dump itself was open for picking. That would change, and now it's heavily monitored, with bound bags tossed into gaping bins and falling far from anyone's reach. (Even the name has changed from Town Dump to Transfer Station.) But during my childhood, one simply threw garbage and broken objects onto open mounds. Naturally, the dump reeked, and one could count on flocks of loud seagulls, or, as we'd call them later, Dumpster chickens.

My father adored "picking the dump," and I can't recall a single time when he didn't return with salvaged goods to replace our tossed household trash. The size of these treasures ranged from a nut or small bolt to the rounded hood of a '50s Ford. I'm not exactly sure why I frequently tagged along. I disliked the smell, and I didn't participate in the picking. Most likely, I simply wanted to spend time with him, a man who didn't go to the beach or play catch or do any number of standard father-and-son activities. He'd wake, go to his studio, come to the house for a brief lunch (reading throughout), then start painting again until dinner. But during a dump run, he was mine, and I think he liked having his boy for company.

In Agnès Varda's marvelous documentary, *The Gleaners and I* (*Les glaneurs et la glaneuse*), the interviewed artists speak rather directly to the ambiance of my upbringing, a world where art and junk united in a bizarre helix. "All these objects around here are my dictionary, useless things," explains the artist Louis Pons.

People think it's a cluster of junk. I see it as a cluster of possibilities. Each object gives a direction, each is a line, picked up here and there, indeed gleaned, and which become my paintings. The aim of art is to tidy up one's inner and exterior worlds. [Pons runs his hand over a piece.] These are just crayons, children's crayons. Here we have tins and spools. . . . This is the tongue of a small bell. I make sentences from things. A cricket on a heap of trash. Cages are interesting too, a bit like boats, like violins and things whose . . . shapes at first are very simple and the same, but the possible variations are infinite.

Pons points to windshield wipers from cars and insists on an identity far removed from our standard labels, where objects escape narrative definition and become pure form: "For me they are streaks. I have to balance the streaks. That's a statement. Horizontal statements, nothing else."

Earlier in the documentary, Varda interviews a fascinating collector whose alias at that time (1999) was VR99. (The alias changed number by year; apparently, he collected names as well.) In the film, he defines an important term, "loading up," as "retrieving heavy objects people get rid of." Soon thereafter, he talks a bit more about his identity and passions:

> I am, among other things, a painter and a retriever. . . . I make images from salvaged material, frames from wood. I use food packages, slates, and then I also recycle my own packets of cigarette paper, and what's good about these objects is that they have a past, they've already had a life, and they're still very much alive. All you have to do is give them a second chance.

Varda and her subject walk into a homemade hut. "I've always liked the world of dumps and salvage," says VR99, "anything that's been sort of discarded by society."

He later adds, "The object beckons me, because it belongs here," and I think my father shared that magnetic sensibility, a belief that abandoned objects belonged on his properties in order to be transfigured, if not reborn. A bureau of many drawers, some missing, could become (and did) the foundation for a semi-spiral staircase, with thick planks (also found on the street) strategically inserted into the gaping openings to become steps. A walk in Manhattan, regardless of location, meant free treats. In some respects, my father viewed the entire world as a dump to be picked. No one I've ever known has matched his joy of "loading up."

So you must understand the deep irony when Dumpsters—used to *return* the decades of dump collecting—became centerpieces in my life, especially to reclaim the nearly impenetrable buildings on the Massachusetts property. The process began in August of 2003, two months after my father's death. The Cape and Philly homes were now my responsibility; the brownstone in New York, and all the cash, were for his widow to use during her lifetime. We agreed to have a memorial service on the Cape in the middle of August. Marleni and I planned to arrive with our children about ten days in advance of this celebratory gathering, which gave my stepmother two full months to collect whatever she wanted and move it to a house she had purchased, right next door.

When we arrived on the Cape, we found that the downstairs had been neatened up a bit—some effort had been made—but the house itself hardly functioned. And it stank. We knew that dozens of people at the memorial would want to come inside, but the house was rank with a miasma of decay. Marleni filled a bucket with bleach and water, and when she placed the mop on a wall by the stairwell, the liquid enlivened black mold that streaked the plaster with bold rivulets; it dripped and pooled like the alluvial blood in Weegee's black-and-white murder photos. One room on that first floor was impassable, crammed with large items (a non-functioning potbellied stove, a huge cedar chest with broken hinges, an entire wall of musty and molded books) and smaller ones, including an assortment of sticks brought inside to burn in chimneys with crumbled grout. If the exposed areas stunned us with filth, what lurked unseen?

Although Marleni and I prided ourselves on our resilience and the energy necessary to tackle significant projects, we felt overwhelmed to the point of inaction. Then, just a few days before the memorial, we were joined by beloved Pennsylvania friends, Jon Bogle and Deb Caulkins, who, among many other talents, gut and rebuild houses. And they saved us, starting with these simple words: "You need a Dumpster."

Taking on the wreckage meant taking on my father. Like cement, my confidence required time before it could harden into a true resolve, and we began the mass removal somewhat tentatively. Always empathetic, Jon and Deb asked permission before tossing even the most broken artifacts, but during this initial effort, I still found myself occasionally paralyzed. I left, for example, a large blue pouffe, stained from humidity and age, which supported a broken wooden duck. (Like so many objects in the house, the duck would have been valuable had it been whole.) We preserved much of the first floor's identity, from the yellow sofa covered in my mother's famous design, Caravan, to the Gramophone bell that functioned as a lampshade over the kitchen hutch table. But that initial Dumpster allowed the first level to be marginally presentable, and it gave me the courage to rent many other Dumpsters; eventually, in full groove, I went through one a day. The man who delivered them finally said, "I just want you to know that I've never had anyone pack these faster or tighter." He still made money off me, he admitted, but nothing like his usual customers. It was a victory of sorts.

The excavation led by Jon and Deb focused most of all on the second floor, and few things thrown from there caused me concern because almost no one had witnessed the upstairs; there would be far less judgment regarding "disrespectful" change. On that second floor, the most daunting room contained my mother's largest loom. In fact, we called that part of the house

The Loom Room, and it was as close to a family room as any other. That's where the TVs had always been, and many summer nights my parents and I retired there: my father at a makeshift desk where he sketched and paid bills, my mother at the loom itself, and me on the lumpy single mattress under the eave, usually drawing or playing invented games. We frequently had the TV running, but the reception was so poor that it hardly captivated us.

Although the room had some size for an old Cape Codder, one would have to call it tiny, or perhaps quaint, when compared to contemporary family rooms, and by the time of my father's death it had become almost solidified. Packed bureaus and cabinets had been positioned beside, in front of, and even atop other packed bureaus and cabinets. Though their contents remained impregnable to the eye, these stuffed containers nevertheless dwelled in possibility for my father. As Gaston Bachelard explains in *The Poetics of Space*, "Chests, especially small caskets, over which we have more complete mastery, are objects *that may be opened*. When a casket is closed, it is returned to the general community of objects; it takes its place in exterior space. But it opens!"

The Loom Room had crawlspaces along the eaves where the roof slanted to just a couple of feet from the floor. The blockade of bureaus sealed off one entrance, but the opposite side remained marginally accessible because of more mobile collections, primarily clothing. The opening had become, in fact, a wild closet, with hangers hanging from hangers hanging from hangers. Many held multiple layers of shirts. Behind them, we found stacks and bags full of dungarees, all purchased for spare change at yard sales and thrift shops. Jon and I took three SUV-loads to the Salvation Army drop. He estimated roughly one hundred per trip. That's right: three hundred pairs of jeans.

This jammed crawlspace also included plenty of rat poison, the same green pellets that speckled many of the room's drawers, and once we'd removed the clothes, I uncovered and pulled out a crumpled shower curtain. My momentum ceased. Obviously, the curtain had become so filthy that even my father and his wife decided to replace it—no doubt a major decision. But he had *stored* this mildewed sheet of plastic, now all the worse from age, with no regard for what it might do to surrounding fabrics in the closet. He simply could not release it.

As I noted earlier, my inheritance comprised two properties, our summer house and the carriage house in Philadelphia. Not remotely wealthy enough to renovate the Cape home, I needed first to empty and sell the Philly property. The Cape house also needed to be stripped clean, but in order to store the few items that I wanted to keep—a schoolmaster's desk, a number of chairs, a blanket chest, a writing desk—I first needed to empty the barn to use as storage. That fall, I had long weekends available to me (I taught my college classes on Tuesdays and Thursdays), and I alternated between the two-and-a-half-hour drive to Philadelphia and the eight-hour drive to Massachusetts.

The difficulty of preparing the Philly home had less to do with accumulation (although the downstairs had been used as a floor-long painting studio with a wall-length still life) and more to do with respecting and maintaining the legacy of Barbara Crawford, my father's second wife. (My mother was his third.) Barbara had been a writer, whose novella, "Day of the Circus," appeared in the first issue of *New Ventures* (1954), which included work by William Carlos Williams, e.e. cummings, and H.D. But she had also been a prolific painter and illustrator, and this home on Chancellor Street housed her collected works; like my father, she didn't sell. So for one of my many trips, I arranged to meet with her "art children"—former students who, to one degree or another, considered her to be a surrogate mother—and offered them any of the paintings that they desired. I took one as well; it hangs in the Cape house for the pleasure of her achievement, and as a gesture of profound gratitude. I gifted the rest of the work to Chestnut Hill Academy, where she taught for almost half a century.

Although she wrote plays and stories throughout her life, "Day of the Circus" represented her first and last major publication. It begins with surreal images created by a character who thinks "the room has shrunk" into "the black of caves at the end of black tunnels":

> "The rooms—the rooms—the rooms—
> 'Now march along, sonny, go on.'
> 'Yes, Father.'
> 'Go on to your room.'
> 'Which one is mine?'
> 'Why the one that is yours.'
> 'That one is not mine, Father, that's the one you gave me; it is filled with old furniture that creaks in the night carrying on conversations that are never finished, that were begun before I came, that stretch from ceiling to wall to floor like spider webs tripping me up. . . .'

I inherited her box of *New Ventures*, no doubt amassed in part because of my father's urging, and probably own more copies of that debut issue than anyone in the world.

I gave Barbara's baby grand piano to her favorite niece, and I did my best to get the more interesting items into the hands of people who would treasure them. I kept some trinkets and anything painted by my father, including a postcard-size self-portrait and his sketchbook from 1932, when he was only seventeen. These pencil and pen sketches focus on the human anatomy, with a full range of ages and activities, from stargazers to tennis players. One dark, well-worked portrait depicts a man with round-rimmed glasses and a thick mustache, white collar and black tie; he looks like a slightly leaner and more scholarly Teddy Roosevelt. It's more mature than many of the others, and it's inscribed along the collar: "Feinstein 32."

The sketchbook also contains a brief meditation on human inspiration, an outline of ideas far removed from expected, teen-aged narcissism:

1. People painting and carving according to thoughts
2. People painting + carving [according] to vision. Child paints according to thoughts

Beneath this, there's a horizontal line, followed by a parenthetic setting: "(B.C. cave men)." And then another short list:

The discoveries + inventions of importance
1. Use of seeds (harvesting of grain)
2. Domestication of dog cattle sheep goats + pigs
3. Cooking—making pots

The last, obviously, invokes art (pottery), and it's no surprise to see how quickly his thinking moves from practicality to creativity.

Almost everything saved from Philadelphia had and has meaning for me, most especially the paintings and this sketchbook. I also value the letters Barbara had saved from my father's Army years, correspondence that made their marriage, which ended years before my birth, all the more real for me. I kept two brass conquistador stirrups that she had mounted in the bathroom to hold small towels, as well as coal irons used as bookends, and a wicker crate with jewelry that my father had hammered out and given to her over the decades. Other things, too. But, very much in a cleaning-house state of mind ("Moving: Everything Must Go"), I chose selectively.

The contents of the Cape Cod barn, on the other hand, provided just about nothing of great value or even marginal sentimentality. I saved some tools—the unbroken hammers, the rust-free wrenches, even some dull saws—and one of the multitude of rusty nail collections, this one in a Chock Full o' Nuts coffee can. I enlisted help from people who could recognize things of consequence (for them, not for me); after an overnight visit, my cousin returned to his house in Maine with a truckload of "treasures," including broken pottery to make a mosaic, the inner workings of an old coal bin, and a zip line that probably worked. I can't tell you how pleased he felt, the expressed glee, because of that zip line. For him, it represented a form of freedom.

For me, freedom arrived in letting go, in giving away things that others would love, from the baby grand to steel wire, and releasing the structures from their punishing interiors. In that relatively small barn, some of the items hidden from sight included a broken pool table and a selection of thick tree trunks. I could not begin to itemize the contents, but I can tell you that, in addition to my cousin's haul and many other charitable handoffs, I eventually disposed of fifteen tons.

Packing a Dumpster well, which is to say as air-tight as possible, requires a sense of space and the strength to destroy. It is a skill, not an art, but I'm grateful to have learned the skill from Jon, a sculptor; lost in a world of junk, I felt bolstered by his creative spirit. He showed me how units with drawers or significant cavities could be broken down or stuffed solid. Flat and near-flat objects (boards, doors, table tops, tiles) must be stacked and weighted down. Save cloth and cushions for the hard-to-fill spots. With the Dumpster as your mold, you reconfigure the contents to make them as liquid as possible. You become, in effect, a hydraulic-less trash compactor.

While there's little creativity involved, I found the results satisfying, and after a series of intensive efforts, I became almost euphoric at the sight of the barn's walls. Its history returned. Look! That's where the horses had been, near the boarded opening used for feed; in a notched post, a thick rope used to tether the animal still threaded its groove. The walls themselves seemed to be in relatively good shape, surprisingly solid and unbowed. They'd been lightly whitewashed at some point, and that thin coating had kept the powderpost beetles from ravaging the wood, the way they had the joists supporting the upper-level's flooring. The barn *could* be salvaged, and I felt both proud and vindicated.

On the Cape property, the most astonishing collection had been hoarded in the barn, where my father had free reign. In the house itself, the most daunting space was the attic, roughly twenty-four by twenty, with eight feet from the floor to the rafters' peak. The thin steps leading to the attic slant precipitously—a classic New England death trap—and at the top, my father had left a two-foot path leading directly to the far window. On either side hung walls of clothing bags. Beyond that: the unknown. Even Jon, who had fearlessly gutted far-larger structures, stopped at the landing and said in rapid succession, "Oh my God, oh my God, oh my God."

The bags of clothing were the easiest to eradicate, given the many off-loading sites for the Salvation Army and other charitable organizations. After that, I removed some of the larger pieces of furniture, only one of which I ended up keeping: a desk with spiraling legs and florets carved into the drawer. I salvaged a few other items as well, but the vast majority—and I assessed *every* item—ended up in the Dumpster. Even without the heaviest pieces of furniture (laboriously brought downstairs to be evaluated), I threw out over three tons from the attic space alone.

Nor was there a direct route from the attic to the Dumpster. I started the job by removing the main window from its sash, and then tossed the refuse two stories down until the lawn looked like the crash site of a small plane. Later, I hauled the contents around the side of the house, across the front lawn, and, finally, into the Dumpster. Although a great many items fractured and dispersed after each toss, making the second haul all the more time-intensive, the alternative—carrying everything down the stairs and out of the house—was unthinkable.

The only item that I knew had some history—and, therefore, personal interest—had been stored in the northwest corner, near the open window sash. The bed had belonged to my grandfather. This is the story:

My grandparents, then living in Philadelphia, had invited their friend Louis Mankowitz and his wife to stay for the weekend. Unbeknownst to them, the previous weekend, their boys had accidently damaged the guest bed and patched it together, badly. Late that evening, after saying goodnight to their guests, my grandparents awoke to a mighty crash in the adjacent room. All four congregated in the hallway, at which point Mr. Mankowitz explained that the bed had collapsed. My grandfather threw his arm around his buddy's shoulder and exclaimed, "Louis, what a man you are!"

From then on, that bed was known as the Louis-What-a-Man-You-Are bed, a hearty frame with several broken slats. I'm sure it ended up with my father because his family replaced it. In any case, I estimated its location in the attic and knew I would salvage it, not for personal use but to give away or trade as a bargaining chip for people hauling off post-Dumpster remains.

No surprise, the bed had been embedded: piles rose from mattress to ceiling, and from floor to slatted frame. Meticulously, I pulled out the contents from beneath, which included large sheets of blank drawing paper, stained both by age and a healthy smattering of those green pellets, some still holding shape, many just dust. I brought a bandana to my mouth, and almost stopped inspecting the papers. Thank God I didn't. In the center of the mess, I pulled out a mixed-media abstraction that my father had matted (himself) and signed, gestures that meant he had shown the piece at one point. Then he'd stored it "safely" in the midst of these other papers, tucking everything beneath the famous bed before burying it all like the stone-closed entryway to a tomb.

Unlike most of my father's work, this piece shows best under artificial light; direct sunlight causes the slate grays to pop, as though elevating the contrast in a Photoshopped image. At the same time, dim lighting forces the regions of black—and there's more black here than in most of his works—to recede. The colors lose nuance. No painting in the house changes more dramatically during the day.

But how do we judge the merits of abstract expressionism? More often than not, people prefer the comfort of not being challenged, a sensibility my father railed against his entire life. In writing, sentiment arrives in its most immediate gesture—and least emotional meaning—through generic cards bought at grocery stores or pharmacies. Taste requires context: Would we accept the world's strongest cheeses, for example, if we were blindfolded and told the substance was rotting flesh? Music in its most insipid form greets us when we're put on hold or while we wait in dentists' offices. (We call it "elevator music," but the elevators of our lives keep expanding.) And paintings relax viewers when imagery brands them with irrefutable identification: seagulls on the beach, deer in the woods, mother with child, someone's house, a dining room, a tea kettle.

Abstract expressionism, on the other hand, requires the viewer to relinquish narrative and absolute context. Like writing constructed by metaphor (as opposed to chronological time), these paintings—or at least the best abstract works—ask the viewer to experience aesthetic emotion on a purely visual level. Just as a jazz musician's improvised solo must tell a story (to quote Fats Waller), so must these non-contextual paintings treat the vibrancy of color and movement of form as a cohesive, emotional journey.

The debut issue of *New Ventures* with Barbara's novella also includes two essays by my father's mentor, Hans Hofmann. In "The Resurrection of the Plastic Arts," Hofmann asks rhetorically, "What is Plasticity?" He responds with an urgent insertion of capital letters and italicized phrasing, a passionate attempt to explain when an abstract work has achieved its own lasting identity:

> *Plasticity means to bring the picture surface to "automatic" plastic response.* The picture surface answers every plastic animation "automatically" with an aesthetic equivalent *in the opposite direction of the received impulse. Push* answers with the corresponding equivalent of *Pull,* and *Pull* correspondingly with *Push. A Plastic animation "into the depth" is answered with a radar-like "echo" out of the*

depth and vice versa. Impulse and echo establish two-dimensionality with an added dynamic enlivenment of created breathing depth.

To me, my father's recovered work from the attic embodies Hofmann's concept of "Plasticity" and "dynamic enlivenment." One might also say it visualizes the spirit of Shakespeare's fourth acts from his major tragedies, including Lear on the heath. Storming and elemental, the gestures surge vertically, the brightest patches in this horizontal work breaking open the bottom left and top right. Balanced streaks of light lime punctuate the composition, yet, like strands of algae floating in a dark tide pool, they're so overshadowed by the chiaroscuro of soot and ash that one hardly registers their green individuality. This holds true for moments of pastel turquoise and slaloming sky blue. Color here functions like the moody highlights on iridescent fish navigating the depths of Mexican lagoons.

The moment I held it to the light, I knew where it would hang in the house; like the storming energy in the work itself, the vision of its future location charged into my consciousness with a thunderous immediacy. And, indeed, it hangs precisely where I envisioned: above the antique schoolmaster's desk. It's now framed in dark cherry, with a plum mat just a few shades darker than his camouflaged signature.

.

CHAPTER THREE

~

Notes in a Time of War

On March 13, 1943, exactly twenty years prior to my birth, the *Reading Eagle* published a report that brought sorrow to the City of Brotherly Love: the Philadelphia Zoo announced that their beloved Josephine had died. "Thousands of children are mourning," the *Eagle* proclaimed, noting that she had given rides to roughly 175,000 kids. "She was publicized nationally as a 'pygmy elephant' when she arrived here in April, 1925—but she grew to weigh three tons." The paper quickly added a sense of mystery to the story: "Science now says there is no such thing as an elephant pygmy." Both the star of their show and an enigma, the wondrous Josephine also had attitude. In 1940, as a gesture of thanks for her popularity, the zoo constructed "an ultra-modern cage" as a new home: "She didn't like it and began a three-week sit-down strike." Eventually, she succumbed to modernity, but not before a late-night rampage, in which she "knocked over stands and ate tree foliage," and "went AWOL."

I learned about this "pampered pachyderm" not from *National Geographic* or the Blabla doll company (which featured Josephine the Elephant in two cuddly sizes) but through a correspondence between my father and his second wife, Barbara Crawford. They had married in 1942, the same year he enlisted in the army. From then until his discharge in the summer of '45, he mainly worked in art-focused units (camouflage, for example), first in Carlisle, Pennsylvania, and then Fort Meade, Maryland, with an important, six-week interlude in Astoria, New York. When Barbara died in 2003, a few weeks before my father, I found among her belongings a handful of notes that he'd mailed to her from the barracks. Still later, in the miasma of junk stored in the Cape attic, I found several army mail bags stuffed with her letters from that time. He'd kept every one. I stopped counting at 250.

The year of Josephine's sit-down strike (1940) also brought Republicans to Philadelphia for their national convention, which endorsed Roosevelt's tedious opponent and proclaimed Josephine to be their mascot. By September, yellow stars pockmarked the war-wrought landscapes in Europe. For my father, the year brought a good deal of personal change as well: His first marriage ended after only two years, and he moved into a loft on Cherry Street, which he and Barbara rented for about a dozen years before purchasing a home. Judging from photographs, and given how dramatically he impacted subsequent houses, this loft looks startlingly spacious, allowing individual shapes—a small rocker; a hutch table; a bulbous, floor-standing glass jar—the dignity of pure exhibition. He strung a wagon wheel to the rafters, all spokes intact, as an ornamental base for an overhead light. (The ceiling appears to be twelve to fourteen feet high.) On one wall, he displayed a rooster that he'd cut from dark sheet metal, a giant cock that would later be placed above their bed when they moved to Chancellor Street.

Still more eye-catching, however, was their potbellied stove, commonly known as the Red Cloud, after the Sioux Indian chief. It stood about three-and-a-half feet from base to stovetop and featured an attractively ribbed, cast-iron belly. But its flamboyant presence had less to do with the artifact itself and more with the venting that flowed like the tentacle of a giant squid: Black piping rose about six feet above the stove (still several feet below the ceiling), turned ninety degrees, ran horizontally for another ten feet, then dropped down about a yard before venting into a painted chimney beside their exposed refrigerator.

Red Cloud stoves had a reputation for strong heat and were primarily utilized in places that required maximum output, so it suited the loft's challenging architecture. Still, the height and length of that one-room apartment could not possibly be heated appropriately by a single source, and in February of 1943, Barbara sent this short note to her husband stationed with his camouflage unit: "Good morning. There was ice in the narcissus bowls. If it kills them you'll be sorry. And this time I mean it. Who freezes these herbs freezes me."

The following month, along with a personal letter, she mailed him the newspaper clipping about Josephine's death, and in response, my father penned one of his longest letters to her. (Sometimes his notes were barely longer than a fortune cookie's slogan, such as this post from Fort Meade:

"Crawford, I am wearing the itchiest underwear in the world.") It begins with mock formality and meanders to the point: "Telephone, if you will, the Zoological Gardens and reserve the body of Josephine the elephant. We in Cherry Street have great need for an elephant."

He accompanied the jocular letter with a whimsical, inspired drawing of Josephine's body fully connected to and working with the Red Cloud pot-belly. Her trunk dips down through the removed cooking lid on top of the stove to deliver an ongoing supply of coal from the pachyderm's upper body. The lower half of the carcass collects ashes. And riding the contraption in a bathtub that looks like a dingy is Barbara, one leg flirtatiously lifted toward the rafters.

"Let me explain the diagram somewhat," the letter says.

> Josephine is a three ton elephant. One ton of my coal can be chuted directly through the funnel (shown on the diagram, marked FUNNEL) and stored in the upper half of her. A strong platform separates the coal from the lower section of Josephine, which is preserved for ashes (see the door so marked, please). Think of it, my dear, two tons of space for ashes alone! The trunk of Josephine is coated with asbestos and slipped into the top of our stove. Through it, and impelled by a tilting of the platform (see the tail connection—one merely lifts the tail) the coal hurtles into the roaring flame. It is almost perpetual motion! And—
>
> atop her broad and sturdy back, and like a veritable maharani, you, in your newly-placed bathtub, can gambol to heart's content. You know we are not happy with the present location of our bathtub, my dear.

Before signing off, a final plea: "Make haste to communicate with the zoo, my pet, ere it be too late. You *know* how 'House and Garden' steals our ideas."

The irresistible zaniness of his vision becomes all the more captivating in the context of his life: Who else would make the visionary leap from elephant carcass to coal burner? And his attention to detail seems meticulously conceived. The trunk is "coated with asbestos." The hundreds of coals in Josephine's upper region have been drawn *individually*. He included a ladder for Barbara to reach the tub, and a drainage pipe to release the water. It's a world of both whimsy and surreal practicality.

Other sketches from the army also displayed mobility and charm. In April of 1943, for example, my father encountered the writer William Saroyan, also stationed in Astoria. Just five days earlier, Saroyan had claimed to be sick—not just with back pain but from unrecoverable sickness of the army itself—and considered desertion. Talked out of that poor option, he made an appearance, and my father created a sketch.

One of Saroyan's complaints about his service duties had to do with pride and fame: He had won a Pulitzer three years earlier and considered himself one of the greatest American writers. (His parents came from Armenia, but he was born in Fresno, California.) Why, he brooded, was a man of his prestige forced to do menial chores as a private? So it's all the more entertaining to see the sketch of Saroyan from behind as he carries, one-handed, a small trash can. It's a truly jaunty caricature, with the writer's right foot angled almost parallel to his torso, left hand splayed maniacally, butt and clutched bin swinging left, with his jacket flapping away from his body like a curtain in a stiff wind.

On the paper, Saroyan himself wrote, "Picture (good) of Pvt Saroyan on Barracks Orderly April 19, 1943 by." My father added his signature, folded it up, and mailed it to Barbara with a note:

> I send you a sample of Saroyan's handwriting & mine own at his request. What is your name? he demanded. Write it down, he said, I want to see how it looks. And he wrote his little piece up to the word "by" and said, Now you write *your* name, Sam.
> The Armenians may be starving, but not for nice manners.

Although separated by ten years, all three Feinstein brothers served in the US Army during the Second World War, and my father, the eldest, saved all of their correspondence. Surprisingly, none fought overseas, and the letters from my youngest uncle, Al, express far more frustration about inactivity than fear of war. Simply put, he was bored. As an aspiring doctor with off-the-charts intelligence, he felt burdened, much like Saroyan, by the futility of inaction. (On October 12, 1945, he wrote: "Very, very disgusted and disheartened and quite fed up with the army, which has so damned much trouble making up its absence of a mind.") With the passing months, his letters very clearly sketch the most ineffectual characteristics of military bureaucracy and his blistering contempt for wastefulness. He wanted out.

It's telling that my uncle turned to his eldest brother for help, and at this time in their lives, they may have been closest. Ten years my father's junior, my uncle Al would become an innovator in the field of epidemiology, especially clinical biostatistics. He published several books and over four hundred articles, and he received a Sterling Professorship, Yale's highest academic honor. As I gravitated toward academe, and with my mother's family all in Sweden, he became my closest relative. But his independence and lavish success seemed to cloak my father's interest in him, and, as always, my father could not hide his contempt. He started referring to him as "a prestige digit." My uncle never fully gave up on the relationship, though he said to me, repeatedly, "Once you're on Sam's shit list, you never get off."

Like the histories behind most family rifts, their increased distance had many factors, including the ideology of materialism. My uncle was by no means a spendthrift, but he appreciated and enjoyed high-quality merchandise. He'd treat me to expensive meals at restaurants with individual fireplaces and chandeliers and dramatic waiters. He introduced me to venison tartar, escargot, sweetbreads, and scallop roe. He delighted in the role of rich uncle, stoking a bourgeois sensibility that my father eschewed.

During my childhood, Al was married to his second of three wives, a woman whose propensity for snobbery and condescension threatened me more than her cavity-filled mouth. But she had smarts—as I recall, she made great strides in the pre-computerized world with punch cards, or something of the sort—and, perhaps most important for the marriage, she had earned gourmet status, her culinary gifts showcased in the years when we'd stop overnight as a respite for our summer trip from New York to Massachusetts. Dinner inevitably began with a wine tasting. My uncle would emerge with two bottles, each elegantly wrapped in a towel to obscure the labels.

"One is really quite expensive," he'd explain, "and the other is much, much cheaper."

He'd pour two glasses for my father, and we would await the verdict. And without exception, my father preferred the cheaper wine. The adults would laugh, and I would laugh, too, although I wasn't sure why. Nor can I tell you, even now, what their laughter meant. Did my uncle want to mock my father, who had mastered the painter's palette but who had none for the culinary arts? Did he want to mock himself for spending more on wine than he should? Was it a combination of the two? Nor will I ever know if my father threw the results intentionally in order to mock his brother. (He joyously embraced deception.) And why conduct this kind of test, annually no less, with a completely uninterested and uneducated participant?

Years later, my father again found himself at a dinner party where the conversation turned to wine. The host and at least one other guest had small but impressive cellars, and they enjoyed the language of a sommelier, though with no intent to sound snobbish. Conversation segued from what had been served to verticals of wine—tasting the same type of wine from the same vineyard, but from different years. Turning to vinegar with boredom, my father impatiently waited for a pause. Then he leveled the conversation with six words: "I've had a vertical of wives."

He liked the line so much that he repeated the story frequently—to me more than once. Everyone chuckled, knowing that he had three almost-twenty-year marriages. Some people, though not many, also knew of a brief, first marriage to a fellow art-school student. In my father's vineyard, she was the vintage not to buy. In fact, she remained quite a mystery to me during my father's life. Her name alone made me laugh—Beryl—because I not only heard "Barrel" but I imagined a similar torso. Whenever I pushed for details, he'd provide the same rehearsed retort: "She said she loved me enough for the both of us, and I had to marry her to prove her wrong."

But, of course, he saved her letters, starting with one from 1934, when he was only nineteen, and her correspondence created not merely a glimpse into their romance but a sense of humanity that she deserved. The ones from '37 appeal to me the most. "Darling," she wrote in the middle of September, "it won't be long till I see you again—and will I be glad, you hateful thing. And do you know what I intend to do when I see you? Well, this is getting me nowhere at all." At the end of that month, she sounds all the more grateful for his company and guidance: "Dearest, you're the swellest guy I ever knew. You seem to know just what to do to keep my chin up. . . . I guess I'm a silly twerp but I at least know enough to appreciate a real pal." By the middle of October, she's found a soul mate—"There is so much beauty in life. You've put it there for me"—and by the end of that month, they've gone beyond courtship: "Hello Lover."

These letters and some photos made Beryl real to me, and wonderfully so. The rest of his "vertical of wives" I knew well: Barbara Crawford, and then my mother, and then his last wife. But his jocular quip seems strangely ac-curate when looked at metaphorically: Just as a vertical of wines become part of a collection, so did this vertical of wives (especially two, three, and four) marry into my father's collective nature.

Consider this fact alone: From fall through spring during his marriage to my mother, he'd leave every Sunday for Philadelphia and stay in the carriage house, which he still co-owned with his ex-wife Barbara. He'd teach two private classes in Philadelphia, both on Monday, then take the bus to Princ-eton, New Jersey, where he taught a third in a private home before returning to us on Tuesday night. (In New York, he taught classes in our basement on Wednesday nights and Thursday mornings.) Only once do I recall my mother weeping over the attention Barbara still received. And I must admit that, during my childhood, the arrangement didn't seem all that strange to me. Like most kids, I accepted family eccentricities as normal. Only years later, after my mother's death, did I seriously contemplate her hardship of being in a marriage while, weekly, her husband returned to a house shared with his former wife.

Did my mother believe, as I did at the time, that he needed to leave in order to support the family? That was always the forceful claim, although it's by no means the entire truth. What he earned as a private art teacher—especially after subtracting the cost of travel from New York to Philly, Philly to Princeton, and Princeton to New York—amounted to very little. I suspect one extra class in Manhattan would have yielded about the same.

And I hated his travel because I idolized my father, invariably fixed by his commanding eyes (made all the more penetrating by thick, black eyebrows) and by his position as a consummate artist. It's easy to idolize, after all, when the reality of presence becomes replaced by a very present absence. It was enough to know that he'd arrive for meals, and that he continued to create masterpieces. I felt proud to be his son, and when I woke on Sunday mornings, my body felt gray with the knowledge of his afternoon departure. In fact, that sadness had already begun to settle by Saturday night.

Looking back, I can't quite understand why his complete absence bothered me so much more than his household absence. Perhaps when he left for Philadelphia, his distance at home became real; perhaps I'd just grown used to minimal presence and cherished it to such a degree that absolute departure created an overwhelming solemnity. Whatever the cause, I'd wait anxiously to hear him open the front door on Tuesdays, late afternoon, after I'd returned from school. I was like a dog to its master, bounding across the brownstone to throw my arms around him. Maybe that's why he used to call me Little Mutt.

And I know his paternal distance depressed my mother because, with frequency, she'd ask, "Do you wish your father spent more time with you?" At the time, I could not understand the question, even for its most simple implications.

"He doesn't *have* the time," I'd say.

"If he did, would you like to spend more time with him?"

"But he doesn't have the time." I remained bewildered. Again, what you're born into seems normal, or at least fated. She might as well have asked if I wanted my father to be a horse.

As someone consumed by the arts, I had been blessed to have two artists as parents, and I idealized their marriage. I assumed that his controlling nature had everything to do with a father's dominance over an untrained son, never imagining that my mother—or Barbara, for that matter—had also been suffocating from his wisteria-like nature. After his divorce from Barbara, she said she could not even pay a bill; she had been so controlled that she felt incapable of the most mundane errands. I learned of this long after my father's death, roughly the same time when I was told that my mother, a year before her cancer diagnosis, considered leaving him.

When my mother died and my father remarried for the fourth and last time, he continued to travel to Philadelphia once a week. He also tried to get dealers interested in my mother's art, and to arrange shows of her work. When I'd visit, he'd frequently refer to his latest wife by my mother's name. A vertical of wives indeed. In my mind, it verged on polygamy.

If, in these pages, I neglect to speak in depth about my mother, it's largely because I concentrated on her in *Black Pearls: Improvisations on a Lost Year*, a memoir inspired by unexpected memory. As I've made clear, she raised me and doted on me, primarily from a mother's love but also, I'm pretty sure, to make up for my father's distance. Her death, when I had just turned seventeen, remains the most pivotal experience of my life, a trauma so profound that I blocked out memories of her illness for twenty years. And then they began to return. *Black Pearls* tries to braid the extreme realities of that time, when I simultaneously collapsed emotionally and grew with artistic vision. Very briefly during that period, I kept a dream journal. Had I kept a daily journal, *Black Pearls* may never have been written; part of the drive behind that book had to do with the reconstruction of months (September 1979 through April 1980) that had shattered.

I knew my father, however, had kept notes: At some point during my mother's illness, or perhaps just after she died, he told friends that he had kept a log, a daily reporting of her events and his thoughts. I frequently wondered about his notes, especially years later, when I struggled to create *Black Pearls*. But I never asked him to share, and he never offered.

I encountered the annotated log after his death and the publication of my memoir. He had used lined paper and squeezed in the cursive text, two lines per ruled space. (He did the same with his checkbooks, minimizing the numbers until the artifact looked more like World War II code than a standard, easy-to-use document. No space should be wasted, after all.) Because I had erased so much of that year, I wanted to know if his scratched-in log would clarify memory. But I also turned to his notes like the speaker in Anne Sexton's "All My Pretty Ones," investigating what has been left behind by her deceased parents, including her father's scrapbook and her mother's journal: "How did they view my existence," Sexton asks implicitly, "and how did they interpret horror?" In her poem, the speaker finds no mention of herself in the father's scrapbook, which features people she can't recognize and clippings of international events, and in the mother's journal she finds more evasion than tough recognition of the family's hardships.

My father's notes begin in September. On October 3, the day after my mother's forty-seventh birthday, the hospital starts chemotherapy treatment. My father mentions me for the first time on October 8: "I sleep over at 311 [the New York brownstone] instead of going to Phila. Go early in A.M. Sascha at home." On November 12, he writes that my mother learns radium treatment will be necessary and is upset, but that he "was in Phila teaching that day + didn't find out until that night." He also notes that her consistent vomiting is "in part, psychological." I'm mentioned again on January 17: "Sascha concerned about effects on his studies," but the Assistant Headmaster assures him that "this will be taken into consideration." I find my name again on the first of March, when my father writes most extensively about me: "Sascha has done relatively well in school: his marks have held up and so has he. He faces the college-hunt business that occurs at this time in his grade, and we hope for the best. A lovely young man." The entry for March 13 begins, "A birthday present for Sascha," but it's only news that my mother has moved her bowels.

These daily notes on my mother's illness include only one tiny illustration. It accompanies an entry from April 3, 1980, twelve days prior to her death:

We have been going day by day in this fashion. Anita, very weak and gaunt, has been unable to use her legs. I have obtained a wheelchair and a hospital type bed for her. We have also worked out ways for her to urinate while in bed. I have, among other things, fashioned a kind of bedpan out of a kitty litter box [illustration] so that it can be slipped under her and urine passes down to a hole which empties into a receptacle held under it. Anita has been subject to depression at her immobility but is now past that.

In my memory, the apparatus was placed snugly in the wheelchair, not the bed—but I only saw it when he unveiled his transformed cat box. He seemed so pleased with himself, grinning the way I imagine he smiled when writing the description about Josephine and the coal stove, as though his pleasure at "fixing" the problem could create happiness for my mother—whose depression had most decidedly *not* passed. She cried when she saw it. I left the room.

If I were to assign a color to this memory, the cat box hue would be exactly appropriate. Originally a sea-foam green, it had faded into something like an over-washed hospital gown. Theodore Roethke once wrote, "I have known the inexorable sadness of pencils"; I have known the inexorable sadness of old plastic.

My father's satisfaction with adaptability and invention eclipsed any sensitivity for my mother's dignity. Why subject your dying wife to a used kitty litter box? How can such a gesture avoid commentary? And why had my father *kept* the plaster litter box? My cat Robin—the only pet we ever owned—had died four or five years earlier. Stricken by Robin's death, I insisted we not get another cat, so there would be no "normal" use for this box. And perhaps this explains my father's bizarre delight in his makeshift bedpan: Even a container that was pissed and shat upon could be, in his eyes, transformed into something positive.

It's possible I left the room because I could not bear the implications of the gesture, but it's more likely I didn't even try to psychoanalyze my mother's tears. From early childhood, moments when she wept caused me anguish to the point of disorientation, as though the supporting walls of my life were about to give way, the ceiling crushing us both. I'll never know what she felt, or if she ever voiced those feelings, nor does my ignorance betray desire.

But I can say with some certainty that my father would have aggressively dismissed any suggestion of debasement. Objects were materials, not labeled artifacts. He would have felt no shame about this, as is evident from his notes, where he made no effort to avoid the phrase "kitty litter box." The fact that he drew it as well speaks to a sense of pride: "What the world abandons for superficial and wasteful reasons," his notes and illustration imply, "I will embrace and transform."

As witnesses, he and I had survived a year of terminal cancer, horrors that far surpassed any traumas he experienced during the war years in the army. And suddenly I'm brought to the poetry of Yusef Komunyakaa—not his astonishing war poems, actually, but the famous close to "My Father's Love Letters." The abusive father, trying once again to coax his beaten wife home, stammers for language, "almost / Redeemed by what he tried to say." Even after decades of rereading that poem, the word *almost* hangs at the line's end like an unexploded grenade.

CHAPTER FOUR

~

Monsters among Trees

One Wednesday in the fall of 1980, the start of my high school senior year, I returned home within minutes of a dump truck's delivery: an entire load of cement chunks piled like a ransacked Maya ruin. The deposit filled an empty space by a fire hydrant just a few yards from our New York brownstone. My father stood wide-eyed before the mass, and I walked to his side.

"Put your things inside the house and get back out here," he said. "We've got to get this the hell outta here before the police come."

In my typically slavish response, I didn't ask many questions and got to work quickly. (If the mountain will not come to Mohammed, Mohammed will go to the mountain.) I feared the police—or rather, I feared the thought of my father being charged with a fine—and his mortality influenced my young adulthood immeasurably. Just half a year earlier, my mother had died of cancer at the age of forty-seven. My father was sixty-five, and although he retained the driving energy of a Ukrainian immigrant, my image of him as an indestructible force had faded to sepia three years earlier when he suffered a massive heart attack. Lifting and lugging chunks of concrete could threaten his life.

But he insisted we remove the wreckage before his art students arrived at seven that evening, and I knew his tone: no discussion. So I dumped my book bag and began the vigorous schlepping. Being New Yorkers, few people seemed particularly intrigued, although a Jewish woman down the block stopped in front of the heap, glanced up and down the sidewalk, and asked, "Ver did it come from?" It was a reasonable question, but I didn't have the time or knowledge to answer what no doubt would have been a series of follow-ups had I engaged her: "Ver are you going to put this?" "Vut are you going to do vit it all?" How many times would I have to say, "I don't know"?

But I could answer her now. A block away from our home, my father had spotted workers jackhammering the sidewalk and loading their dump truck. The moment coincided with plans he had for building a wall at the far end of the courtyard behind our brownstone. He wanted sheer bulk to defray the cost and time of shaping fresh cement, so he asked if they'd be willing to deliver part of a load. "Sure, Mister." And why not? It would save them a trip to the landfill and the dumping fee. He had planned to limit the deposit, but the truck had tipped its bed before releasing the back flap and belched the entire haul onto the city street.

Reaching the courtyard would have meant moving each hunk another sixty or seventy feet, and we didn't have the time. Instead, we piled each piece in a semicircle outside the brownstone, an entryway used in other buildings for a stairway to the second floor. Fearing the strain on my father's heart, I focused on the largest pieces, some the width of my body, most of them three or four inches thick. I'd been physically active that summer, swimming and playing tennis daily, but I began to tire before we'd made a significant dent. And then, like an apparition, one of my father's students arrived—he'd been telephoned—and his presence renewed my resolve, even my strength.

We finished before dark. I washed up and started dinner, but before we ate, I asked my father to take a Polaroid of me sitting in the center of the reshaped rubble. My hair's long and full—shoulder length—and I've retained the summer's tan. My body's two-toned: brown socks match my brown shirt; blue sneakers match my jeans. The walls of broken cement rise as high as six feet behind me, and I'm smiling broadly, my elbow casually positioned on an accidentally constructed armrest. I could easily be digitally transferred onto a sofa.

The following morning, after I'd gone to school, he checked the dumpsite for sharp remains that could puncture tires. He said a Chinese man walking a small dog stopped by the hydrant and stared at the dusty gutter. The man looked up and down the block, and he looked straight up into the sky before turning to my father and asking, "Where did it go?" For years, my father said the whole story could be summarized by the Jewish woman and the Chinese man: Where did it come from? Where did it go?

Eventually, most of the rubble got hauled to the courtyard, and by the spring of 1982 (according to my slide's date) my father had positioned the chunks so that they surrounded four large slabs of rusted metal: an old, steel water tank that a neighbor had blowtorched into pieces for the sake of removal. The top and bottom parts were perfectly circular, with the two sides somewhat resembling massive medieval shields. Exposed now to the oxygenated environment, the concave parts rusted into a thrilling radiance that reminded me of my father's work. But, of course, rust evolves like slow-motion fireworks, bursting until it burns itself out. In an effort to sustain the color, he covered the flaking steel with a coat of clear acrylic, but rather than preserve the sunniness, the paint deadened the metal to a fairly homogenous brown. Eventually, he added a layer of cement to the concave steel, creating a row of impressive geometric forms—something akin to the impact of Easter Island heads—but, ultimately, depressingly sterile in hue.

My early childhood memories of the courtyard may be partly romanti-cized, but I can say with absolute certainty that the great majority of stored junk arrived after my mother's death in 1980—which is to say, from my late teens onward. My mother had kept much of his collecting in check, limit-ing his obsession to the basement (where he taught and which therefore included wall-to-wall still lifes), his fourth-floor studio, and, also on that top floor, two side rooms, which he packed as though challenging air to move. She also *respected* the courtyard, brightening its back border with yellow tu-lips and keeping clutter out of sight. Brick paths framed a central crabapple tree, and, yes, that solitary tree with its charming red fruit looked Edenic.

Springtime for me meant Tonka trucks rumbling on the bricks and toy steam shovels plowing small patches of earth left raw for my delight. In April, my mother speckled the ground with colored eggs (a nod to Easter like our nod to Christmas—events celebrating childhood wonder as opposed to religious conviction). But her death brought with it a kind of liberation for my father, whose found objects leached their way into the home and garden as easily as water dripping through a cracked toilet tank. And he announced two projects—the cement wall and a roofed enclosure for the first dozen feet—that consequently "justified" the determined efforts to salvage massive, discarded objects. He stacked lengthy pipes and rebar found at demolition sites and in Dumpsters, metallic bones to be used as foundational supports. Along the northern border, a bathtub overflowed with ceramic roof tiles. The crabapple tree, set off by an expanse of cement wall, became surrounded by clusters of building material, a scene reminiscent of the one described by E. L. Doctorow in his novel, *Homer & Langley*:

> We had no victory garden, our backyard had been given over to storage—
> things accumulated over the years that we had bought or salvaged in expecta-
> tion of their possible usefulness sometime in the future: an old refrigerator,

boxes of plumbing joints and pipes, milk-bottle crates, bedsprings, headboards, a baby carriage with missing wheels, several broken umbrellas, a worn-out chaise longue, a real fire hydrant, automobile tires, stacks of roof shingles, odd pieces of lumber, and so on.

On Cape Cod, the backyard—which is to say, the area between the house and his small studio—also became the site for cemented projects. I've already discussed the stone table, for example, and the hundreds of pounds of hardened cement that ringed the rhododendron. Diagonally across the property, he had begun what he called a barbeque pit, though, in truth, it bore no resemblance to such a thing. (Had the cement been stone, it would look like a natural formation in Utah: two parallel but uneven pillars, very roughly constructed.) Grates for the middle had rusted out and been removed. The curious gray forms simply marred the natural landscape.

And the beauty of that area mattered to me. In the center rose an enormous oak that I'd climb, almost to the top, to survey the land the way red-tailed hawks now use our trees. (As John Berryman writes in his first "Dream Song": "Once in a sycamore I was glad / all at the top, and I sang.") That soil nourished the greatest cedar on the property, as well as a small apple tree that looked both charming and arthritic. When my cat Robin died prematurely, we buried him in that yard, not far from a spruce I'd helped plant in 1967 when I was four. The tree must have been hardly more than a sapling then because, annually, when we'd first arrive at the summer house, I'd run to gauge who had grown taller over the winter. In the course of forty years, it outgrew children, adults, shacks, houses.

Then, four or five years after my father's death, we returned to the Cape house to discover the massive spruce had fallen, though not from vines like so many others. A nor'easter had penetrated its rich foliage, the way a good storm can invert even the strongest umbrella, and wrenched the massive trunk from its sandy soil. Defeated, the spruce spread its still-green branches across the crabgrass and pine needles.

Witnessing the tree's carcass initially gutted me, yet I soon felt strangely relieved—not from a sentimental past but from the realities of physical space: without the tree's hearty, expansive branches, the backyard seemed to triple in size, and the possibilities for spatial transformation elated me.

Before my father's death, I'd never used a chain saw, but in the process of cleaning out the barn, I discovered an old Stihl with a long blade. He must have acquired the tool in the '70s because I remember the purchase: a yard sale item, of course, sold cheap because the owner had lost the key for the electric ignition and didn't have the strength or patience to operate it by pull-start. My father had rarely started that chain saw, perhaps because it actually worked and was a great brand (something, therefore, to be saved more than used), and as it hibernated in the barn, I forgot its existence. But with gas, oil, and a new chain, the saw revved up with fresh-out-of-the-box urgency.

The revived Stihl became invaluable as I addressed what we called the back forty—the second half of the property, which had been consumed by poison ivy. (I dropped tall, completely dead oaks and used them as walk-ways.) I saved a number of trees by amputating massive dead branches, and, after eradicating the poisonous ground cover, I used the saw to chain-up fallen trunks. The decades-old tool churned through cords of dead oak, pine, cedar, and locust, allowing me to save healthy hardwoods and liberate the property from the odor of rotting pulp. What did it matter that its ignition kicked in from a pulled string and not an electric spark?

Given those summers of practice, I rather easily cut up the branches and trunk of the fallen spruce. But the stump and tentacled roots required far greater power, so I hired a fellow named Brian, who owned a Kubota tractor, and, after severing the roots, he plucked the tree's core from the ground with the ease of my childhood Tonka trucks digging up small stones. He began to rip the massive roots from the soil. But then he shut off the engine and said, "Uh oh—"

Those two syllables triggered a horrific image for me. My cat's grave had not been on my mind, but within seconds I flashbacked to his death in 1975, painting a cardboard box in my mother's studio because she thought I'd have more solace if I decorated Robin's coffin. And she was right: It felt ritualistic, Egyptian. I worked on his box most of the day until finally she suggested that I should let it go.

Now I imagined it ripped open by the Kubota's claw. Dangling, shattered cat skeleton . . . I couldn't look.

"Gas line," Brian said. Few phrases could have relieved me more, though for excavators on Cape land, few images create more concern.

Just as I'd forgotten about the chain saw, I'd forgotten about the gas line, but its canary yellow ignited memory: My father had buried the forty-to-fifty-foot pipe not for gas but as a casing for an electrical line to run beneath the expanse of lawn. At each end, he connected a lengthy extension cord, one from the juice's source in house, the other to his studio in the woods. The electricity powered a cheap radio so he could hear music while he painted, although he never seemed to notice or care if the station turned to static.

Brian stepped out of the Kubota's cab.

"No problem," I said.

Brian winced. "It's a gas line."

"Yes, but there's no gas. My father buried it."

And then we both started laughing, hard, for different reasons.

The bright yellow was just a plastic coating. Within: back-breakingly heavy stainless steel. And suddenly I recalled how my father bragged to my mother and me about his victorious burial, that it looked *much* lighter than it actually was, that the task had required enormous strength. Frankly, I didn't care at all; he had buried a pipe—great. But I now understand his bravado. After the Kubota twisted and snapped off a third of the length, I dragged the remaining line a few yards downslope toward the barn, and it took *all* my strength to do so.

During the many stages of the Cape restoration, I received more than a few incredulous looks from workers. Most have managed to suppress their immediate surprise, although one arborist inspecting the property involuntarily exclaimed, "What the hell is *that?*" The cause for his alarm was larger than the failed barbecue pit and much more confrontational than the stone table or, for that matter, any other sculptural project that my father left behind. It marked the center of the property, standing guard like Cerberus. My father called it The Monster.

Two large metal objects formed The Monster's foundation: a small coal stove, which formed a gaping mouth, and a tubular hot-water heater placed horizontally, the bulk of the creature's belly. I'd forgotten about the heater, in fact, until I found a sheet of drawing paper with five sketches scratched out with a blue Bic pen. The sequence of drafts demonstrate how my father's imagination progressed from totally inorganic, geometric form—angular stove, cylindrical heater—to something alive with fluidity, a bodily transformation from skeleton to muscle, flesh to expression.

What inspired the initial vision? He told many friends and visitors that he wanted to create a whimsical sculpture for children to play on, and he'd point out small stepping points (to call them "steps" would be a stretch) to aid in the climber's ascent. And, indeed, a great many people had photographs taken astride the beast's back, from candids of my buddies goofing around to semiformal family portraits. That said, his sculpture could never be labeled "child friendly" (among other reasons, its hide includes chunks of sharp slag) and so I never accepted my father's line about entertaining children, or, more to the point, entertaining me. I think his proclamation allowed him to construct a dramatic sculpture—one that commands the whole yard the way Maurice Sendak's Wild Things command their forests—without being judged for his childlike imagery.

Because it's largely cemented, it has rhinoceros-like "skin." When first glimpsed, many people, not just children, become disconcerted by such an anomaly in the woods. Till today, The Monster retains its otherworldly strangeness, often leaving people silent and wide-eyed. They're startled all the more as we anthropomorphize the creation: its gaping mouth and bright red eye. To the right of its cavernous mouth, he embedded a vertical cluster of shattered glass the color of thick seaweed. But it's the glossy burgundy eye—for its disproportionate size and bright finish—that hypnotizes the viewer. The ceramic bowl had been discarded by his friend, Harry Holl, because the shape had lost its symmetry.

Materials from the Prue Foundry proved to be essential for its exterior finish. Each summer, my father brought the owner a bottle of rye and in return gleaned what the foundry planned to abandon: bits of unusable slag and, primarily, heavy crucibles. Roughly eleven inches in diameter and thirteen inches tall, the crucibles had been cemented into the stone table and strewn throughout the property, with a massive heap stacked behind the barn. He collected them whether cracked or shattered. The whole ones, when turned upside down with the rounded bottoms up, bear a stunning resemblance to the unhatched eggs from the *Aliens* series.

Chunks of slag and fractured crucibles define what one would have to call The Monster's nose. Beneath that nose, a front leg with three stone toes juts forward. In some respects, it seems more like a gigantic head with four legs and a tail—a thick, snaking tail of cemented rocks. The form rises over six feet from tail tip to back foot, a rough beast slouching toward Provincetown to be born.

He built The Monster halfway between the house and his studio, and as the years passed, the foliage around it thickened. And then my mother died, and we planted two trees, the first, a copper beech, located just behind the house. He wanted to place the second tree, a cypress given to us by a long-time student and her husband, near The Monster, though not to adorn his work, nor for some symbolic, marital gesture. "This is a very special tree," he told me. "We need to hide it."

As usual, I said nothing. I just helped dig, drag the bag of peat moss, and run the hose. The loss of my mother had deadened me in crucial ways. The first tree had felt ceremonial and important; the second seemed like a superfluous gesture, and I really didn't care where we put the cypress. But I've come to think of my father's statement as almost quintessential. He felt nothing in the world could be trusted, and so expecting the worst was the wisest point of view. And he believed that things of value should not be used *because* of their value. He never wore new shirts, for example, that we gave to him as holiday presents; they'd remain pinned, boxed, and buried in drawers. The most expensive pallet knife he ever owned, enthusiastically given to him by a beloved student, I found still in its package long after his death. Yes, if it was special, hide it.

In the decades that followed my mother's death, the copper beech thickened quickly and rose far above our house. (Part of its dramatic growth, we all suspect, had to do with the broken septic system, which apparently leeched nourishment into the yard instead of the tank.) But the poor, hidden cypress struggled beneath shadowing oaks and pines. The year we took over the Cape property, I hacked away brush and wisteria from its trunk, then cut overhanging branches from neighboring trees to create direct sunlight. It was so sad, something worthy of *A Charlie Brown Christmas*: a tree with about three tiny sprigs of growth. While the copper beech had a circumference of fifty-six inches, the cypress, planted at the same time, had barely surpassed six.

I have failed to save a great many hardwood trees on the property, many of them consumed by wisteria, poison ivy, and other strangulating predators. But one can try, so I began fertilizing the cypress each season, and while the trunk's growth has been minimal, it keeps pushing out new branches, new life. And beside that struggling life, The Monster's red eye demands our focus like the terrifying and revered countenance of the goddess Kali, forever balancing madness and salvation.

CHAPTER FIVE

~

Children of Paradise

I grew up in an age when movie theaters didn't kick you out after a showing. In fact, when my mother and grandmother took me to see *Yellow Submarine*, we watched it two-and-a-half times in one stretch. This policy changed nationwide during the mid-1970s in part because of *Jaws* and other blockbusters, where people would have regularly stayed for multiple viewings. On his own, my father rarely arrived on time for a film. (With my mother, he tended to buckle and watch movies properly.) He'd catch the movie in medias res, watch to the end, wait a few minutes for the next showing, then stay until he'd caught up to where he began. He insisted this approach created more interesting and lasting imagery.

I accepted his attitude the way I accepted all his proclamations. Later, I found it utterly strange and, frankly, disrespectful. How could a man obsessed with art not respect the artistic construction and unity of film? It makes no sense—except that, in his worldview, it makes absolute sense. His approach to watching movies reflected his philosophy on just about everything else: Unless the subject had to do with masterpieces—and here I'm talking about the visual arts—he preferred to interject his own creative manipulations into his daily experiences. And he assumed any son of his would feel exactly the same way, which is why the story I'm about to tell took place.

My parents never took me to kid movies. In general, they treated me more like an adult than a child, and, for the most part, I preferred it that way. I saw my first Disney film while overseas, at the age of twenty-nine, and by accident. (The theater in Singapore hadn't changed the marquee; I thought

I had purchased tickets for *My Cousin Vinny* and instead saw *Aladdin*. Talk about a whole new world!) Growing up, I mainly attended the movies my parents wished to see. Usually, this took place during summers on the Cape. They'd place blankets in the back of the Volvo station wagon, cruise to the local drive-in, and encourage me to sleep, which happened swiftly. But occasionally during the non-summer months in Manhattan, they'd take me with them to a matinee, and I remember in particular an experience from the fall of 1971, when I was eight. The three of us walked to the theater around the corner on Broadway—The New Yorker, long since defunct—and my father bought tickets to a movie whose title held some promise for me: *Children of Paradise*.

Director Marcel Carné had filmed and produced his masterpiece in France during the Second World War, from the summer of '43 through January of '45. Set in the 1820s, the black-and-white movie starred the popular and attractive Arletty (one name, like Cher) and the brilliant mime work of Jean-Louis Barrault. Most major film critics have slathered the film with praise. Pauline Kael described it as "a sumptuous epic." Roger Ebert wrote: "Few achievements in the world of cinema can equal it." Leonard Matlin called it a "Timeless masterpiece of film making. . . . Wise, witty, and completely captivating." In his notes for the 2002 Criterion edition of the film, renowned critic and biographer Peter Cowie refers to it as "the ultimate exemplar of classical filmmaking, great acting, and a perfectly constructed screenplay."

My father, who had seen the movie many years earlier, would later explain that he recalled images of street performers and dancers during carnival festivities, as well as Barrault's achievements as a mime, and that he thought those qualities of the movie would appeal to me. I was, after all, a Pisces—an introverted, sensitive lover of the arts. In the past, I had had no difficulty finding ways to engage myself in my parents' activities.

And so the movie began, with its dramatic orchestration of drums and trumpets, and, to establish one of its primary themes (all the world's a stage), a closed theater curtain. The credits began to roll. I saw the name Pierre Renoir and perked up. I loved Renoir—the painter, that is, Pierre-Auguste Renoir—and had hopes that the black-and-white curtain would shortly give way to lush, romantic imagery. I'd spent considerable time looking at the Renoirs in the Metropolitan Museum of Art, and in a flash my memory brought me back to fleshy, peach nudes and that wonderful, large canvas (*Madame Charpentier with Her Children*) where the woman looks like her big, fluffy Newfoundland.

I peered up at my mother and asked, "Is this movie about Renoir?"

"No," she said.

I knew I'd seen his name. "Is he one of the actors?"

"No, it's not the painter."

The credits, which last for almost four minutes, continued to scroll, and I felt I had time for a follow-up. Plus, I thought I had something on my mother, that she had missed it. I leaned past her and whispered loudly, "Dad. Is this about Renoir? I saw his name."

"No," he told me. "It's his son."

"Is he a painter, too?" I asked.

"He's an actor." My father moved his hand in the air as though petting a cat. "Watch the movie."

Then the black-and-white curtain rose onto a black-and-white street fair in Paris. A tightrope walker hovered a few feet over the crowd. A shirtless man in leopard Tarzan shorts raised an iron bar, each end weighted with cannonballs. A clownish figure wearing tuxedo tails and boxer shorts guided a monkey that walked on stilts. Children swung in a carousel of swans. This wasn't so bad. There was a lot of crowd noise, almost enough to silence the musicians at the fair. And then the people started speaking in French. And then my life ended.

The whimsy of the street fair soon enough gives way to a tangled love story, and with every passing minute—with every grainy segue—I found myself disappearing into a black hole of boredom. After twenty minutes, when some man's watch gets stolen and Barrault mimes a reenactment of the crime, I knew I didn't have a shot at comprehending the drama. And what if I had? What if I had known French—would an eight-year-old boy care about a mime and a messy love story? Of course not. But not having language made the movie all the more intolerable since I couldn't follow the narrative or even weigh the importance of characters. When a blind beggar turns out to be a charlatan, regaining complete vision once he enters the town bar, how could I possibly understand his importance as a purely thematic figure? I wanted to know about the new plot twist.

"I thought he was blind," I whispered to my mother.

"He was faking."

"Why?"

"To make money."

I doubt that I actually asked how he fit into the plot; by that point, I had no idea what anybody was doing. It didn't help that Barrault as a white-faced mime seemed to be a different character entirely without the makeup. Nope—didn't put that together. And that's when I started a series of requests to know the time, to know exactly how many minutes had ticked away. The questions weren't well received. After the fourth, I knew I had to stop, even though this verged on child abuse.

I don't know how old one needs to be to embrace metaphor and theme over linear plot, but I couldn't do that at eight, nor did I find ancient footage of amorous desire the least bit enticing. An hour into the movie, Barrault and Arletty stroll the Parisian night in a scene of heightened French romanticism. He expresses his love; she leans into him, her heart-shaped silver earrings flickering in the evening light. They kiss deeply. I remember saying, "Oh my *God*—" Like Barrault later in the film, I had suicidal thoughts.

So you can imagine my euphoric relief when, after an hour and forty minutes, the curtain that opened the movie finally folded downwards from the top of the screen to the bottom. My whole body released itself the way it does when a raging fever subsides after days of punishing discomfort. "*Finally*," I said, exhaling and drawing out each vowel to make the word count, the thought heard, the feeling *known*.

That's when my parents explained this was the end of Part I.

Before setting out, my father—and my mother, too—must have assumed that I would make my own sense of this foreign-language film, translating words and narrative into my own story. In a bizarre, backhanded way, their decision complimented my own creative abilities. Still, I never forgave them, or, more accurately, I took pleasure in recounting the criminally boring experience, although not to the kids my own age, since they didn't seem to care. No one in my third-grade class had been subjected to a foreign film. They already considered me something of "the other," what with my parents being artists; this simply solidified their evaluation that we were weirdos. At school, I had no audience. But for my parents' friends, I'd mock the mime, mock the French kisses. I'd have the group howling. I wanted the whole world to know that I had been subjected to cultural torture and would stop only when my father said, "Okay, that's enough."

In the summertime, my parents dragged me to even more movies—*Roma*, *Fiddler on the Roof*, *The Omega Man*, *Patton*—but these were at drive-ins, and I could fall asleep in the car. The back of the '58 Volvo station wagon, in fact, made for quite a nice little fort. They'd pad it with blankets and pillows. I really dug it. I slept easily and deeply.

The only unfortunate experience occurred during the summer of '72 when we drove to see *The Godfather*. I had spent the afternoon with my friend Eric, playing in the underbrush behind his house in Brewster. The movie began, and I remember the sweeping orchestration, the fanfare, the warm Coppola browns, and the private meetings with Brando. It did nothing for me, and I nodded off. But I woke up because I kept scratching my ear, and as I regained consciousness, I realized I'd pulled off a tick.

On the screen, James Caan is about to learn that his sister has been beaten again.

"I've got a tick," I said from the back of the car. My parents hadn't expected my voice at all.

"What's that? Go to sleep."

"No, I just found a tick in my ear."

My mother sprang to attention and told me to climb over the seats so she could take a look, while James Caan drove like a maniac onscreen, completely focused on pulverizing his brother-in-law.

"I think I've got two," I said.

"Let me take a look. Come over here."

"I think I've *three*," I added, climbing over the seats. I handed her a tick, which she tossed out the window. "I know I've got more."

Caan's car paused at the toll booth. My mother started picking at my ear with her fingernail, checking my hair. And then the machine guns opened fire, and I wanted to watch, wanted to see the action. The windshield cracking, Tommy guns blasting their castanet rhythms, the side of Caan's car fully ventilated ("Hold still," my mother said) as Caan emerged from the sedan. My mother kept shifting my hair, checking my ear ("Was it your left or your right? I don't see a thing"), Caan now writhing on the asphalt in an electrified dance.

"Keep your head down," my father said.

I got sent back to my nest and woke up again sometime later, insisting I'd found more ticks in my ear. By the last count, I'd plucked five or six, but we never found the others. I kept crawling to the front seat, but we couldn't find those ticks.

From the drive-in experiences, I remember the starts of many films (George C. Scott standing in front of the huge American flag, Charlton Heston cruising the postapocalyptic city streets in his fancy red convertible) but I didn't finish seeing them for many years, and that's been an interesting experience—particularly this last week when, almost four decades later, I made myself watch *Children of Paradise*. Truth be told, the first half still lagged for me, and there's something to be said for Desson Howe's *Washington Post* review: "Its 188 minutes don't exactly jet by." I fought fatigue. But I suspect that had something to do with the unusual amount of expended energy: while reading the subtitles and watching the movie, I tried to interpret the film simultaneously in the present and the past. What would have bored me the most at eight? What do I appreciate now?

Recalling my first experience, I laughed when the curtain dropped to mark the end of Part I, but I also wondered if I had the energy and focus to launch directly into Part II. I decided to go for it—not to worry about remembering my eight-year-old self and just finish the experience—and a curious thing happened: I got into the movie. In fact, I loved it. I don't know if I'm sorry or pleased that my parents aren't alive to know this.

We returned to The New Yorker theatre in the fall of '72 for yet another foreign film. I was nine, now—still scarred from *Children of Paradise* and actively irritated at the thought of another soul-crushing afternoon. If my mother offered a bribe of sorts, I can't recall the agreement; it's far more likely she simply pointed out that they didn't do this often and would appreciate my understanding. *Children of Paradise*—or *Children from Hell*, as I called it—ran over three hours; this film didn't even last two. It had color, and my mother insisted that the Italian actor, Giancarlo Giannini, had a wonderfully expressive face. So, unhappily but dutifully, I joined my parents for a screening of Lina Wertmüller's *The Seduction of Mimi*.

Although I had no concept of the plot at the time, being still limited by the speed of my subtitle-reading skills, I can now provide a brief summary of the action through the first eighty minutes. Giancarlo hates his life, and for good reason. He's got a lousy, backbreaking job and a wife who's so frigid he can barely stand to touch her, even though she's fairly hot and he badly wants a child. He loses his job, heads for Turin, finds employment, falls in love with a babe, and knocks up his mistress. Now Giancarlo's a very happy man. To keep up appearances of matrimony, he makes a rendezvous in Sicily—only to find that his wife's pregnant! Giancarlo's out of his skin with anger. Rather than separate and enjoy individual lives, he allows his furious, Sicilian sense of revenge to overwhelm logic: His singular option, he decides, is to knock up the wife of the man who impregnated his no-longer-frigid spouse.

I think I would have enjoyed this film had I understood the plot. My mother tried to fill me in from time to time, but she had to concentrate, too; in her defense, it's not easy to simultaneously read subtitles, watch the film, and explain the action to a child while you continue to read and watch. So I couldn't enjoy the ridiculousness of Giancarlo Giannini's plan to cuckold his cuckolder, but the proposition scene slays me now. Dressed in a sharp dark suit, black fedora and shades, he awaits his prey outside a school building. He's shaved the corners of his mustache to a classy triangle. He's dressed to kill, and when she emerges from the building, he moves behind her with catlike dexterity.

"You're beautiful," he purrs in Italian. "You drive me crazy."

The object of his feigned desire is built like an Italian tank. She rotates her machine-gun mounted turret and dismisses him without a second thought as she grinds forward with children in hand. Her hulking physique's pressed into a suit the color of steel, and when she rounds the building's corner, we see for the first time an enormous boil-of-a-beauty mark—larger than a nickel, smaller than a quarter—implanted on her right cheek. Unfazed by her staggering ugliness, Giancarlo unleashes his overtures, and as the camera zooms to her face, the lens activates the mole's dimensions, widening its circumference and plumping out its girth. She snarls and snaps at him—*Niente!*—and suddenly, the camera films her from behind: one could set a bottle of Chianti on her buttocks. Then the Italian chase music kicks in—half tango, half screaming banshee—as she torments the city streets with her fat shoes. Giancarlo's relentless, whispering so close to her ear you can almost smell her through his nose.

In the next scene, probably the following day, he enters a sewing sweatshop and finds her working solo in the back. "I'm burning for you," he says. Then he takes off his glasses to give her sex eyes, but she remains obdurate and implacable, her nostrils flaring within a monumental head capped with wiry black hair. Finally, though, she cracks: if he'll leave, she'll meet him tomorrow at four in the afternoon.

It's an hour and twenty-five minutes into the film. I still have no idea what's going on and am bored beyond complaint; I'm a nine-year-old corpse seated in a cushioned coffin. They're now at a church, and I don't care one bit—although she's mercifully covered up: black dress, black blouse, black hat with veil, even large sunglasses. She's bickering about her wretched husband, although to me she just sounds like a chattering monkey. Yes, it's another *Children from Hell* experience, one made barely more palatable because of color, but Dantean nonetheless.

A minute or two later, they're tangoing outside a rental shack on the shore, the music as corny as their footwork. She continues to prattle ceaselessly, and I am ready to call my own time of death—but my parents, to my amazement, have been chuckling ever since the hunt began.

"What's so *funny?*" I asked, irritated both by the movie and the fact that I couldn't understand the humor.

Then Giancarlo grabs her and tries to force her carcass into the love shack. Much screaming ensues while he clutches her waist and wrestles with her the way a man might tussle with a wild boar. Still hollering in a soprano screech, she falls right on top of him—and *that*, I remember vividly, made me laugh. It hadn't been worth the ninety minutes of drudgery, but, yes, I laughed.

From the floor of this sleazy love nest decorated with a menagerie of Catholic art and trinkets, Giancarlo strains to winch her body across the mattress, a welterweight taking on a Sumo. I'm laughing and laughing harder as she tries to stop him. Finally, she grabs his collar with both hands and consents, her bubbly mole almost erupting in the camera's close-up.

The tango music returns as they begin to undress, lustfully glaring at each other. She pulls down her shoulder straps and stands, all the while staring him down. For a moment, the camera pans to the holy Mother Mary and baby Jesus in the springtime painting that blesses the bed, and then we're back to the seduction—to one of my favorite moments in motion picture history.

Having removed her scarf and blouse, she stands with her back to the audience and pulls her black dress overhead to expose circus-tent underpants. Giancarlo's eyes widen. No bra, just a huge expanse of back. And now the panties come down, revealing the most wrinkled ass I have ever seen. I'm *howling* now, utterly apoplectic, my preadolescent voice ringing throughout The New Yorker. Wertmüller, knowing the shot's a winner, repeats the footage three times so that the wrinkles tumble and unfold over and over and over again. My body's convulsing, my diaphragm seizing up; my mother's placed a hand over my mouth. She's laughing, too, but she's a bit embarrassed because I'm the only kid in the audience.

At the sight of her colossal glutes, Giancarlo blinks—four times, hard, each one seemingly longer than the last. The woman messes with her hair and turns her head in profile, highlighting the mole like a tumor on a CAT scan, and Giancarlo, after deciding with resignation to leave his sleeveless undershirt on, crawls into bed and clutches the sheets with both fists. And then, in a moment of cinematic genius, Wertmüller switches to a dramatically wide-angled lens so that the sheets at the bottom of the screen sprawl like an expansive desert, with tiny Giancarlo way off in the distance.

Enter an albino hippo. She crawls onto the bed so that all we see at first are her planetary butt cheeks. They fill almost 50 percent of the movie screen.

By now, my mother has me in a headlock so both her hands can cover my mouth, but I'm ripping them away partly because I need to breathe. Every time her fingers slip, I squeal and scream, snorting as I catch my spastic breath, my ribs aching, my face now completely wet with tears.

The tamed beast peers at the cowering Giancarlo and says, "I'm not used to this. What should I do?" Seconds later, her panoramic ass fills the screen again. Then, from below, the camera highlights her fleshy breasts, and she lands on him like a WWF wrestler making a final slam. Giancarlo's gasping for air; I'm gasping for air. It was a highlight of my childhood. For those few minutes, and for the days that followed, I'd found Paradise.

CHAPTER SIX

~

Cheap Seats

Baseball played a brief but passionate part in my childhood, and I've retained my first baseball memory: my father standing in front of the small television, his body awash in the flicker as he says to himself, "They're actually going to do it." October 16, 1969. I was six and stood by my father's leg. I asked what was happening, and he told me to be quiet. I'd never seen him watch baseball before—any sport, actually—but now the TV mesmerized him, his arms folded as he gave the screen his undivided attention.

Years later, I placed names to the players from that broadcast. Jerry Koosman, who'd pitched all nine innings, now faced Baltimore's second baseman, Davey Johnson, who connected, his ball soaring into left field toward Cleon Jones's glove. "Get it!" my father yelled, and then, even louder, "Yeah!" Soon, I heard car horns and shouts from the street. The entire island of Manhattan had been focused on their Amazin' Mets, and the city went berserk.

The '69 World Series victory didn't turn me into a baseball fan, perhaps because I didn't know the rules of the game. That changed after third grade. My class had gone outside for a springtime treat and the athletic department provided us with softball equipment. Since I didn't know how to play, I lay in the field and watched. I felt content, much like Ferdinand the bull from a favorite childhood storybook, but my ignorance of the Great American Pastime enraged at least one of my classmates, Paul, who happened to be positioned not far from me in left field. He glared and said, "I hate your guts."

Over the years, I've gotten a lot better at retorts, but the only words that came then were, "I hate your guts, too." That's when Paul, stocky but short, charged and leapt above my body. He no doubt planned to land with his fists in my face, but I retracted my legs and sent him flying backward, his arms hammering the wind. It was straight out of the movies; I can still see his body against the sky. And he would have cleaned my clock had he been given a second pass (I was a loner, not a fighter), but the kids and our teacher broke it up. Then my mouth soured as I imagined being sent to the principal's office, but our teacher just smiled admiringly. "You sure know how to defend yourself," she said, twice. The relief made me mute. She was so wrong—I'd just gotten lucky—but I felt great all the same.

That summer of 1973, I learned the rules of baseball and proclaimed myself a Mets fan. This turned out to be both a good and heartbreaking year for such a declaration. For the first time since '69, the Mets returned to the World Series, this time facing the Oakland A's, defending champions with the coolest player names in major league sports: Catfish Hunter, Vida Blue, Rollie Fingers, Sal Bando, Blue Moon Odom. They had Reggie Jackson, for crying out loud. It just wasn't fair. Still, the Mets managed to win three of the first five games. They just needed to win one of the next two. They didn't. And they didn't return to the World Series until 1986, when my interest in the game had long since withered.

Growing up, I heard stories of my father's softball games in Provincetown during the 1950s, a decade or so before my birth, and a particularly vibrant time for the arts. Provincetown became a favorite summer location for artists in all fields, and with some regularity they'd get together for a friendly game. (In one of the photos from those years, my father's walking onto the field to arbitrate a dispute. He said Franz Kline was furious!) The story I'd ask him to retell—one I've written about before—featured the painter Herman Cherry pitching to tenor saxophonist Zoot Sims. Cherry lobbed it in slowly, and Zoot connected with *all* of the bat. At that point of contact, Sims must have felt like Willie Mays. Then the ball exploded: The day before, a couple of the artists had carefully painted a grapefruit. Flesh and juice burst around home plate, the painted remains sailing down the third base line.

On weekends or after school, I'd often entertain myself with a tennis ball and a mitt. In New York, we had a small, gated area outside the brownstone about five feet by ten that had a three-foot wall at one end. (This is where, years later, we stacked the chunks of jacked-up sidewalk.) I would throw the tennis ball so it skipped from the cement ground to the base of the wall, arcing back to me until it popped into my glove. I created entire games from my own odd rules. Every catch was a strike. A dropped ball was a base hit; if it got by me, a double. If it bounced out of the area, a home run. I'd play all nine innings—the Mets versus the world!—and I could be Jerry Koosman or

Tom Seaver sweating on the mound, feeling the pressure of New York fans, my cap's hot orange letters emblazoned against blue cotton.

Of course, in my role-playing fantasies, the fix was in, and the Mets never lost. Somehow the opposing pitcher always tried something a bit too fancy, and the ball would soar over the low wall to the neighboring property. But those victories created a weird complication because it often meant an encounter with the landlady next door. She lived in the basement. Mrs. Walker. She was insane, yet seemingly aware of every pitching error.

I realize I'm entering the world of cliché here—the madwoman next door, the house of terror where friends enter on a dare, the landlady from a standard *Scooby Doo* episode—but, clichéd or not, Mrs. Walker lived. She'd emerge in the afternoon, almost always wearing a dirty nightgown, even in the winter, so that the shape of her body was unknown, at least to a kid who didn't want to stand close. She had wrinkled, papery skin and thinning hair, and she reeked of what I termed "old age." Even at a distance, and I always kept a distance even though she'd creep forward as I stepped back, the odor overwhelmed me, the way wet clothes smell when they've been left in a plastic bag. Nocturnal, she'd scold me for waking her up, and then she'd tell me stories of the night. And I had to listen because I'd been caught.

"They were changing license plates at three in the morning," she once said. "I walked out. One man, a colored man, had a screwdriver, and the other one told me to get the hell inside." Another time she described pouring steaming buckets of water onto the sidewalk in the middle of the night because of all the dog shit. (I remember this vividly in part because the word *shit* surprised me. I had tender ears.) "Hours," she said. "I cleaned for hours." It never occurred to me that she could have been lying, living in some whacked-out fantasy world; in New York, most stories end up being true, even if they begin as fiction. I'd stand before her, paralyzed, not knowing what to say, or how to escape. Then she'd slap me lightly on the cheek, a couple of times, and say, "Go play—but stay on your side."

In March of '74, I received a baseball bat for my eleventh birthday. I'm convinced my mother suggested the gift (she took care of holidays) but I strongly suspect my father picked it out because of the unusual color: forest green. In fact, I suspect my mother had hoped the bat would entice my father to join me in the park where he could pitch to me, and although that never happened, it *did* send me to Riverside Park for pickup games. On one of my first trips, three guys, all much older and larger, asked if they could check out my unusual present. I hesitated, and they smiled knowingly. "Hey, don't worry about it," the tallest one said. "If I'm gonna steal somethin', I'm gonna take, like, a million dollars, you know? I ain't gonna steal a *bat*!" This made sense to me, and they made no moves. I felt better about the world.

But the thought of actually attending a game didn't grab me until the year after I received my green bat, 1975, a time when the Dairylea milk company printed coupons on the back of each carton with varying points, depending on the container's size. Collect enough points and you could mail them in for a free Mets ticket. *Free.* I couldn't believe it. And if I got two, I could take my father. It would be my treat to him.

I became obsessed by this challenge, but I found myself in something of a squeeze play. The sale began in the spring; we always left for the Cape at the end of May. Also, my father could only go out on three nights of the week. As I've said, he'd leave for Philadelphia and Princeton on Sundays, returning, tired, Tuesday afternoon or early evening. He taught art classes in our home on Wednesday nights. This left Thursday through Saturday. It's even possible that Dairylea didn't offer weekend tickets (I can't recall now), but I had a three-day target at best, and I had to amass the coupons quickly in order to mail them off, have them processed, and receive the tickets. It could be done, but it would be tight.

I enlisted my friend Alan, who had no interest in baseball but adored milk. We became an impressive duo, consuming carton after carton of the requisite gallons, sometimes shoveling in malt-flavored Ovaltine, sometimes going pure. We milkaholics celebrated every dead soldier, and I can still feel the scissor blade puncturing the containers to create entry wounds, and the sound of the coupon being snipped into my awaiting palm.

My mother, I might add, didn't entirely shine on this plan, partly because she had to keep replenishing all this milk but also because she didn't feel food should be consumed in such a way. Usually I retreated at her slightest reservation, but I had my eye on the prize and just didn't care. I suspect, in fact, that she told my father just to buy the damn baseball tickets, but that he dismissed the suggestion. He would have admired the ambition and, even more, the goal (something free). As a child growing up in Philly, he had scraped metal from grates and sold the scraps for pennies. And I can't help but suspect he also would have weighed the odds and doubted my success: if we didn't get the tickets in time, he could talk to me about the limitations of sports—how athletics can't compare to the sustained, religious nature of creativity—and that it ultimately would be a disappointing experience. I heard such talks a lot growing up.

I should add that while we didn't attend sports events together, or other recreational outings, I spent time with him in galleries and art museums. One year, for example, he agreed to organize a monthly meeting with a group of women who wanted guided tours of downtown art galleries in Manhattan; he would scope out possibilities in advance and construct a highly selective list. Then they would congregate in our home for a discussion. I believe I was in eighth grade at the time because I recall telling my art teacher, Satish, about the experience: We zoomed through forty galleries in a single Saturday. Forty. It hardly seems possible, but I took a flyer or brochure from each place and counted them on my return.

A different day, we left for the Gruenebaum Gallery, where the proprietor had featured his own work, a gesture that could easily have been a narcissistic disaster. But I responded to his paintings; I thought they swung.

"I like this show," I said.

"Yeah," my father replied, slowly, quietly. "He knows how to get into the paintings. He just doesn't know how to get out of them."

I've since thought a great deal about that statement—and similar ones by Robert Frost and others—especially in the context of my writing, and my teaching, and my appreciation of jazz. Like a goldsmith, one must begin with fire and bright metal—the flames of inspiration and materials of substance—but then we must have the wisdom and skill to craft something lasting. Ultimately, mere excitement and energy are not enough.

Of the museums, I had favorites that will surprise no one: the Met, the Modern, and the Frick. One of my most searing memories with my father, however, took place at our only visit to the Hispanic Society of America in Spanish Harlem. Royal portraits introduced me to "the Hapsburg jaw," which I found as unsettling as images of deep-sea fish. And we spent a fair amount of time studying the museum's centerpiece: Goya's *Mourning Portrait of the Duchess of Alba*, better known as *The Black Duchess*. Goya completed the portrait in 1797, and historians wondered for over 150 years why the duchess's right hand pointed so unnaturally to the ground. Then, in 1959, after a cleaning that involved some removal of varnish, language emerged from the brown canvas patch: "Solo Goya." The world had its answer.

Or at least *an* answer. As my father explained the story, Goya and the Duchess had been romantically involved. *Solo Goya*, he explained, meant, *Only Goya*, as in, a woman who had love for Goya alone, despite her royal status.

"Had the Duke of Alba learned of their affair," my father said, "Goya would have been beheaded on the spot."

This version, I'm sorry to report, has more sexual intrigue and passion than the probable truth. The relationship between Goya and the Duchess remains ambiguous at best. Even the inscription, "Solo Goya," has been translated in various ways, including "Lonely Goya," suggesting a completely unrequited attraction.

But what interests me more than absolute narratives, whether torrid legacy or forlorn resignation, is the revelation itself: Did Goya ever imagine the word *solo* becoming public, and at what point did he decide to create and then bury the caption? I'm reminded yet again of Gaston Bachelard's statement, "He who buries a treasure buries himself with it." But, of course, I'm thinking as well about my father—not because I suspect he left any messages beneath the paintings' outermost layers but because I'd love to know what he expected me to do with, say, the vast tonnage of stuff in the Cape barn. What happens when private burial becomes public? Was he anticipating a kind of shrine, and, if not, what did he imagine my thoughts to be as I relinquished a legacy of junk collecting? Would I judge the outrageous accumulation to be the work of Only Sam, or Lonely Sam?

I loved all the museum and gallery outings, even our thoroughly exhausting forty-in-a-day marathon, and I'll forever be grateful for an upbringing saturated in the arts. Still, I craved that baseball experience, and Alan and I drove for the finish with one final, milk-intensive weekend. The tickets arrived roughly a week prior to the game, a Mets/Giants matchup scheduled for May 13, Alan's birthday. But it fell on a *Tuesday*. I couldn't believe it. I had written in bold letters that I couldn't go from Sunday through Wednesday. I cried, but my mother said she'd speak to my father, and, later that day, he said he'd make it happen. He would come home a little early, have a nap, and we could go out. I remember feeling guilty, and I told him it was okay, that we didn't have to go. But he said he'd make time.

On the day of the game, my father said we had to leave early (we *always* had to leave early) because we needed to walk seven blocks to Ninety-Sixth and Broadway, take the IRT to Times Square, and then switch trains to get to Flushing Meadows. "Better to give yourself lots of time," he said, and I delighted in his words; the longer the trip, the more time we'd have together.

It had rained very early that morning and the evening air still held the humidity. And I was overdressed. The temperature was in the mid-sixties, but my father told me that baseball stadiums got cold and that sitting in the bleachers was the perfect way to catch the flu. "Better to be overdressed," he said. I perspired a bit as we headed for the IRT, although it could have been from sheer excitement. Jerry Koosman was scheduled to start that night, and I couldn't believe I was actually going to see the man whose pitching prowess had so fully captured my father's attention six years earlier. I had a ceremonial baseball card of the last game in the 1969 series. Primarily gray, it read "The Sporting News" on top and, on the bottom, in caps bordered by yellow: "KOOSMAN SHUTS THE DOOR!" I'd held the card so many times that Koosman became for me the iconic image of a pitcher: left hand cocked, left leg stretched until his knee just about touches the mound, his right bent perpendicularly toward home plate. My father and I had seen that pitch thrown on TV; now we were going to see the pitcher—live.

I had equal excitement about many other players, especially sweet Bud Harrelson, Number 3, who'd also been part of the Amazin' Mets from '69. (In the 1973 National Championship series, he got into a brawl with Pete Rose. "I got in a good shot," Bud later reported. "My eye to his fist." I've detested Rose ever since.) Jerry Grote, Ed Kranepool, Félix "El Gatito" Millán, Rusty Staub—they'd all be there. And about a year earlier, the Mets had acquired Dave Kingman—"Kong," they called him—who stood six foot six and had more power than anyone on the roster. In fact, by the end of '75, he'd chalk up thirty-six dingers, a club record. Kingman averaged a home run every five games, and he hadn't connected in the last three. My odds weren't bad.

"Do you think Kingman will hit one out of the park?" I asked as we entered the station.

"Oh, don't get your hopes up," he said. I could have anticipated his every syllable. I grew up being told that expectations only led to disappointment. "I'll just be happy if it doesn't rain."

We approached the turnstiles and my father took out a token, worth thirty-five cents at that time, and dropped it in for me. We were on our way! Suddenly, I felt intense pressure in my solar plexus, my breath wrenched from my body like a dry heave. Simultaneously, my back seized up from pressure, and I stumbled through the turnstile, almost jettisoned, feeling bruised and bewildered. I turned around and bumped into my father, who stood just inches away. "Keep walking," he said. Beyond him, on the other side of the turnstiles, a guard leaned against the wall. He'd seen my father jam his body against mine so we could enter on one token, and I watched the officer shake his head, although he didn't say anything or step forward. Then I didn't know where to look.

"Keep walking," my father hissed.

When we reached the platform, I said, "You know, that guard saw you."

"He didn't arrest us, did he?" My father winked. Normally, I would have laughed—I always laughed when he behaved badly—but my stomach hurt.

While on the train, we didn't say much because of the subway noise, but when we waited for the train to Flushing, I asked if he'd ever been to a baseball stadium, and he said, rather dismissively, "Oh, sure," as though he'd gone every weekend. "I once saw Ty Cobb steal home." I recognized the legendary name, and as he told the story with all of its drama—Cobb at the end of his career, no one expecting such a daring move, the crowd exploding as he crossed the plate—I had the sad, strange feeling that nothing could happen at Shea Stadium to remotely compete with that experience. Not Kingman knocking one out of the park, not Koosman throwing a shutout.

Still, the arrival at Shea felt otherworldly, as though an enormous spaceship had landed before us. My father handed the Dairylea tickets to the attendant, and we began to ascend the steel inner-workings of the stadium. When we passed a public phone, I said, "Wait. I have to call Alan. It's his birthday."

"Make it quick," my father said. "We're almost at our level."

We had plenty of time before the game so I didn't feel any rush, and when Alan picked up the phone, I spoke loudly, rushing through my words, overwhelmed by the actuality of being at Shea Stadium with my father. And Alan had helped get me there. All those gallons of milk!

"What are you doing?" I asked Alan.

My father hissed: "Hurry up."

And then I had trouble hearing my friend. My father puffed his cheeks, and for a moment I thought he was spitting. Later he'd explain that he'd heard the drops of rain and wanted me to at least see the field while we were there. But I felt too excited to interpret urgency. Then the skies must have opened because the stadium echoed with a crushing, steady rhythm. It sounded exactly like people stamping their feet overhead, rattling the bleachers as they cheered. Koosman had probably taken the field, I thought, and I imagined thousands of New Yorkers celebrating the way they had when the Mets won the series in '69.

"I've got to go, Alan. The game's started. Happy birthday! Happy birthday!"

I beamed at my father's scowling face, not caring that I had missed the team taking the field, not comprehending the rainout. The whole stadium seemed to be cheering not just for their team but for the mere fact that we had taken a trip together, and I felt drenched in the sound of the bleachers roaring their metallic thunder.

CHAPTER SEVEN

~

Eternal Machinery

The situation required magic. 1976. The Boston Red Sox had dropped ten games in a row—their worst losing streak in sixteen years. In the previous season, they had won the American League championship, and their success, according to Sox pitcher Bill "Spaceman" Lee, was launched by the incantations of Salem's official town witch, Laurie Cabot: "In 1975, Laurie danced on the roof of the Red Sox dugout during a rain delay in Cleveland," Lee explains. "After that, our team won fifteen out of seventeen games and went on to meet the Cincinnati Reds in the World Series; I considered her magic potent." Now it was May of 1976, and the AL champs looked like a farm team, but they were back in Ohio, and a Boston television station decided to fly Cabot to Cleveland Municipal Stadium so she could cast a victory spell.

Cabot explained to anyone who asked that she knew almost nothing about baseball. She also insisted that her powers had no connection whatsoever with satanic ritual or black magic and went so far as to call her professional activities "pure science." She spoke of energy fields, explaining how each person (and, therefore, each group of people) generated specific kinds of energy. In the context of failure and dismay, those energy fields could become fractured like a severed, sparking electrical line. In essence, she wanted to rewire and amplify the team's source of power.

Dressed in a flowing black cloak, Cabot arrived early for the Red Sox batting practice and later sat directly behind their dugout. Her presence was not entirely welcomed. Carlton "Pudge" Fisk, the Hall of Fame catcher who had made iconic leaps during his winning homer in game six of the '75 series, his arms waving the ball fair as though he controlled the wind, felt she jeopardized their professionalism. And maybe this influx of negative energy slowed down her powers because Boston and Cleveland remained tied through eleven innings. (Herschel Nissenson from the Associated Press referred to her as "A slow-starting witch.") But then the Sox scored in the twelfth and sustained that lead. Shazaam! The streak was over.

I learned of the story that June, after my parents and I arrived on the Cape for the summer. We had a guest staying with us: Thorpe Feidt, a former student of my father's and my godfather. Today, Thorpe sports a trimmed Van Dyke and smartly cropped hair, but in '76, he remained all '60s in his appearance, his beard triangulated but full, his brown hair a raucous, curly frizz spreading outward and across his shoulders. In addition to being a brilliant painter, he was well read in matters of the occult, and he spoke joyously, with sweeping gestures, about this fusion of baseball and witchcraft.

I had offered to mow the lawn, and my father said he'd start the machine. I accepted. Starting the mower was more of an achievement than actually grooming the lawn—if, that is, one can accurately use the word *grooming*. Since we only returned to the house in the summer months, the fall leaves and winter snows compacted the compromised grass, but enough survived to rise knee-high by June. (Our lawn was decidedly not like the one described in a Coltrane poem by William Matthews—"plush as a starlet's body"—nor, I might add, is it now.) Also, the Jacobsen required a gas and oil mix, but he estimated proportions, which might explain why the mower belched smoke until the whole front lawn seemed engulfed in fog. From a distance, at least, the grass appeared more fumigated than cut.

My father had purchased this Jacobsen, the color and essence of rust, secondhand—auction or yard sale, I can't recall—and, from its purchase in the late '50s or early '60s until his death in 2003, we never owned another. In my adolescence, when I'd suggest a replacement, he'd spit the same reply: "Do you know what mowers *cost* these days?" I never did, nor did I ever consider arguing or suggesting otherwise; I had no hope for a reasonable conversation. He despised spending money to replace something that could be found, fixed, or purchased at a yard sale or flea market. It never bothered him that his hardcore philosophy almost always meant fierce struggles for simple accomplishments. And as an adult, when I could have given him a new one, I knew the gesture would not merely be dismissed but held with contempt. Once, for example, I gave him an expensive book on Rembrandt after he'd returned from the hospital. His whole countenance became a wince.

"Why the hell did you *do* this?" he asked.

"Because I knew you'd be so grateful."

He didn't thank me, but he did chuckle. It was one of my few wins with him.

The Jacobsen lasted decades thanks to a retired Cape local, Mr. Richardson, who repaired things simply to stay busy. He seemed charmed, or at least amused, that my father refused to let it die. That attitude probably spoke to New England frugality. "Good old machine," Mr. Richardson would say, smiling broadly. When we'd pick it up, my father always called him a genius and offered money, but Mr. Richardson steadfastly refused. So one summer, my father offered to draw a portrait of him or a family member—from a photo, not a studio session—and Mr. Richardson provided a cherubic photograph of his granddaughter. With dime-store pens, my father created a near-photographic rendering that astounded his good-natured friend.

As a gesture, the Richardson gift wasn't unique, and one good story concerns a garbage collector in New York, a man named Harold. He'd come across a box filled with oil paints, as well as a small, stretched canvas, and rather than crush them in the truck, he rang our doorbell to drop them off. (As I'm writing this, I wonder how Harold knew my father's profession. What kinds of exchanges, no doubt focused on trash, did they share?) Moved by this overture—and probably, too, by the sensibility—my father asked for a family photo. Instead, Harold returned with an eight by ten of Martin Luther King Jr., which my father very faithfully reproduced on the salvaged canvas. Harold almost wept when he saw it.

My father also created meticulous pen-and-ink portraits to help secure my position as a professional. Late into my graduate school years, for example, he drew a sunny portrait of my dissertation director, Bob Gross. (When I saw it displayed, Bob said, "He actually made me *handsome*.") And when I began my tenure-track job, he created a regal drawing of the novelist G. W. Hawkes, my older brother in the department. He actively liked both men, but he also, quite clearly, wanted to do what he could to ensure his son's independence. I've never forgotten that.

Prior to these, he drew a color, pastel rendering of Yusef Komunyakaa, one that appeared in 2005 for an issue of *Callaloo* that celebrated the great poet's artistry. It also included my short essay titled "Portrait of Gratitude":

My father, Sam Feinstein (1915–2003), would have enjoyed seeing his portrait of Yusef Komunyakaa on the cover of *Callaloo*, even though this particular work does not reflect the general nature of his paintings. Well trained in realism, he nevertheless found himself moving away from direct portraiture by the mid-1940s; in 1949, he began studying with Hans Hofmann, and his work turned more completely to abstract expressionism. Speaking of the principles solidified by Hofmann's teaching, he once explained to me:

You had your direct experience from the world around you, and simultaneously you were creating a direct experience not simply *on* the canvas, but *out of* the canvas, seeing the rectangular flatness of the canvas as a countenance in itself, or as a body in itself, which had to be brought to a vibrant life.

In the half-century that followed, my father created large, symphonic paintings responding to the dynamic range of nature and human emotion.

But as this cover reproduction makes clear, he never completely abandoned realism. I recall a number of times in my teenage years when he would pick up a cheap Bic ballpoint and photorealistically sketch his left hand ("Just to keep my hand in it," he'd say). He also completed several pen-and-ink portraits based on photographs, and those were almost always made gratis for friends or acquaintances who had done personal favors: one pal who frequently fixed our decrepit lawn mower and who never accepted payment, or an old family friend who used to repair our 1958 Volvo station wagon. These friends, I should add, appreciated this kind of art *far* more than abstract expressionism, and perhaps my father felt a certain amount of satisfaction in demonstrating to the community his prodigious academic skills. But in private, he dismissed those works as being "merely a coordination between the hand and eye."

So the portrait of Yusef is something of a curiosity, partly because the impulse to make the piece was not generated by such a specific or mundane circumstance. (As far as I know, Yusef has never repaired any of our gas engines.) In this case, the gesture had to do with a father's gratitude: I first knew Yusef as my mentor, then we became collaborators on books and good friends. In fact, the development of my relationship with Yusef in many ways paralleled my father's personal history with Hofmann, and so he fully appreciated both the invaluable knowledge that I received as a student and the depth of friendship that followed.

The moment of my father's inspiration arrived unexpectedly when he encountered a poster on Broadway advertising one of Yusef's readings. Struck initially by the shock of familiarity—seeing the face of someone he knew fairly well—my father then became captivated by the photograph itself (taken by Don Getsug and later reproduced on the back of *Thieves of Paradise*), which he found far more animated and suggestive than most publicity headshots. He later obtained a copy of the poster, and that became the basis for this portrait, although he took great liberties as well: the drawing incorporates what the photograph provided (facial features, details of the glasses) but also what he was responding to *in* that photograph (warmth, wisdom, movement), as well as his own memories and associations from their several encounters. In the photograph, for example, Yusef stares directly into the camera's lens; in my father's piece, he looks away from us—head slightly lowered and turned, eyes glancing upwards. Those familiar with Yusef's profoundly shy nature will agree that the drawn portrait more accurately reflects his demeanor and spirit.

I should add that the friendship Yusef enjoyed with my father extended beyond my relationship with them individually, and it seemed grounded by a mutual admiration for each other's art as well as genuine personal respect. While my father did not know a great deal about contemporary poetry (despite my efforts!), he admired writers and writing, and he knew, of course, Yusef's astonishing accomplishments. He was also well aware of Yusef's complex personal history: that he had grown up in a deeply segregated America and had lived through the terrors of racism in the South; that he had served and survived the war in Vietnam; that he had, in effect, experienced the extremes of mankind and had opted *not* to embrace self-pity—or self-aggrandizement, for that matter—and had instead, with humility and brilliance, concentrated on being a poet. It was the kind of dignity and class, fused with a celebration of art, that my father admired as much as anything else in the world.

Conversely, Yusef knew that my father and his family fled Russia in 1919 and spent two years on a journey to America that included kidnapping and bribery, conversations at gunpoint, and ransomed jewelry. He knew my father's family had lost all its money when the Russian currency changed during their immigration, and that they lost everything once again when the banks collapsed during the Great Depression. And he knew that no one in my father's family valued painting—that, much like Yusef, he had pursued art without family guidance or support. In short, these two men may have grown up in different decades from different backgrounds, but they shared a remarkable resiliency and integrity, as well as an ebullient creative drive with a genuine vision of their art.

I mention these general but significant similarities to frame an important point about the portrait itself: my father never dismissed this rendering the way he did so many others. This is not to lay claim that the portrait achieves, say, the radiance of his grandest acrylic canvases, but it conveys far more than "merely a coordination between the hand and eye." In the evocative gaze through moon-round gold rims, or the complexity of the lips not quite parting into a full smile (what has caught Yusef's attention, and how has he already begun to interpret the moment?) my father's portrait evokes some of the gorgeous polarities that resonate in Yusef's poems, such as the closing lines of "Anodyne":

> I love this body, this
> solo & ragtime jubilee
> behind the left nipple,
> because I know I was born
> to wear out at least
> one hundred angels.

I own several of my father's realistic pieces, including his first draft of Mr. Richardson's granddaughter, which he felt had become too dark so he started over. (It's beautiful; the revision was better.) And I also have a self-portrait that he made by request of a favorite student, Bonnie Warwick, whom he loved. His consent astonished everyone, but he came through with his promise, albeit not a contemporary portrait: It's of little Sam, roughly three and still in the Ukraine, with soft dark eyes that would make the entire rendering tender by nature were it not for his dramatic widow's peak and, in his right hand, a whip.

What is the nature of portraiture? Is it not to keep the spirit alive—and, as soon as one considers that premise, isn't the innate oxymoron (body vs. soul) an evident failure? Since childhood, I have been eerily attracted to the portraits that adorn Egyptian mummies, those innocent faces in no way betrayed by the mortality of flesh. And yet, why did the frightening Hapsburgs commission paintings? At what point does our vanity—our desire for eternality—overshadow the reality of death?

Mr. Richardson died in 1995 at the age of eighty-one, and somehow my father kept the Jacobsen smoking until his own death eight years later. To his credit, he kept a lot of things going, and, of course, he hoarded so much that one came to expect some kind of resolution when faced with challenges requiring tools. (He never used a typewriter, much less a computer, but in the barn I found an antique Royal Corona and, for that matter, a printing press.) He used dull loppers to trim the privet hedge—as well as an electric meat carver. And once during a visit to New York, when my wife asked if they owned a hair dryer (despite my caution), he sprang from the kitchen table and descended into the cellar. He eventually emerged with an avocado-and-yellow contraption worthy of an *I Love Lucy* show: a helmet with a hose that (good luck!) plugged into the wall. He had gone to so much trouble that Marleni couldn't refuse. The contraption began to hiss with lukewarm, musty air. "This is great," she yelled as she gassed her head.

Radios with broken antennae became Calder-like sculptures with aluminum foil and metal coat hangers (even wooden sticks!) positioned to inspire a better signal. The only new radio he ever purchased was given to me for my thirteenth birthday. (I'm not ashamed to say it's in the barn and still in use.) In my father's final years, he had two yard-sale toasters on the kitchen counter because each could only warm one slice; you'd depress both machines, see which sides glowed, then drop in your bread.

The Cape barn housed a tremendous number of garden tools and handyman items. If you required a metal scraper, he would emerge after a hunt and bring you a bucketful. (He took great pride in finding things within the chaos. "Like a homing pigeon," he'd say.) Ten or twelve handsaws hung on the southwest wall. Tools could always be found—but *sharp* tools did not exist. Why? Because what he owned had been previously discarded and happily sold on the cheap at yard sales. Even shaving razors would be used for years, so dull that he would walk around the house, "scraping my face" as he'd put it, until the blunt metal eventually tackled his Ukrainian stubble.

Tools that did not have edges and objects meant to assist in projects also required adjustments and safety awareness. The medium-sized ladder, for example, was missing a bottom claw; the forty-foot extension ladder didn't lock properly and required ropes to secure the center lest it collapse beneath you. You can imagine the acrobatics required to saw an elevated tree limb. (In retrospect, it's astonishing that neither of us broke any bones.) While I rarely pruned the foliage, the combination of rickety ladder and dull tools shaped my adolescent summers: each year, I'd be assigned a side of the house or barn to scrape, prime, and paint.

My buddy G. W. likes to say, "It's a poor worker who blames his tools." I now confess that I was a poor worker. None of the assorted scrapers and chisels allowed for fine craftsmanship. One had to press the dull edge with unnatural force to chip the clapboards clean. Often this resulted in an awkward slip and gouged wood. Hours elapsed with minimal results, and no effort ever induced an encouraging "Nice job." Given the ongoing decay of both the house and barn, the summers always demanded a farcical facelift. It was Sisyphean.

In the introduction to *In Artists' Homes*, Roberta Kimmel writes:

> An artist's sensibility leaves its imprint everywhere. The home, especially, offers not only a glimpse into the aesthetic that shapes an artist's work, but often the inspiration behind it. When the same decision making and thought process an artist uses to create a work of art continues beyond the studio into his or her home, the result is a space that reflects—sometimes directly, sometimes more subtly—the spirit, feeling, and character of the artist's work.

While there's plenty of truth to this, general claims stemming from that assertion would suggest that every artist creates a *Better Homes & Gardens* abode. My only hope of making a personal connection seemed to be Kimmel's chapter titled "Collecting, Amassing, Accumulating" about the artist Arman, who moved from France to New York City because he "fell in love" with Manhattan's "paradise of accumulation." The title of the chapter came from the artist's voice: "One thinks about three categories: collecting, amassing, and accumulating, which are translated in my work. It is a pack-rat instinct that is embedded in my mind, and I use it in my work as I use it in my home." But what he collected was obviously *collectible*; in the photographs, his home looks like a somewhat overcrowded museum as opposed to a true pack-rat's den. Kimmel describes the experience of entering the home: "Two full suits of traditional seventeenth- and eighteenth-century Japanese samurai armor greet visitors with their fearsome intricate beauty, and more headpieces fill the hallway shelves. One of the world's largest groups of brass Bakota sculptures from Gabon hold court in the dining room, and Arman's third-floor office is home to his collections of colorful Bakelite and Fenolite radios, crammed edge to edge on shelves. All are objects of function, past and present."

And there it was, the defining separation: "objects of function." My father almost eschewed functionality. The shape of something mattered more than its original intent. Beyond that, something semifunctional yielded more interaction with the user and therefore provided greater enjoyment for him. Consider television, for example. In his lifetime, he never purchased a TV in a store. In New York, the TVs of my childhood had been discarded on the street by people who had lost patience with bad reception or had upgraded to color. (Not until my college years did I find out that Victor Fleming had filmed most of *The Wizard of Oz* in Technicolor. The yellow brick road was yellow; the ruby slippers, ruby!) This meant that watching a show began with challenge: you *worked* with the television—pivoting the set; expanding, contracting, and redirecting the rabbit ears; connecting the antennae to coat hangers, broken hasps, and other metal objects; repositioning your own body, for that matter, sometimes standing so close you appeared to be counting the electronic snowflakes—until you coaxed a reasonable image out of the grain. A program didn't just mean entertainment; it meant triumph.

Yes, clarity meant success, but he deemed too much clarity (something we never worried about) "offensive." This was in keeping with his thoughts about entering a film midway through: the viewer should be a creative participant, not just a passive audience member. For this reason and others, he refused to install cable TV. (He also insisted that men would damage the roof, although we all knew it had more to do with saving money.) On the Cape, the last television I saw him acquire arrived in 1982, the summer after my freshman year in college, and it was a real '50s-style behemoth. Although the tube itself was only twenty-two inches, a wooden console encased the TV. Of course, since he'd purchased it at an auction on the town green, we had no way of knowing its quality, and it turned out to be somewhat inferior to the smaller, existing set. But after lugging it across the lawn, onto the porch, into the kitchen, up the back stairs, and across the house—and after making room for it by adjusting bureaus and other heavily settled artifacts—we weren't about to switch. We'd make it work, goddamn it.

Like all other Dennis town auctions, that one had been a success for my father, and I have photographic proof of the haul. In the slide, the items spread across the lawn seem smaller than in my memory, and listing them may decrease their size all the more. The TV's a centerpiece of sorts, but it's surrounded by a radio and a few house shutters; several pairs of shoes, sneakers, and boots; books and records, including Paul Weston and His Orchestra's *Music for Memories*, featuring a pastel, "come hither" gal on the cover; various garments and towels; two or three carpets, at least one of which has substantive length and width; something that looks like a drying rack near a low-level wooden table; a large jacket with a bright, hunting-orange interior, as well as a ceramic vase that looks vaguely Mexican; one old sewing machine attached to its table; a big bag of nails (as I recall) and several hernia-inducing boxes labeled Florida Tile. The shutters and tables obscure plenty more.

To be fair, some of this was mine: a pair of leather boots, and the Paul Weston record, which I purchased for its cheesy cover. And, also to be fair, I loved these events, and the zany thrill of watching a master scavenger in action. I loved that he was *known* there, one of the town's great characters. It never crossed my mind that, one day, I'd be responsible for the aftermath of his maniacal collecting.

Of all the mechanical things requiring upkeep, the largest was our car. My parents had purchased a 1958 Volvo station wagon secondhand in 1959, four years prior to my birth. In '59, my mother was twenty-seven, my father forty-four. She knew how to drive; he did not—although he would receive a driver's license with that car and never drove another. Like the Jacobsen mower, the Volvo remained on life support until his death.

The Volvo (a 445 Duett, I've learned from online sources) was dark blue with gray trim around the windows, with a bulging rounded hood and wheel wells. It had two doors, as well as two doors at the very back that opened for a spacious storage area in lieu of a trunk. In our town of Dennis, and for most of the Cape, no one else drove that vintage, and its presence became all the more rare (and therefore defining) as the decades rolled by. The Volvo announced my family's return as loudly as an air-raid siren.

The Volvo was kept alive by Danny Walker, who ran a Getty Station around the corner from us on land that's now a well-groomed grass lot with benches, though no one spends time there. Again, my mother did most of the driving, and she had both great beauty and charm. (One spirited holiday party, Mr. Walker admitted to his niece, "That gal has great legs.") After her death, maybe out of respect for her spirit or perhaps simply because of the challenge, Mr. Walker continued to repair the vehicle, often improvising parts when the appropriate replacements were unavailable.

Even those who didn't identify the Volvo with my family benefited from its significant size and unusual presence on the road, and that's because I've never known a worse driver than my father. This has a lot to do with his late start (my mother taught him to drive when he was about fifty) and limited exposure (she continued to do the vast majority of the driving during her lifetime, and they only used the car during the summer). But it also had to do with his nature: He drove the way he walked the streets of Manhattan, with the determination of Moses and an unflagging belief that the sea of oncoming vehicles would part for his dramatic entrance. He literally turned *into* oncoming traffic, calmly explaining to me during these kamikaze maneuvers that the drivers would inevitably let him through. Stop signs were optional. As Mr. Walker once said, "He should paint that car red so people can see him from far away and pull over."

What *didn't* my father hit with that car? People, thank God. But he backed into poles and trees and fences. He backed into his last wife's car (with her in it). He even got busted for a hit-and-run: The cops telephoned the house because someone had witnessed the crime. Not surprisingly, it took place in a parking lot outside a thrift store.

"I had no idea I hit anything," my father said to me, shrugging and trying to look as innocent as a filler in a police lineup. "I didn't feel a thing."

I nodded, as usual, and didn't challenge his summary. But I knew better. Around that same time, I had gone to the supermarket with him, walking a few steps behind, and saw his coat accidentally brush against and knock off the shelf a large bottle of spaghetti sauce. It supernovaed on the linoleum. He turned around and glared—at *me*, as though *I* had done something—and said, "Come on, let's get the hell out of here!"

I'm convinced he knew very well that he'd struck that car outside the thrift store, but I'm also convinced that culpability and guilt disappeared when he considered financial retribution. And while he always blamed something or someone else for his accidents, he could not dismiss the reality of the dents themselves. So he experienced enormous pleasure when Danny Walker introduced him to a product that allowed one to smear a metal compound that acted like quick-drying cement. Now the car became a sculpture to repair. It required finesse, as well as a finishing coat. Yes, even the car had come to require his nurturing.

I don't recall if the major dent repairs took place during the summer when he repainted the entire Volvo, but I do know what happened when he next drove to the Getty station for gas. Danny Walker stepped out to the pumps and eyeballed the revitalized exterior.

"You got a new cah," he said, dryly, knowingly.

"No," my father replied. "I just painted it."

Mr. Walker scanned the Volvo's expanse, and nodded. Then he said, "You're an ah'tist, ain't ya?"

"Yes," my father replied.

"Hmmm. Why didn't you paint stripes, or butterflies?"

I never saw the car again after my father died. It was sold for cash, or maybe just scrapped—I don't know. But the Jacobsen lawnmower remained in the barn, and, yes it's true, I tried to start it up, but I didn't try very hard. My mind began to re-film the scene with Thorpe: my father becoming more enraged as the engine continued to fail him despite sandpapering the out-dated spark plug and adjusting the choke in all positions. From time to time, Thorpe would thrust his fingers in the direction of the machine like Cabot trying to adjust the energy field. Bare chested, my father pulled and pulled and pulled until he swore a final time and we all went inside.

The Jacobsen ended up in one of the many Dumpsters, and I learned what a new mower costs these days. It didn't break me. Now, at the start of each season, I wheel it out of the barn and fill the tank left dry for the winter. And when I pull the engine cord, without expending much energy, without the anxiety of my father's fury, without psychic intervention from witches and spells, it starts, and I release the choke.

CHAPTER EIGHT

~

Exotic Dennis

I can't recall when they first landed on our property, nor can I tell you how quickly they took over. I can tell you that we'd battle them each summer, and each summer we lost ground. By the time my father died, the backyard had completely yielded to the bamboo's tenaciousness.

My father planted the tropical stand because he wanted a natural fence between our Cape house and a gravel lane used by neighboring homes. He claimed to have been misinformed; some strains of bamboo merely clump instead of spread, and that's what he thought he'd planted. When the growth became rapid and consuming, he chose not to rip it out but to tame the growth—the same way he planned to tame a willow tree in the front yard and transform it into a "willow bush."

"Lopper the stalks as close to the ground as you can," he'd instruct me, referring to the growth nearest the house.

The philosophy behind that low-to-the-ground severing was twofold: It meant a clearer walking passage, but it also created the longest length of bamboo—which, of course, he began to collect. The goal of a bamboo fence never materialized, though the second floor of the barn quickly relinquished its pockets of oxygen to the drying stalks. At one point, a New York student of his, an outstanding classical musician, told him that oboists paid large amounts of money for bamboo reeds. "I thought I'd found my fortune," he'd tell friends. But again, alas, his turned out to be the wrong strain.

How hard is it to kill bamboo? Almost as hard as saving a sand castle against the tide. This type spreads through rhizomes extending as far as a hundred feet from the plant. In the process, it creates clusters, hubs of new roots, then spirals from each cluster into new clusters. It travels like connections on the Internet: the underworld wide web. Thus, you cannot spray a stalk and kill its offspring; even if you manage to poison one shoot, the node-like structure stops the poison from reaching even the first cluster. Ripped from the ground, the root balls look surprisingly similar to the just-hatched offspring in *Aliens*—"facehuggers"—an inescapable image, actually, if you know that monstrous form. (For the facehugger dissection scene, the production team manipulated sea creatures that could have come from the Cape: a horseshoe crab with oysters.) Acid for blood. An outer layer of protein polysaccharides, and shedding cells replaced by polarized silicone. Isn't that the same as these vicious rhizomes that some people claim can be killed with glyphosate herbicide only to fail, to the have the yard consumed by these—

Stop me. I want to tell you everything I know about the evils of bamboo. I want to bore the crap out of you the way Melville forces his readers to experience every layer of a whale.

I am still at war, although of late I'm winning major battles. After the house passed to me, I hired a young guy with a California spirit and a Bobcat to excavate the yard, leaving a five-foot swath of bamboo along the property line. Then we sank a thick, specialized liner along our side—because my father was very right to this extent: a natural green fence sure beats an artificial one, or a lack of privacy.

And, truth be told, as a teenager, I found the wilderness of bamboo exotic. I knew of no house on the Cape that featured such a tropical expanse, and I'd not been to, nor even dreamed of visiting, Asia. (My marriage to a Singaporean, and subsequent travels throughout the region, took place years in the future.) We were an anomaly. Sure, it was tedious and completely unsatisfying to keep hacking at the bamboo, but the forest itself was pretty cool.

And it became all the more cool with the addition of a pool table. That's right: a full-sized billiard table. It had gone up for sale at the Dennis Town Auction but no one bid, mainly because the bumpers were in really poor shape and most of the cues had warped. And, of course, it had to be moved; I can't imagine many people expected to leave with something the size and weight of a pool table. My father offered three bucks, plus fifty cents for a Ping-Pong table. Sold! Then somehow we loaded it into the back of the Volvo and, once home, wheeled it on my childhood red wagon, balancing and heaving until we reached the back of the house. The folding Ping-Pong table lay across the top, and then we covered the layered union with an oil tarpaulin.

Leveling the table required strength and finesse, and a good rain could easily betray a hard-earned win. As I said, the bumpers had been abused, one section so smashed that balls hit and thudded to a stop. Although we lopped bamboo to create a reasonable circumference of space around the table, one inevitably had to negotiate one's cue with the stalks. None of this concerned me. I loved being out there—loved the challenges, and the anachronistic nature of the whole setup. Who but my father would have envisioned an outdoor pool table on the Cape, surrounded by a bamboo enclosure?

By this time in my life, I had begun to purchase jazz albums, and the annual town auction in Dennis proved to be a great fishing ground as I trolled for old recordings. Around the auction tent spiked into the Village Green—just a short bike ride from our house—church volunteers presided over fold-out tables stacked with donated goods, including LPs. Most of the music bins got log-jammed with soporific sessions by Engelbert Humperdinck, Andy Williams, the Ray Conniff Singers, and others, but every now and then I'd find a recording of lasting quality, even an indisputable gem. One August, for example, I paid ten cents for Count Basie's *Basie Land*, which, unless it's an outstanding forgery, the Count had autographed. As a teenager, I filled in my collection—and, yes, this was *my* collection—with artists who wouldn't have been on my radar had I not found them accidentally, like trumpeter Jonah Jones or even the great Dinah Washington. At a dime or a quarter apiece, the sales allowed me to purchase work I knew I wouldn't love but wanted for the sake of my growing library: recordings, for example, of big bands led by Glen Gray, Glenn Miller, or the Dorsey brothers. Despite the poor odds of finding something extraordinary, the auction unfailingly filled me with joyous anticipation.

I bought new LPs not so much for historical breadth but as extensions of live experiences. At fourteen, I heard Ella Fitzgerald with the Oscar Peterson Trio, a time when Pablo Records pumped out sessions by those artists. Even through mediocre stereo speakers, the sounds of Joe Pass brought me back to concerts where I'd heard him live—the rush of human experience—and transformed the LPs from artifacts to mementos. But so many great musicians had died before I started listening with real knowledge, and I by no means limited my purchases by actual encounters. I had never heard Thelonious Monk, for example, but I had more records by Monk than anyone else.

I realize now that my efforts to accumulate LPs subconsciously reflected a desire to connect with my father's nature, and that my own impulses to accumulate stuff sold for pennies might inspire parental pride. But mainly, of course, I purchased albums for knowledge and pleasure. In my late teens, I played the clarinet and saxophones seriously enough that I imagined a career as a jazz musician. Nothing in my life provided greater joy and freedom.

As my record collection swelled, so did my identification with the musicians' careers and lives. I pored over liner notes and bought books to supplement my knowledge of the sound. The wider my expanse of records, the happier I felt; eventually, I began collecting obsessively, often with a completist state of mind: How could I *not* have everything waxed by, say, Charles Mingus? In some respects, records served a purpose similar to my Legos in childhood. Unfailing. Limitless. Friends. "Is it so wrong," asks Nick Hornby in *High Fidelity*,

> wanting to be at home with your record collection? It's not like collecting records is like collecting stamps, or beermats, or antique thimbles. There's a whole world in here, a nicer, dirtier, more violent, more peaceful, more colorful, sleazier, more dangerous, more loving world than the world I live in; there is history, and geography, and poetry, and countless other things I should have studied at school, including music.

In addition to my search for music of lasting value, I got perverse pleasure in acquiring the wackiest stuff I could get my hands on. I can't fully explain this urge, except to say that, for whatever reason, I'm still pleased to own such albums as *Phantom Foley Plays Piano Rolls*, with the Phantom's maniacal laughing on "When You're Smiling," or *My Mother the Ragtime Piano Player Mrs. Mills*, with the enormous, pasty Mrs. Mills herself on the cover, smiling as though she's consumed her eighth dessert. (The host of Australia's radio program "Get Out Those Old Records" frequently refers to Mrs. Mills as "the greatest piano player in the world.") I also enjoyed finding LPs that had no doubt been donated by disapproving Cape parents whose children had finally left for college. I'm thinking now of David Peel & the Lower East Side's *Have a Marijuana* ("Recorded Live on the Streets of New York"), or Country Joe and the Fish's *I-Feel-Like-I'm-Fixin'-to-Die* ("Contains Giant Full-Color Fish Game Complete with Instructions"), its cover showcasing the musicians dressed as a wizard, a Mexican bandit, a hippy soldier, a pope from outer space, and a roast pig. I found a copy of *Their Satanic Majesties Request*, with its glued-on, eight-by-eight 3-D image of the Rolling Stones dressed in psychedelic, we-can-outdo-the-Beatles garb. I bought Julie London's *Make Love to Me* featuring "Go Slow," a tune that includes her plea to "take it easy on the curves" and concludes with a passionate whisper: "You make me feel so *good*." And one summer, fishing through the bins, I landed an LP that made me feel like a lucky Ahab. The cover featured a trumpeter donning a frayed straw hat, both his neck and horn draped in festive pink leis, the title itself inked in passionate purple. Bobby Hackett: *Hawaii Swings*.

Many articles on Bobby Hackett begin with the disclaimer that they're talking about Bobby, the thin cornet and trumpet player, not Buddy, the hefty comedian. Consider my disclaimer made. But this is not to say that Hackett was a stiff. Quite the opposite. According to everything I've read, and the conversations I've had with those who knew him, Bobby Hackett was a sweet, good-natured person who could bust up a room with his sense of humor. In *Jazz Anecdotes*, Bill Crow recounts several splendid stories, including the time when a friend, knowing that Hackett never criticized anyone, challenged him to say something about Adolf Hitler. Hackett replied, "Well, he was the best in his field." Another time, a Canadian customs agent pointed to Hackett's trumpet case and asked, "Is that a musical instrument?" Hackett said, "Sometimes."

Hackett recorded *Hawaii Swings* over three days in April 1959, less than a month after my personal favorite, *The Bobby Hackett Quartet*, with pianist Dave McKenna (his close friend and a fellow Rhode Island-born Cape Codder). Glancing at the cover image, one would assume that some hokey producer latched onto the concept while vacationing in Honolulu: after five or six umbrella-speared rum drinks beneath a Hawaiian sunset, the suit thinks, "Let's get little Bobby to blow some horn with these hula bands." Not so. Bob Carter, a bassist and arranger who'd been born Bob Kahakalau, concocted the idea after a trip to his homeland. And, as Dan Morgenstern has pointed out, "the idea was neither new nor far-fetched." Nor was this an unprecedented or unique concept album. I'm thinking, for example, of Martin Denny's wildly popular *Exotica* from 1957, and *Taboo: The Exotic Sounds of Arthur Lyman*, and Augie Colon's *Sophisticated Savage*. (Flip through Jennifer McKnight-Trontz's *Exotiquarium: Album Art from the Space Age*. It's a gas, baby!) In fact, record companies pressed Hawaii tribute LPs throughout the '50s and '60s. Many capitalized on the thought of a dream vacation, with vibrant sunsets across a wide expanse of water. Even Jimmy Rowles, one of my all-time favorite jazz pianists, joined a group called the Surfmen and waxed *The Sounds of Exotic Island*, also released as *Tradewinds Romance from Hawaii to Tahiti*. Buddy Collette, a well-respected jazz saxophonist and flute player, joined the Polynesians for *Aloha to Jazz*, the vinyl itself colored a vibrant, Hawaiian blue.

In the early '50s, the album that remained on the Billboard bestseller list for 153 weeks (a record yet to be equaled) was *Music for Lovers Only*, which sold an astonishing half million copies. Conceived, funded, and produced by comedian Jackie Gleason, this utterly nonthreatening, saccharine LP with arranged orchestration was antithetical to Hawaiian exoticism. The cover zooms in on a table with the remnants of a romantic encounter: two wine glasses; a man's hat; a woman's sparkling purse and white glove; a single key, perhaps for a hotel room; and two lit cigarettes (one with lipstick), facing each other in the ashtray as though they're about to hump. On the back of the LP, the liner notes read, "A wisp of cigarette smoke in the soft lamplight, the tinkle of a glass, a hushed whisper." (Gleason himself said, "The only thing better than one of my songs is one of my songs with a glass of Scotch.") Not everyone could get to Hawaii, but anyone with booze, candles, and a turntable could turn a bland apartment into an exciting getaway.

The Gleason LPs that followed his triumphant debut bore similarly provocative titles: *Music to Make You Misty, Music to Remember Her, Music to Change Her Mind, Music for the Love Hours, That Moment,* and *Music, Martinis and Memories.* The mood music albums saturated the homes of suburbia and revved up the repressed hormones of the mid- to late 1950s. His LPs became the make-out music of the time, and Gleason made millions on the sales. The pre-elevator-music string arrangements created a cushion for romance. But the key ingredient—the addition to the orchestra that Gleason himself insisted upon—came from the single brass instrument on those sessions for Capitol: the soft tone and mellifluous phrasing of Bobby Hackett. If you have a deeply generous ear, one that can somehow ignore the feathery background, the sweetness of Hackett's horn almost makes these musical come-ons listenable.

In an interview with Whitney Balliett from 1972 conducted at Bobby Hackett's Cape Cod home, the trumpeter talked about his wife: "They said it would never last with Edna and me. We met in Providence, where we were both born, when we were ten—at a Halloween party. I even left my ukulele at her house to give me an excuse to go back and see her." When I first encountered this profile, I assumed that Hackett had attended the party dressed as a Hawaiian, but I later learned that his earliest instruments were the ukulele, banjo, and violin. (He got his first cornet at the age of twelve; his mother, he told Balliett, kept trying to hide the instrument because she disliked the noise.) Could it be that a Hawaiian influence coursed through his artistic blood decades before Bob (Kahakalau) Carter suggested making the hybrid album?

The day after I purchased *Hawaii Swings,* I brought the record across the street to my Cape neighbor, Allan Perry, the grandfather I never had. (My mother's father died in Sweden when I was a boy; I met him a few times but only remember one childhood visit. My father's father died before I was born.) Allan had traveled with the Casa Loma Orchestra and had rolled joints for that band; having never tried marijuana, I found that *so* cool! He knew and exchanged letters with Louis Armstrong, and in his living room hung a studio portrait of Duke Ellington, signed to him "with deep affection." His heart belonged to the swing era, and he adored Bobby Hackett.

In the jazz tradition, encountering the previous generation can yield a deer-in-the-headlights thrill. I'll never forget the jazz producer Hank O'Neal saying to me, "I got a summer job as a plumber's assistant. I mean, I had to carry the slop from the basements. And I thought this was the most ignorant, buffoonish guy I'd ever seen in my life—until I found out that he had actually *seen* Bix Beiderbecke at the Alhambra in Syracuse, and that he had *seen* Django Reinhardt in wartime France."

So you can imagine how I felt: instead of being an apprentice for a "buffoonish guy," I touched the past with a neighbor I *adored*. I hooked and netted every story I could. Allan treated me like a grandson—like a son, really—and when he died, his wife, Ruth, who never cared much for the music, gave me the signed portrait of Duke Ellington. "This was part of your world with Allan," she said, "not mine." The photograph hangs in my office next to one of Dizzy Gillespie, a signed print of a portrait I took. But Ruth's gift remains among the most moving I've ever received. To this day, I can tear up looking at it.

Allan loved Bobby Hackett's tone and phrasing, the purity of his sound, and I couldn't wait to see his expression when I placed *Hawaii Swings* in his hands—for the humor of the cover image. Sure enough, he squinted his cheeks into a wince. "Aw Jesus . . ." he said. But then he added, "Well, it's Bobby. It can't be all bad. Put it on." So "Kohala March" started up, and we chuckled. And the *twang* at the conclusion of "Orchids from Hawaii" made us laugh. But by the fourth cut, "On the Beach at Waikiki," we'd both found a groove. The self-conscious fusion of cultures had given way to spirited swing. (What other music lovers can claim such forgiving assessments?) We had to admit we'd been prejudiced by the image-projected concept. It wasn't fabulous jazz, but it wasn't just a gimmick, either. Like Julie London's sultry shamelessness on "Go Slow" ("You make me feel so *good*"), the ridiculousness somehow turned into charm, the way a clever craftsman can transform kitsch into something not merely attractive but sought-after—or the way my father gave renewed life to that broken pool table.

Later that afternoon, Allan introduced me to the art of crabbing. He'd told me to wear shorts and the worst shoes or slippers I owned, and when we reached the creek, we walked a ways through the muck, our soles sucking up sand with every step, until we reached his favorite spot. That's where we baited fishing lines with half-rotten chicken necks, tying off the free end to poles jammed into the sand. Soon the lines began to move laterally, left and right. Then, with our nets almost flush to the creek bed, we slowly reeled in the blue crabs, so greedy for the flesh that they refused to release their claws until we scooped them up. Like the shock of blue vinyl emerging from the sleeve of Buddy Collette's *Aloha to Jazz*, the blue shells and dangerous claws magically emerged from murky waters until we'd caught a bucket full.

Before we returned home, Allan took me to a local joint where we ordered his favorite dessert, Mississippi Mud Pie. He'd had all sorts of surgeries by this point in his life and wasn't supposed to eat that lavishly—"Don't tell Ruth," he instructed me—but somehow the illicit nature of the treat made it all the more satisfying. I thanked Allan profusely for taking me crabbing, and he seemed to find my great enthusiasm quite charming; having crabbed and fished for most of his life, he viewed my naïve delight not with skepticism, exactly, but with bemusement, as though the simplicity of catching blue crabs couldn't possibly bring so much pleasure. And yet, I'd never had the opportunity to fish for my dinner—had never done anything remotely like this with my father—and the experience of collecting these bright, primordial creatures from the blackened water locked into my boyish delight in finding treasure. (How had Balliett described Hackett?: "a born-and-bred city slicker who lives in the woods on Cape Cod.") For me, this was exotic.

I visited Allan frequently, listening to music, hearing stories, and occasionally catching a Red Sox game. (Being able to *see* the ball on the television screen made such a difference!) I sought him out for his kindness, for his gentle demeanor that warmed the retelling of his memories and gave his bits of advice, which he sprinkled upon me in subtle asides, the challenging comfort of knowing I could grow slowly into an adult life.

So it's no surprise that I walked across the street for his guidance in the summer of 1980, roughly three months after my mother had died. I had returned to our house—maybe earlier than expected, I can't recall—and heard a woman's laughter from behind my father's closed bedroom door. I suddenly felt bewildered, lost in my own home. From the locked room, my father called out my name in the form of a question ("Sascha?"), and I said I was going to Allan's.

The woman had been a student, of course, and the tryst didn't last beyond the summer because she lived off-Cape and, oh yeah, she had a husband. But it ignited a sexual fire that inspired a rampage of "conquests," collected much the way he collected everything else. One of the few women close to his age had once been the lover of the famed underwater explorer, Jacques Cousteau. (My father said she made great eggs, and from then on, I only referred to her as Eggs.) But most were decades younger.

He wanted me to *know* about these women, at times providing graphic details—and not merely to demonstrate his prowess. In one case, for example, he knew I fully distrusted the woman, and he wanted me to like her, even to care about her. So he'd share her intimate secrets about, say, agreeing to her former husband's request that she sleep with another man while her husband watched. I suppose my father thought I'd feel more pity than disgust at her self-imposed degradation, but it didn't work.

The following summer—about a month before I left for college—he had a week-long affair with a student who happened to be the cousin of a current girlfriend. She stayed in the house; nothing was veiled. But the familial complexity of this situation, for them both, shadowed and invigorated their lust, much like the illicit romance in Howard Nemerov's poem "The Goose Fish": "And for a little time they prized / Themselves emparadised." So I was stunned to learn that he agreed to bring her, during the day, to the beach. (To quote Nemerov's poem again: "They stood together on the sand / Embarrassed in each other's sight / But still conspiring hand in hand.") My shock was twofold: First that he would go to the beach at all, and, second, that he'd risk being seen.

But apparently they snuggled and laughed like honeymooners in Hawaii, and I learned of their beach visit from someone else who had spotted them and wanted to know the dirt. Who was the woman, and was this serious? Sensing my discomfort, the man said, "It seems about right. He's had a year of mourning," and, after a momentary pause, I guffawed and replied, "You think he's been mourning for a year?" It seemed as though he cut notches on his bedpost as fast as I could collect records.

Perhaps narcissistically, I had expected a lot of private time with my father after my mother's death, but his panic and ego deposited me to the side. So I left for college with a sense of relief, actually—relief and great trepidation because I knew nothing about the college experience. With my domestic scene so disjointed, I didn't investigate my future with much focus. Both parents had attended art school—no touchstone there. I selected the University of Rochester because of its strengths in English and music, but had no idea what a dorm would be like. I imagined and planned on a hotel environment, so I failed to bring such necessities as towels. I boarded a bus on the Cape and sat through many hours of travel until I finally landed in Upstate New York.

Only then did I realize I had no idea how to get from the bus station to the campus, but, miraculously, the university had sent scouts, and someone offered to give me a lift. He'd been instructed to ask the green newcomers about necessities, and when he found out I hadn't even packed soap, he took me shopping. I borrowed towels from my new roommate, but then called my father and asked if he could send some. (It never occurred to me to shop in a department store. We'd never done such a thing.) So the box of *new* towels stunned me. Soon after, he mailed this short note: "I assume that by now you have received the towels I sent you. Don't give them away; towels cost a lot more than I've thought."

My records remained on the Cape, and I'd return to them each summer, reuniting with these old friends and eager to expand that circle. I purchased full-price, new releases slowly and with care, but I bought used records indiscriminately, especially at events like the everything-must-go tables on the grounds of the town auction—a collector's enthusiasm that may well have matched my father's (although my obsession had far greater focus). Like the root system of bamboo, one purchase could lead to countless others, including wildly unexpected discoveries. From the shores of Kitch-a-roony, just a mile or two from Cape Cod Bay, the twelve-by-twelve image of Bobby Hackett in Honolulu somehow landed in my hands. Not up to his greatest sessions but certainly worlds better than the Gleason LPs, *Hawaii Swings* makes me smile. "Music is supposed to be fun," Hackett once said. "No seriousness, no self-consciousness. Just blowing, and to hell with the musicology." A quarter of a century later, I can still recall the sound and feel of LPs as they flipped across my fingers, and the ticklish joy of the hunt itself.

CHAPTER NINE

~

Unrecognized Prophets

The scene's dramatically fractured and crisscrossed. From the bright sun's emblazoned shadows, we know the second floor and ceiling have flamed away. The shadows themselves seem more substantive than the physical remains, with one portal leading to another: a charred doorframe open to a second doorframe, open to half a wall. In the second door-less rectangle: a veiled dancer, her head completely blackened by shadow. Her right hand stretches heavenward as though unscrewing an invisible light bulb; her left, angled to four o'clock, splays fingers across a charred beam.

But whose hand thrusts itself into the photo's right edge, filling most of the gap created by burnt lattice? As with so many surrealist photographs by Clarence John Laughlin, the many questions about narrative—What happened here? Who is this skirted woman frozen in a plié? Who leaned the beam in the doorjamb as a prop?—taunt our imagination and, ultimately, become superfluous when experiencing the aesthetic drama of form itself. Firelight and now the sun's light shatter and splice the house into a Franz Kline. 1941. Beams lattice fingers. Plaster blasted. Looping, dangled electrical line transforming into snaking plaster crack. Ruin and celebration of ruin. *Día de los Muertos.* Within the solidity of the photographer's rectangle: relentless, ordered chaos. Laughlin titled the photo *The House of Hysteria*, a variation of *Spectre of Ruin (No. 1)* and part of an astonishing series called *Poems of the Interior World.*

The image recently appeared in a slim but thrilling book called *Haunter of Ruins,* in which Laughlin discusses the series:

> I tried to create a mythology from our contemporary world. This mythology, instead of having gods and goddesses—has the personifications of our fears and frustrations, our desires and dilemmas. By means of a complex integration of human figures (never presented as individuals, since the figures are intended only as symbols of states of mind); carefully chosen backgrounds; and selected objects, I attempted to project the symbolic reality of our time, so that the pictures become images of the psychological substructure of confusion, wants, and fear which have led to the two great wars, and which may lead to the end of human society.

But the New Orleans photographer also acknowledged the sheer aesthetic power of his imagery, quite apart from narrative: "For those not interested in symbolism, these pictures can be seen in terms of their basic level of meaning, which is design in terms of light and dark." That experience seems much more likely than his specific intent, describing the photograph as "A projection of the mental milieu of hysteria resulting from all the stresses and repressions to which contemporary men have been subjected, and which formed fertile ground for the wiles of the totalitarians."

Spectre of Ruin (No. 2), a companion photo from the same shoot, appears in *Clarence John Laughlin: The Personal Eye.* Here the first doorframe has been more centered, and the gaping hole is without an extraneous hand. The female figure stands straight and holds in front of her face something strung like a tiny loom, the reeds tight enough to once again obscure any specific features apart from her eyes. "From a scorched and partly demolished building," Laughlin explains,

> with its walls webbed with tortured and foreboding shadows, emerges a phantasm of ruins—a figure which intimates that there is an urge toward death in human beings, and that it is slowly gaining ascendency over the urge toward life. It seems to flaunt its entrails in madness. And between a blackened beam and the upper right of the furthest door, there appears, seemingly, a tiny head of Hitler (composed of parts of broken buildings).

In the chapter "House and Universe" from *The Poetics of Space,* Gaston Bachelard explains that "a house is first and foremost a geometrical object, one which we are tempted to analyze rationally." Without relying on fire to cause a visionary change, he asks us to reconsider the spirituality of form: The "prime reality" of a house is visible and tangible, made of well hewn solids and well fitted framework. It is dominated by straight lines, the plumb-line having marked it with its discipline and balance. A geometrical object of this kind ought to resist metaphors that welcome the human body and the human soul. But transposition to the human plane takes place immediately whenever a house is considered as space for cheer and intimacy. Independent of all rationality, the dream world beckons.

The publication of *Clarence Laughlin: The Personal Eye* appeared in conjunction with a 1973 show at the Philadelphia Museum of Art. Both the show and the book would have been significant markers in Laughlin's career, so it's telling that he chose to include *Spectre of Ruin (No. 2)* over *The House of Hysteria*. For Laughlin, I suspect, the emphasis on the mysterious figure—and, yes, the eye moves immediately to her—locked into his passion for mythological narratives. It defies the "basic level of . . . design in terms of light and dark" and almost demands a literary interpretation. But I find myself more enamored of *The House of Hysteria*, and I suspect my father would feel similarly—not because it eschews myth (it most certainly does not) but because it provides a more propulsive geometry. Because the image seems independent of all rationality, the dream world beckons.

Symbolism versus the sheer aesthetics of architecture and form: In how many different ways can one dismantle a house?

In the 1930s, when my father lived in Philadelphia, he created two portraits of a home ravaged by fire. The first, larger and alive with flame, includes a short section of wrought-iron fencing aglow from the heat. The blaze has eviscerated the second floor's exterior wall, exposing dismantled remains of rooms. Rising flames lick the painting's left edge, darkening to smoke that blows so sharply we follow its horizontal path across the entire work.

His next rendering shows greater craftsmanship in terms of detail but feels far more subdued. The bright fencing's been removed. It's the aftermath, the fire and smoke long gone. We witness in exquisite detail the exposed second floor: crisp supporting beams, jagged stairs, glints and reflections in far-off windows. More roughly laid in are an elongated cloud across the top center and a snowbank at the building's base; working together as a kind of whitened frame, these cottony forms enhance our focus on the dramatic collision of interior and exterior architecture.

I discovered the first work in the Philadelphia house after my father's death. He'd kept it in the city that inspired the rendering. But the second piece ended up in New York, and he'd often share it with visitors to his studio, especially those unfamiliar with abstract expressionism, to display his facility with realism—to prove, in other words, that he could draw, too. What's entertaining, of course, is the fact that *what* he rendered looks abstract by nature because we're simply not used to seeing architecture that way. Like Clarence Laughlin's photograph, the painting transforms known iconography into a mythic or dreamlike context.

On cool evenings in late May or early June, my father smoked up the Cape house with fires, and, in retrospect, it's remarkable that he didn't set *our* home ablaze. The house had two chimneys running through its center, a common feature of New England dwellings built in the nineteenth century; with no insulation in their homes, families wanted as much hot brick as possible. One chimney with a Franklin stove had a terrific draw and could thrust heat into the living room for a speedy blast of warmth, but its shallow depth limited the size of sticks, much less logs. The opposite side had a vent into which my father installed a large potbellied stove. But the venting didn't quite match the chimney's aperture; fires in the potbelly meant smoke in the house.

To my knowledge, he never burned cords of hardwood, and I never saw him split a log or saw up chunks. Instead, he'd collect fallen sticks, some stored inside the house in an antique copper bin. Outside, the bulk of his wood got shoved beneath a makeshift addition to the back of the barn, which, as a result, began to rot.

Crammed with sticks, the Franklin's opening raged with god-like fury. In the other chimney near the kitchen, where he could burn larger pieces, he kept widening the hood to catch smoke because of an inferior draw. No one ever inspected or cleaned those fireplaces, and mortar disappeared. Complete replacement would never have been an option; no matter how impractical, adapting to potential disaster outweighed the risks. Our kind neighbor, Ruth, feared the house had become a deathtrap. But, like everything else, the structure managed to hold on until his final breath.

"The house, as I see it," writes Bachelard, "is a sort of airy structure that moves about on the breath of time. It really is open to the wind of another time. It seems as though it could greet us every day of our lives in order to give us confidence in life." And several pages later, he spends considerable time discussing the realm of the fantastic, a discussion that I suspect both my father and Clarence Laughlin would have delighted in. He eschews sentimentality by celebrating eternal possibility:

> Sometimes the house of the future is better built, lighter and larger than all the houses of the past, so that the image of *the dream house* is opposed to that of the childhood home. Late in life, with indomitable courage, we continue

to say that we are going to do what we have not yet done: we are going to build a house. This dream house may be merely a dream of ownership, the embodiment of everything that is considered convenient, comfortable, healthy, sound, desirable, by other people. It must therefore satisfy both pride and reason, two irreconcilable terms. If these dreams are realized, they no longer belong in the domain of this study, but in that of the psychology of projects. However, as I have said many times, for me, a project is short-range oneirism, and while it gives free play to the mind, the soul does not find in it its vital expression. Maybe it is a good thing for us to keep a few dreams of a house that we shall live in later, always later, so much later, in fact, that we shall not have time to achieve it. For a house that was final, one that stood in symmetrical relation to the house we were born in, would lead to thoughts—serious, sad thoughts—and not to dreams.

Bachelard concludes, "It is better to live in a state of impermanence than in one of finality," and I wonder if this is the reason why my father in no way minded his unfinished projects, from the barbeque pit and stone table to his own large canvases, some of which he worked on for decades.

In terms of a dream house, one major renovation remained in the realm of fantasy: For years he spoke of cutting a large, square hole in the Cape house ceiling, the one separating the downstairs living room from the upstairs master bedroom. He wanted to open much of the floor—hinging a trap door—to create a kind of interior skylight. The concept embraced the appearance of great space within the confines of Puritan architecture. He had already made strides in this regard, having smashed out foundational walls. Space and fluidity: As much as he obsessed over free acquisitions that eventually transformed structures into a failed game of Tetris, he simultaneously defined his relationship to the world by the movement among shapes. (Is this why, in high school, he was dubbed Class Prophet?) A hole between floors would allow the eyes to travel not merely across a room but up, beyond the expectations of a house.

I don't know how much structural damage this would have caused or if the ceiling would have collapsed. In New York, he cut an equally large hole through the second floor to make an opening for the semispiral staircase (an enterprise that several architects claimed could not be done), and in Philadelphia, the carriage house had wooden slats covering a hole where farmers used to lower hay. Challenging the standard concepts of barriers—the necessary opaqueness of flooring—had been something he'd lived with, and created, for decades.

So perhaps it's unfair to question his proposal, but I'm pleased the ceiling remained solid. As is, the demolition of foundational walls had tilted the ceiling by several inches; compromising the structure still more could only invite disaster. And if, indeed, the interior had collapsed, we would have listened to passionate monologues of selfless blame—misinformation from others, shoddiness in the original construction, errors made by assistants (probably me)—to punish the thought that the mistake began and ended with his impractical dream.

That said, I love the vision itself and share his lust for space and movement. As Clarence Laughlin's work asks, why resign oneself to square rules when Cubism and myth can be applied? The first four stanzas of Robert Creeley's "The Window" suggest this as well:

> Position is where you
> put it, where it is,
> did you, for example, that
>
> large tank there, silvered,
> with the white church along-
> side, lift
>
> all that, to what
> purpose? How
> heavy the slow
>
> world is with
> everything put
> in place.

And then, as must be inevitable, the speaker's mind reorganizes objects into a logical narrative ("It / all drops into / place"), and what is known shatters the extraordinary magic of vision that turned the mundane landscape into Braque's otherworldly portraiture: "I can / feel my eye breaking."

Although Clarence Laughlin was ten years my father's senior, they met in the army, both stationed in Astoria. Laughlin was an off-the-charts egomaniac, and my father certainly wasn't a timid man. But their artistic passions superseded any personal friction. In fact, many of my father's best army stories involved Clarence Laughlin. Once, for example, Laughlin had been asked to give a presentation on the photographic process. Privates and senior officers congregated in the dark room as Laughlin hammed it up, flamboyantly washing the burned paper in the standard three baths. One of the jokesters, however, had switched around the developer, stop bath, and fixer, and, obviously, no image appeared. Laughlin tried to distract attention from the failure, talking and talking (did he ever stop talking?), and, finally, he stuck a finger into one of the baths and licked it. That's when he realized he'd been hoodwinked.

"Wasting government property," he said, pointing the wet finger around the room.

"Drinking government property," replied the prankster.

In a spirited letter to Barbara Crawford in June of 1943, my father re-creates the essence of their relationship, for all its wacky tumult and pleasure. "Well," the letter begins, "Clarence and I are friends again":

> It was a sudden mushrooming; a fierce and overwhelming rebirth. A booming kindle of boiling sun and literature and art and 10 cents and kitty. It was victor and vanquished.
>
> This morning (yes, this morning) Laughlin and I were enemies. Yea, and when he was washing films and eyeing me with a wispy lidded look, my cold syllables spat upon his presence. "Who," I asked haughtily, "who speaks to you, Laughlin? Not me, to be sure. . . ." "Shaddup" snarled Laughlin, "Shaddup, stoopid."
>
> This passionate indifference lent a monumental stability to our schism. And my airbrush and I were calm, serene, imperturbable.

My father then describes a scene in an elevator, all soldiers except for one Betty "Grable-doll of a blonde pert-piece." Everyone admires; Laughlin ogles. Then someone says, "Clarence is the only one in the world who carries his etching with him." Laughlin replies, "Etchings? Etchings?" before turning to the gal and saying, "You should see my photographs!"

From here, my father retreats for "a placid little lunch":

> an omelet with simple side-pats of vegetables, and light-coffee, and pie, and I repair serenely, in a quiet damp, to the building, oozing in a calm trickle, mentally digesting heredity and environment, and the dry fry of the sun, easy and wet, and balanced—

And at this point, Laughlin arrives with the subtlety of a shotgun in the night, speed-talking as usual with such a relentless delivery that my father relies on strings of run-on sentences to mimic his rhetoric:

> "Hey Kitty, hey look Kitty, at this buy, this book [the novel A *Virgin Heart*] by [Remy de] Gourmont that I just got did you know there was a second hand book store look at it Kitty translated into English and in perfect condition—"
>
> "Listen Laughlin," I say, shaking off his grip, "who speaks to—"

"Shaddup Kitty" says Laughlin, "and translated by Aldous Huxley who wrote Point Counter Point did you know and it cost only ten cents—"

"Listen Laughlin," I say "who sp—"

"And here is a copy of Town and Country," says Laughlin, "which has got an article on Weeks Hall whose photograph I made with his mother's dress framed in the background that moves with a fantastic and inexplainable magic and it is by Henry Miller who was sent to Weeks Hall's by Rattner the painter and I was the guy who told Rattner Kitty, look at it."

"Listen Laughlin," I say, holding off his thrust, "who s—"

"His dog," says Laughlin, settling the matter, "has absolutely human eyes."

. . . .

"Listen Laughlin," I say, "I want to get some candy next door." "Alright," says Laughlin genially, "make it snappy, Kitty."

. . . .

Make it snappy Kitty, he says. Five minutes ago we were not speaking and now make it snappy Kitty.

It is a bright sweat of a day and Laughlin's too too solid friendship is a high, hot collar. Make it snappy Kitty. Give me a day or so with Clarence and Kitty will do him a few mischiefs he will long remember.

They remained in touch after their discharge. A couple of years later, in 1947 while still married to Barbara, my father decided to move to New York City for artistic reasons, returning to Philadelphia only on weekends. I don't know how Barbara felt about this; her saved letters do not portray any sense of betrayal or resentment. And, of course, she had her own life, along with visitors. In January of '48, for example, she wrote, "Clarence has been very kind. He listens to everything I say after I scream shut up to him."

Although I may have encountered Clarence Laughlin as a child, I recall only one vivid visit from the early 1970s. It began with a phone call. I was in the kitchen with our friend Thorpe when my father picked up:

"Hello? Clarence! How are— Uh huh . . . Uh huh . . . Okay, hold on."

My father had already started to laugh before hanging up the phone. Laughlin, whom he had not seen or heard from in several years, had begun the conversation, "Sam? Hi, it's Clarence. Listen, I just realized I have to go to the bathroom. Can you call me back in ten minutes?"

Later that day, Laughlin stopped by and announced, "I'm on the verge of a complete physical collapse." He had divorced his fourth wife and now felt unmoored. But he spoke with dispassionate focus about his second wife, Elizabeth, a marriage that had ended in 1950. (He had two of his three children with her, although he paid attention to none.) Laughlin said she'd moved to a new house that had a bricked, windowless area. He figured he could convert that into a darkroom and thought he might propose.

"I bet he does," my father later said, "and I bet she marries him." And, in 1976, that's exactly what happened. The aftermath has been reported by A. J. Meek in *Clarence John Laughlin*, subtitled *Prophet without Honor*: "At last, he was getting home-cooked meals along with devoted attention. Her patient counsel mellowed Laughlin in his final years and balanced his off-center life and ways. As a joke, she clipped a line from an article in *Vogue* and hung it in their bedroom: 'It Takes Genius to Live with Genius.'" You can decide whether or not she meant that as a joke.

Although only a kid when he visited us that day in New York, I found Laughlin's narcissistic stream of language intolerable and left the adults alone. So while Laughlin spoke of failed marriages and ailments and an emotional descent into hell, I dragged out my large box of Legos and began to build. I had an extensive collection; for birthdays and holidays, I asked exclusively for more Legos. Understand, of course, that I'm talking about the 1960s and early '70s, ages before Lego sets featured reproductions of, say, the Millennium Falcon and the Death Star. The shapes and sizes were cut to reproduce simpler structures, and between the boring final product dictated by the box and my own creative impulses, I felt absolutely no attraction to the design instructions.

(Decades later, in 1992, I visited Legoland in Billund, Denmark, and marveled at the builders' skill. Thai palaces, the Statue of Liberty, a functioning miniature harbor, Mount Rushmore, Egyptian ruins—this was an extravagant tribute to replication, but who had *fun*? Who dreamed?)

I wanted the *parts*, and I wanted the parts to be used in unusual ways. Slanted roof tiles became race car spoilers and sword blades and chutes below retractable trap doors. Large cogs taken off spinning bases became otherworldly spacecraft wings. Blue railroad tracks spun as helicopter blades. Red crisscrossed fencing could be embedded within walls to create prison cells; hinged doors connected to the bellies of submarines and pivoted as rudders. I'd take tires off wheels, attach the axles to the top of airplanes, and then thread long strings beneath the grooves to create zip lines for carefully balanced jets. Platforms meant for house bases became the wings of three-foot biplanes. The addition of a marble allowed for elaborate (albeit super-mini) golf courses. Nothing pleased me more than Legos. From wheeled dragons to fantasy houses, I lived in a plastic world.

For this sensibility—transforming the tame, dictated shapes into endless possibility—I rather obviously must thank and credit my parents. My mother taught me, *very* early on, that boredom was for losers. And while the intellectual depth of my father's teaching, which I witnessed on a regular basis because I loved hearing him teach, sank in most profoundly in young adulthood, crucial aspects of form and function and connectivity made sense to me even as a child. And so using the blocks for alternate purposes wasn't merely a choice; it was the *right* choice, if not, in my mind, the only choice. Yes, I shared my father's desire to rethink and reform the nature of objects. The difference, of course, had to do with proportion: At the end of each day, my Legos returned to their giant box, out of everyone's way and doing no harm.

At one point during the visit from Clarence Laughlin, he, my father, and Thorpe took a look at what I'd been up to. In truth, I don't remember what I made, or what I said, but I apparently took my time describing the creations. Thorpe later explained that I was probably the only person in history who had kept Clarence Laughlin silent for a full five minutes: "Not even Clarence would tell an enthusiastic little boy to shut up."

The related story for me—and this would have taken place a bit ear-lier—involves another artist friend, the architect Louis Kahn, dubbed by my father "the unrecognized prophet of Philadelphia." Kahn spent considerable time with me, asking about the Lego collection and what I made and what I *thought* about structures when I made them. He seemed focused with an almost unnerving seriousness, and I felt intimidated, too, by the significant scarring around his mouth and cheeks—savage results from a fire when he was only three. But his attention and genuine interest overshadowed my trepidation. Open to dreamlike vision, Kahn watched with care and treated me with respect. Whatever I was making that day interested this magisterial architect, undoubtedly not because of brilliance on my part but rather my whimsical youthful freedom.

Not long afterward, Kahn gave a talk in Philadelphia, and one of my fa-ther's students tried to speak with him by using friend-of-a-friend clout: "Mr. Kahn," she said, "I'm a friend of Sam Feinstein." But the famed architect didn't break his stride. "That's a great little boy," he said, and walked on.

A stunning documentary on Louis Kahn, *My Architect: A Son's Journey*, was released in 2003, the year my father died, and I'm saddened that he never saw it. One of the many reasons I continue to be moved during repeated screenings is its equation of art and identity. Created by Nathaniel Kahn, the documentary painstakingly pursues the monuments left by his father. But the son's goal could hardly be more personal and poignant: Born out of wedlock and only eleven when his father dies, Nathaniel tries to understand the mind of his father through other voices and through the art itself. In Louis Kahn's sixty-fifth year, for example, he completed The Salk Institute for Biological Studies, considered by many to be a true masterpiece. "There is something spiritual about this space," Nathaniel says in the film during a visit to the institute. "For the first time since he died, I felt I was getting closer to my father."

Kahn was born in Estonia in either 1901 or 1902, married for the first and only time in 1930, and they had a daughter. In '51, he traveled internationally, witnessing a range of architecture that forever shaped his sensibility. Then Kahn became involved with Anne Tyng, with whom he had a daughter, and another woman, with whom he had his only son, Nathaniel. When he played with my Legos, kneeling on our carpet and giving me undivided attention, he was somehow balancing three different families.

When Anne Tyng became pregnant, she left for Italy to avoid a scandal, but they maintained a steady correspondence, beautifully documented in *Louis Kahn to Anne Tyng: The Rome Letters 1953–1954.* One of his letters explains how he had dinner with my father (and Barbara, who's not named in the note), whereupon he learned of my father's intention to write a profile on Kahn for *Art News.* "They have fixed up their place most ingeniously," Kahn writes, "with the broad approach to space Sam has a real feeling for."

In the context of the fifty years that would follow, Kahn's compliment sounds laughable, but he spoke without any irony, nor was the praise inaccurate. The hoarding had not begun, in part because he had few hiding places and had not launched into his private teaching career in which he could justify junk collecting for the sake of still lifes. Kahn would have experienced a sweep of space—much like the Manhattan lofts where my parents first lived—with a lively array of homemade lamps and unmatched chairs.

When Anne Tyng and her daughter returned to the States, they lived with Barbara and my father until they could find their own housing. Kahn had greeted them when their boat docked: "It was an emotionally charged, happy meeting," writes Tyng as a postscript to the letter collection, "and Lou stayed part of each night with us in New York, returning to Philadelphia very early each morning for several days. . . . I called long-time friends Barbara Crawford and Sam Feinstein in Philadelphia, who very generously let us stay with them until I could find my own place." But one never senses any bitterness. (For how many women involved with self-absorbed artists has this been true?) As she says in the documentary, *My Architect,* "He always said that work was the most important thing, that you cannot depend on human relations, that, really, work is the only thing you can count on."

Nathaniel Kahn closes his film with a trip to the National Assembly Building (Jatiyo Sangshad Bhaban) in Dhaka, Bangladesh. Like the spiritual nature of the Salk Institute, this massive structure—completed only years after Kahn's death—highlights much of the architect's ideology, especially in its fusion of daunting solidity and transcendent shafts of light. "He paid his life for this," explains the Indian architect Shamsul Wares to Nathaniel, "and that is why he is great, and we'll remember him. But he was also human. Now, his failure to satisfy the family life is an inevitable association of great people, but I think his son will understand this and will have no sense of grudge or being neglected, I think. He cared in a very different manner, but it takes a lot of time to understand that."

CHAPTER TEN

~

Stop-Time: An Interlude

In his brown slacks and pale green jacket, the clarinetist Buddy DeFranco looked as though he had stepped out of a smoky '50s nightclub, or perhaps a faded cover of *LIFE* magazine. In a way, the clothes dated him just as he chose, announcing twice during the night that he'd been gigging as a pro for fifty-three years. When he initially approached the microphone, the pickup for his clarinet made the monitors hiss with feedback. "Huh," he said, smiling. And then he looked out and offered his first words of the evening, "Never trust electricity." DeFranco had charm—a word sometimes hard to define exactly, although my father once improvised as good a definition as any. "Charm," he said, "is the ability to make others feel charming." I suppose he could have said, "the ability to make others feel charmed," for as DeFranco slid into "Skyliner" and "Mr. Lucky," row upon row reclined and smiled at phrases that looped and wrapped back on themselves as though the distrusted electricity had gone straight from his mike into his body, his horn, and out to an audience suddenly conscious of how rare it is to experience the splendor of timeless art.

For months after that concert in the early '90s, I thought obsessively about the evening, and, many years later, still try to discern why it resonates so deeply. Part of it, I've realized all along, simply has to do with the sheer magnificence of the concert itself. But that performance has also encouraged me to consider the anachronistic aspects of creativity. DeFranco stopped time merely by his physical presence—bringing to the stage jazz history, a legacy of performances with hundreds of jazz giants—but his fresher-than-ever phrasing simultaneously transported older members of the audience into the past and made the younger ones feel both humbled and more mature. Later, I imagined my father hearing DeFranco in the '50s, and I delighted in the thought of this clarinetist's music linking our generations.

DeFranco's craft and style commanded everyone's attention in seconds, guiding us with his elegance and fluidity, yet there was something about him (his thin physique? the out-of-fashion clothing?) that caused us to feel a little protective of him, in the same way that people hold onto stories passed down from one family member to the next. Or the way many of the oldest buildings in New York City suddenly, in a few days it seems, disappear. I remember a cigar shop on the corner of Ninety-First and Broadway where my father would buy the daily paper. The shop smelled like bubble gum, and I would receive a piece or two for tagging along. The man who owned the store would sometimes stuff a few extra into my pocket, then pat my face with his rough fingers. I couldn't understand why he'd flush with delight when he saw children, how the vibrancy of youth could animate his entire countenance. It took years for me to comprehend more telling details about the man—his thick accent, those numbers inked across his arm.

A cement apartment building later replaced that shop, one of many Upper West Side landmarks to disappear because of mankind's urban plague, and I never found out what happened to the old man. Almost everything in big cities changes quickly, so you hold onto what you can, including aging jazz musicians. It was DeFranco, after all, who had almost single-handedly established the clarinet as a significant instrument in modern jazz, and his history of friendships, which he described briefly but passionately, sent us to the big bands of Gene Krupa, Charlie Barnet, Glenn Miller, Boyd Raeburn, and Count Basie. He became everyone's uncle, commanding the room like the family's best storyteller, for when he reminisced about these musicians and their music it was clear that memory for DeFranco was not a sentimental dream but rather sustenance for living out his life. Among his many anecdotes, he told one of his most popular stories about Tommy Dorsey, who fired him for not repeating his recorded solo note-for-note. DeFranco was rehired not too long afterward, at which point DeFranco gladly, he emphasized, played the solo as required. That made us laugh, of course, even those of us who'd heard it before. In a peculiar way, it was comforting to know the punch line, to know his history and our relation to it, however tangential that may have been.

Buddy DeFranco turned seventy on February 17, 1993, the same day that my son, Kiran, was born. The coincidence pleases me, and maybe all the varied reflections in this chapter really concern my own discovery of fatherhood and what I wish for Kiran, who has innate, infectious charm. In Kiran's infancy, I dealt with expected stereotypical issues, like wanting to absorb the subtle details of growth, to capture each new expression. Later, in reflection—which is to say, as I've stopped time—I've meditated on issues that, while no doubt stereotypical as well, I did not anticipate. Some have to do with fathers and father figures; others explore our desire to share personal history with our children. But all seem to concern time, how it is not linear but rather a continual back-and-forth movement between what has informed our past and how that past affects our present and future.

When I think about DeFranco's concert, I realize that he drew on half a century of practice and experience, that part of him must have hoped his music would swell in our memories, as it clearly has for me. Yet, these could not have been conscious concerns; as with any performance, the actuality of the art—in the immediate present—was all that mattered. In the same way, the immediacy of my son's earliest gestures (and, later, sentences) shocked me into the present, and then clouded into reflective moments of my own childhood, or of my father as a first-time parent, and the complexities of heritage. In repositioning these kaleidoscopic moments, uniting one generation's history with the next, some bewildering yet marvelous patterns have emerged. And while they focus on fatherhood and father figures, they have to do more urgently with the concept of time as something fluid and circular, if not miraculous.

The musical term "stop-time" probably began with tap dancers, and even people unfamiliar with a musician's lexicon know what it means when they hear it: The band in unison plays just one note, usually on the first beat of the measure, then stays silent while the dancer taps a series of rhythms. Another note from the band; more solo tapping, and so on. The same form holds true for jazz soloists. In either case, there's just enough rhythmic support to keep time, to establish tempo and pacing, but the featured player or dancer must lock into and *drive* the time. Rarely in ensemble performances is a musician more exposed and vulnerable.

I probably first heard musicians play stop-time on one of my father's 78s, such as Louis Armstrong's famous solo on "Potato Head Blues" from 1927, but I was first wowed by stop-time on an LP from 1975, the Hanna-Fontana Band's *Live at Concord*, featuring trombonist Carl Fontana. I heard it two years later on the Cape, when I was fourteen. Allan Perry introduced me to the live concert (we used to share new recordings) and on "Beautiful Friendship," when Fontana reenters the ensemble after the piano solo, the band cuts out—stop-time—and he swings even *harder* unaccompanied. I can still feel Allan's sofa pressing itself into my back.

Maybe that's the thrill of stop-time, that only the most accomplished soloists can sustain the urgency of rhythm while maintaining their sense of lyricism. It's the thrill of witnessing an ice skater's triple toe loop followed by a double axel—a combination of technical skill and daring, facing a potentially disastrous performance but gliding through the challenge as though the body's movement merely replicated human breath. Spotlit and boogie-jumping across minimalized accompaniment, the jazz soloist places the flurries of sound into the unforgiving air. How can a crowd not go wild?

And yet, my metaphor extends only so far: skaters replicate "perfection"; jazz musicians improvise new twists, leaps, and landings by the second. (The distinction defines the reason DeFranco initially left the Dorsey band.) In fact, the term "stop-time" might be considered a misnomer; more accurately, the rhythm section "marks time" while the soloist textures the air, and in that sense, stop-time reminds me of family histories, the downbeats acting as markers for years—1923, '66, '82, '93—and within those progressive years we improvise our lives. People emphasize the years because dates mark time, yet everything memorable, all our achievements and failures, falls above and below the dates. No one lives a life strictly delineated by year after individual year.

In the late 1940s and early '50s, more than a dozen years before my birth, my father studied painting with Hans Hofmann, first a mentor, later a friend and confidant. Hofmann's influence on my father cannot be overstated; one might say Hofmann became a father figure. (My grandfather apparently never fully understood or supported the notion that art could be an honorable profession.) Growing up, I heard many more stories about Hofmann than I did about my father's relatives, and when I look at the one photograph of Hofmann and my father and me (cheerfully sitting on my father's shoulders), it strikes me as a generational family portrait.

For Hofmann, paintings became his children, and he loved each equally, regardless of any qualitative discrepancies. According to my father, Hofmann felt entirely pleased with a work so long as a portion of the painting captivated his interest (a concept that amused but did not influence many students) and that satisfaction reflected his tangible enthusiasm both for painting and teaching. "I went to Hofmann to get recharged," my father often told me, recounting how his work had moved more and more toward abstraction and that he needed someone to nourish those impulses. He used to explain Hofmann's aesthetic principles but sidestepped any sensitive issues of a need for parental guidance. I think my father had to separate from Hofmann in order to establish himself as an independent artist—a separation, in other words, without regret, ill will, or awkwardness. The two men simply had become less intimate by the time Hofmann died in 1966 on February 17.

I was just shy of three then, and although my father worked almost exclusively with abstraction at that time, he drew a realistic portrait of me. I framed and hung it over Kiran's crib, and some mornings my son would mesmerize me as he lifted his eyes over the rim: Two expressions—one filled with motion, the other more permanent but inexplicably changeable—hanging in their vertical balance. At that time, already living the future, I envisioned Kiran disregarding the generational magic until he was married, perhaps, with children of his own.

We need years to understand years. My father used to joke repeatedly that his former lofts in Manhattan had been plowed under to make parking lots. He'd point to the air as though he could reconstruct whole buildings with expansive rooms and chilly wooden floors on which I crawled. (I saw nothing beyond the nothing we faced.) He'd detail serious issues that caused penetrating anxiety—failed heat in winter, evictions by corrupt landlords—and yet I'd listen to his stories without experiencing any visceral fear or sadness. ("What did I know," wrote the poet Robert Hayden, "Of love's austere and lonely offices?") Was the lesson for a child simply that we live in a rickety world?

There's no reason my own son should care about the cigar shop on Ninety-First, though I've pointed out where it used to stand and mentioned its owner who disappeared from my eyes but not from my memory. Structures lost in time can't be reclaimed from the air. So why, I keep asking myself, is it important for fathers to share their past? What's the source for this tradition? Maybe we recount stories of our youth in order to stop time, if only in our minds. We need to bear witness to experience, to talk of journey, to explain that one does not progress from a start to an unrelated finish. If we're intelligent, we continually reorganize the past to inform the present. Precise details matter. Maybe it's analogous to the information on jazz albums that necessarily tells us when, exactly, the musicians recorded their improvised melodies.

My first jazz record was Thelonious Monk's *Brilliant Corners*, which featured the pianist's head brilliantly photographed in angled mirrors so that there appear to be five Thelonious Monks sitting shoulder to shoulder in a circle. Still in my early teens, I learned the record by heart and bought many other Monk LPs. His music—which no other students in my high school knew or cared about, much of it having been recorded before we were born—seemed to guide my adolescence. There's no other way to say that. I listened to Monk's long pauses and realized that pockets of silence could be music, too. I stared into his phrases as though the notes themselves spotted the air across the room.

How I wanted to hear him live! But by then he'd stopped performing, wouldn't even play for friends at home, not even for his son, who said there were times Monk would pace for days throughout the house, then collapse from exhaustion. I have no idea what makes anyone, particularly a genius, stop creating; the reasons must be personal and trenchant. But I do remember my sustained desire for one chance to hear him in concert—just one— and then the profound sadness when he died in 1982, on February 17.

So instead, I lived vicariously through my father's memories of seeing Monk at the Five Spot, 1957—just months after he'd waxed *Brilliant Corners*—even though my father recalled more silence than music. Monk, of course, was known for withholding commentary. Earlier in '57, Ira Gitler interviewed the great pianist, a conversation typified by this exchange:

Gitler: "What do you think about the state of modern jazz today?"

Monk: "Oh, it's coming along okay now."

Gitler: "You think the people are beginning to get with it, that they're caught up to it?"

Monk: "Uh-huh."

That night at the Five Spot, Monk appeared aloof, not merely linguistically silent but unwilling to sit at the piano for more than a few brief minutes. Occasionally he'd hit two or three keys and let his eyes dilate with the reverberating sound. But that was all. No complete versions of "Epistrophy" or "Rhythm-A-Ning" or "'Round Midnight." Those who came often and could afford not to worry about lost opportunities dismissed the evening. "Monk's just out of it," one fellow apparently said. "We'll come back tomorrow."

My father had attended the gig with a fellow painter, Herman Cherry, and one or two other artists who frequented the club. He had many opportunities to revisit the Five Spot or other clubs where Monk headlined, but he didn't. Rehearing the story of the failed performance, I never comprehended why my father didn't return to the club, but his response to my queries always amounted to a shrug that acknowledged he and I didn't share a passion for jazz. Still, the music linked our lives like the diagonal that bisects parallel lines in a does-not-equal sign.

♪

"*Criss-Cross*," I said to a taxi driver during a visit to New York when Kiran was still a baby. The cabbie was playing a cassette, and by recognizing the Monk album, I had established the jazz lovers' immediate bond. "People will never understand Monk," he said to me. "They think to themselves, 'Hey, how come this cat can write something as beautiful as "'Round Midnight" and then play all that other stuff?'" I'd never thought of it that way, maybe because I knew that painfully few people recognized the tune "'Round Midnight," or, if they did, knew that Monk wrote it. To me, his music will always sound modern—fresh, captivating—and while still in that cab, I jotted a note to myself: What will Monk's music sound like to Kiran when he's a teenager? I knew, with regret, that my son would probably rebel against my music on principle, but maybe, I thought, the sounds that fill our house will also infuse his spirit. Or maybe, for sentimental reasons, he'll embrace the music of Buddy DeFranco, whose birthday he shares.

A few years ago, I brought Kiran, then seventeen, into my study and asked for his honest reaction to selections from *Criss-Cross*. He listened with patience, and had similar responses: the compositions themselves—the heads—sounded "a little obnoxious," "unnecessarily in your face." But once the solos began and time loosened up to a steadier, boppy swing, he felt the music sounded "sharp" and "kind of cool."

So we talked a little about jazz and his generation. Kiran felt that unless you grew up with the music, kids his age wouldn't give it a shot. "Jazz is an acquired taste," he said. "In my school, everyone likes the obvious."

"And you?" I asked, putting on a 1954 recording with Buddy DeFranco in which he devours "The Bright One," his choruses shimmering like the dazzling filigree on a Selmer sax. "You obviously like what you're hearing—but not enough to download it on your iPod. Is that fair to say?"

"Yeah," he said. "That's about right."

I smiled and nodded to assure him his feelings were cool by me. The desire to share history and to show a connection through history does not equal a desire to have history repeat. Maybe that's partly why fathers share their stories: because we know our sons are working on their own.

"I wanted you to hear this clarinetist," I said, "because you two share a birthday."

Kiran smiled back. "Huh."

♪

The night I heard DeFranco, he performed "Cherokee" as his encore, a tune he used to play in all twelve keys, "but it used to take too long," he explained, "so we'll keep it to four." DeFranco applauded the work of the band, said it would be just as tough for them, and launched into the melody with spirited verve. Oh, what a close! DeFranco soared from one key to the next, lipping his slurs into the upper register, popping brilliant high-notes to punctuate his passages the way the brightest stars form constellations. A short breath, then back in with the band, floating above their rhythms and counter-melodies. He had showed us what a great concert can achieve: teaching the audience about the music's history, making bodies move to its swing, slowing down the collective pulse with beautiful ballads, and leaving a crowd coursing with energy and admiration. As he exited the stage to a photographer's flash, and as the audience rose, I couldn't help but feel not only joy but relief, for some might say he had been flawless.

So when he came back onstage, clarinet in hand and ready to play, I considered leaving because there was no way for him to improve on the evening. A slower tune would sound anticlimactic, and an equally fast one would be overkill. DeFranco made no announcements this time, nothing to clue us in to what he had in mind. And then, quietly but with a compelling and confident rhythm, he opened with solo clarinet, the famous motif that introduces Thelonious Monk's "'Round Midnight" and teases one's ears into melody. What a clever idea: play the entire introduction with no accompaniment, a showpiece for his lyricism and elegance.

At the song's theme, we expected the rhythm section, at the very least, to join him, but even the bass player sat out and listened. DeFranco played the entire tune, and an improvised chorus, completely solo, yet he never lagged in phrasing or rhythm. At each turn, he explored the chord changes like clouds forming and reforming in Midwestern skies. DeFranco returned to the theme, played a brief but resonating cadenza, and left the stage for the final time, leaving us the way anyone would like to be left—on our feet again, utterly charmed, laughing at the magic of time: each mellifluous glissando rolling back the years to his youth.

CHAPTER ELEVEN

~

Temples of Inscription

Under normal circumstances on a Wednesday at 8:30 in the morning, I would have been home, but on April 11, 2012, I found myself halfway through an English department meeting, part of the required ten-year review, so I didn't feel our house shake as though hit by lightning. My mother-in-law certainly did; she'd been attending to our cockatiels in the dining room. Upstairs, my wife also felt the explosive jolt, although it took her a couple of minutes to figure out where it had occurred. My fifteen-year-old daughter, however, slept in teenage unconsciousness for her last morning of Easter break.

I'd been dreading the departmental meeting, not because of the early hour but because my skepticism of academe almost always creates worst-case scenarios. I was physically worn-down, too. (My throat hurt more with every breath, and I'd begun to cough and wheeze from a steady "discharge." I knew these signs: A massive sinus infection had begun to take hold.) Our department's outside evaluator, although primarily a scholar of fiction, had written an encyclopedia entry on an energetic yet relatively minor poet, and I envisioned aggressive challenges, such as, "Why isn't this poet taught in your Modern and Contemporary Poetry course?" From there, I began to parry more standard lunges about dead white men and the canon. I'd have to defend the inclusion of such anti-Semites as Ezra Pound and T. S. Eliot, even though, for their politics, I hope they're eaten by rats in the afterlife. I'd have to point out the great diversity in the course, not for the sake of artistic depth—my central criteria—but to justify my teaching. And, because this was a literature-track review, everything would focus on that one annual course rather than my poetry workshops. Christ. Everything seems to break down when your territory is under attack.

My swelling concern, of course, had no foundation: I'd never met this professor and knew her only from a curriculum vitae—one of world's most common introductions, and one of the most antiseptic. And less than ten minutes into our meeting, I silently mocked myself. She was a joy: smart, fair, focused, and genuinely helpful. I had made judgments about this scholar based purely on a general distrust of academics, many of whom would rather run down a colleague than celebrate successes. So despite the oncoming illness and the knowledge of a second, one-on-one interview with the evaluator scheduled for that afternoon, I returned to my office feeling grateful and relieved.

I wasn't even rattled by the phone message from my wife, which asked me to call home immediately, because I assumed she simply wanted a report about the meeting. That changed quickly.

"Hey, Hon," she said when I returned the call. "Something's happened here. A car drove into our house."

I arrived home five minutes later. The driver, a woman who lived across the street, had been questioned by police and had returned to her home, but the crumpled Honda Accord—dark green, two door—remained on the lawn. Ripped from its body, the back bumper extended perpendicularly like a tentacle. The severed muffler and exhaust pipes snaked across our walkway. Most of the shattered back windshield spread across our porch, its aquamarine glass sprinkled in painterly patterns among severed rhododendron leaves and pink azalea blossoms.

Slowly and surreally, the details fell into place: Challenging everyone's sense of plausibility, the vehicle had rocketed across the road, over the thick curb, onto the sidewalk, then up and across the pitched lawn before smashing into the stone foundation. And it had done so while in *reverse*.

Later that day, the police shared an alarming discovery: It looked as though someone had tampered with the accelerator. Our home had suddenly transformed into a crime scene, with one mystery explained (the speed and trajectory of the Accord) and a larger one just beginning. My imagination took off like the vehicle itself. If the car had indeed been rigged, why, and by whom? The more we shared the story with friends, the wilder the speculation: two of my friends jocularly suggested that I had been the target.

Almost as surreal was the damage itself. The compact car, one would think, would be no match for rock, but it hit hard enough to dislodge stone steps, each one foot square and as wide as six feet. It had completely demolished an entire stone structure—a low wall demarking the entrance—transforming cemented blocks and ornamental slate into geometric debris. The crash had repositioned other parts of the stone foundation, creating huge fissures and threatening the porch's integrity. Had that Honda accelerated into the house itself, hitting the softer brick, it probably would have reached the living room.

When I look at my photographs of the dismantled stonework, I'm reminded of so many ancient ruins, including a seminal archaeological find in 1949, when Mexican archaeologist Alberto Ruz Lhullier discovered the moveable stone on the temple floor in Palenque and directed a team to start excavating the impacted stairwell. It took over three years to remove the rubble. The bottom initially seemed to be a dead end, but then, on June 15, 1952, Ruz's team loosened and removed a massive triangular portion of the wall, and the burial chamber opened for the first time in centuries.

The discovery also caused experts to wage battle over identity: Was this indeed the skeleton of K'inich Janaab Pakal, the first great leader of Palenque, or did it belong to a much younger man? Certainly, the remains had been hidden with the care afforded royalty, and the tomb's lid, intricately carved with hieroglyphs detailing Maya cosmology and the afterlife, led to a reasonable conclusion. But some thought the skeleton itself would not have matched Pakal, an octogenarian. Does authenticity of a body matter more than the artistic environment? Eventually, the world's contemporary scholars concurred that the corpse must be Pakal (AD 603–683). What had literally been written in stone could now be trusted.

I'm no historian, but various accounts explain that Pakal must have commissioned the temple a few years before his death. Laborers and artisans worked uncounted hours to manufacture his sarcophagus from white limestone. The lid itself depicts his moment of transition, the cessation of his "white flowery breath" (to quote a translated inscription). My first book on Maya art, *The Blood of Kings*, notes somewhat casually that once his burial chamber had been sealed, "five or six sacrificial victims were killed and laid in a small chamber in front of the plaster-covered door." In the very long and shifting stairwell from the tomb to temple floor, the Maya placed an airshaft for the Vision Serpent to ascend, as well as an assortment of ceremonial offerings. But they filled the vast majority of that space with worthless rocks— ton upon ton of stone—until the entrance became impenetrable.

Like so many ancient cultures, the Maya fused everyday life with art, symbols with creativity, direct messages with aesthetic presentation. For a ruler and for the community, the hours sacrificed for ornamental stonework—materialism at its most majestic—became justified through ceremony. Forget ego. The spirit rises through the path for the Vision Serpent. The art and artifacts bless the ground, but not human eyes. For the Maya at Palenque, this tomb's art was meant to be as temporary as a Tibetan sand mandala.

But for archaeologists, the inscription on the unearthed tomb now afforded a very different kind of rebirth. How much can we know of a person from the art, and is it worth disturbing the dead? In terms of materialism and identity, how much can we comfortably relinquish?

After the mid-1950s, my father stopped signing his name to canvases. My mother, too. Quite consciously, they wanted to sidestep the ego, eliminating signature for the sake of a complete composition. They understood that none of the Maya—or those from other ancient cultures—personalized their art. Whether out of religious conviction or a reason far more mundane (relatively few workers on the pyramids and other phenomenal artistic sites were devoted artists), the nature of their achievement eclipsed any personal aggrandizement.

Part of this difference has to do with the replication of iconography: from Egyptian hieroglyphics to standard depictions of Indian gods, the power of form depicting myth often supersedes artistic independence. And with independence (for better or for worse), iconography gives way to personal identity. My parents may not have signed their names on the majority of their work, but their styles and sensibilities thrust forward almost as conclusively as fingerprints.

Which is why I am certain (and bewildered by the fact) that my father signed my mother's name on a couple of her paintings for a posthumous show of her work. The lettering, *Anita Askild*, bears a close resemblance to her signature—on written correspondence—but it's a little off, and there's no way she would have placed her signature on the canvases at that time in her career, or even in those *places* on the canvases. I cannot explain why he felt the urge to do this—some sense of authentication? one final gesture of absolute control?—but I know the paintings are hers and the signatures are his.

In August 2009, the Provincetown Art Association and Museum hosted a show co-curated by the museum's executive director and titled "Modern Vision and the Provincetown Drawing Practices of Hans Hofmann Students." The traveling exhibit included a booklet, *Search for the Real: Drawings by Hans Hofmann and His Students*, later reproduced online. And it included a drawing (c. 1952; twenty-five by nineteen inches) credited to my father.

It's a nude, somewhat Cubistic in feel, and memorable primarily for its savage treatment: In an effort to show formal dynamics, Hofmann (one presumes) razor-bladed a section in the center to elevate the torso; poor draftsmanship by the student, it seems, caused the hips to be too low. The cheap tape used to reposition the severed paper slip has now darkened to a rich tea.

The marks around the figure seem disjointed, inharmonious. One can argue with ease that the importance of the work has more to do with artifact than art, an example of Hofmann's technique as a teacher.

And one can argue, with equal ease, that my father did not create this work. Yes, I have more than one advantage here: He told me directly that Hofmann had never cut his drawings ("Not that I would have minded," he added) and that he had kept a couple of stranded pieces by students who no longer wanted them. But, far beyond that, there's *nothing* in this drawing that suggests my father's hand, by which I mean style and artistic sensibility; I don't believe that an artist's personality necessarily radiates from the art. (How many cruel men have nevertheless created beautiful works?) More often than not when assessing a masterful artist, style emerges with DNA-like clarity.

For that reason, I remember being astonished at my father's memorial when a display of his work included a canvas by my mother—a painting that had been hung upside down. Conversely, I felt great surprise and joy when I sifted through the hundreds of works by Barbara Crawford: In the midst of her lifetime collection, eight or ten canvases appeared that were undeniably my father's. The discovery could hardly have thrilled me more. I knew that the vast majority of his work—99 percent—remained in the New York property and that it would most likely not be shared. (When he died, I asked for three things: the ring on his right hand, a spiral of gold that he crafted for my mother as her wedding ring and that he wore after her death; my mother's urn that he had designed and glazed; and one painting, *Nocturne*, which he promised me when I was a boy. I received my mother's ring the day of his death. The urn took many months. The painting took many years.) But on the studio floor, I lined up a series of oils from the '50s, each three by four feet, stretched, stunning. A couple of them even had titles (they must have been shown), including *Celebrant*.

For me, the music invoked by my father's abstractions corresponds most accurately to classical luminaries—Brahms, or late Beethoven. The parallel seems easiest with his large, brooding elegy for my mother, *Requiem*; the adjective I use most frequently when describing his art is "symphonic." But to my eyes, *Celebrant* evokes jazz. Painted in the '50s at the height of bebop, its angular gestures spring like notes on a shattering staff. The painting strides and jives with far more energy than Mondrian's famous *Broadway Boogie Woogie* or Matisse's charming but cautious *Jazz*.

The connection with jazz, as I've said, is my personal, associative response; after all, the painting was called *Celebrant*, not *Jelly Roll Morton* or *King Porter Stomp*. Had I mentioned my synesthetic connections between *Celebrant* and the music I adore, my father probably would have answered, "If that's what you want to see, fine." This would not have been a put-down, or a completely dismissive response; he seemed pleased when people connected his work to art and nature. But the buoyancy that inspired a celebratory title shares the energized vitality of stride piano and infectious swing. And if the painting *had* been titled after a musician or composition, the analogies would stream forth: rambunctious sound captured with bold color. The two white rectangles above dark blue rectangles suggest a piano keyboard, and a few of the gestures appear like unfurled eighth notes. Like the near-physicality of sound, a swatch of black down the top center floats, *elevated* when it should be sinking, because there's so much harmonic propulsion beneath it. The painting dances, yes, and it dances to a hot band.

During the final stages of coediting *The Jazz Fiction Anthology*, I suggested to the press that they reproduce *Celebrant* for the cover art, and they enthusiastically approved the image, but their award-winning designer couldn't figure out how to make it work. Like most people in his field, he wanted to play with the image. The painting, he felt, had too much vibrancy for text to be superimposed; words would be lost within the artwork's vitality. Rather than frame the work and place text within a border, he began to manipulate the scan, at one point fading out the color so that it ghosted into the book's title. Similar to my father watching movies, he didn't seem to appreciate that great canvases are not meant to be edited. Before the press finally abandoned the cover art, he flailed at samples the way James Baldwin describes musical struggle in "Sonny's Blues": "He and the piano stammered, started one way, got scared, stopped, started another way, panicked, marked time, started again; then seemed to have found a direction, panicked again, got stuck."

My father's title intrigues me not for its most specialized association with the Christian Church, but for a broader sense of spirituality and the very nature of celebration. I say "intrigues" because he pretty much rejected public celebrations, and maybe this had something to do with his birth date being unknown (either February 7 or 27, my grandmother wasn't sure). He married my mother in private. For his last marriage, the only people invited to the ceremony were the two sons (his and hers); we congregated in a small Unitarian chapel in downtown Manhattan, and somewhere I have a photograph of her son sitting among rows of empty pews and grinning like the captain of a mediocre chess club. Years later, when I telephoned my father to announce that Marleni was pregnant with our first child, he said, "I thought something like that might happen." I laughed, expecting him to say something else—right then, or at the end of the call—but that was it. He dismissed the news as though I had coughed.

He did, however, agonize each year over Christmas cards, handmaking each one with rubbings (often from my mother's wood- and linoleum-cuts used for her designs) and enlivening the greeting with flamboyant penmanship. After triple-folding the paper, he'd carefully round the corners with scissors and close the flap with a rubber-cemented seal. He said some people had collected them for years. All I knew was that December meant he'd be lost to card making. They were lovely, but he turned into a factory worker.

Between his obsessive card manufacturing and his unwavering devotion to routine, it's miraculous that my mother convinced him to leave New York during my winter break for a family vacation. She said she wanted to go somewhere—just the three of us—before I grew too old (I was fifteen) and didn't want to do things with my parents. She had saved money from her fabric designs and went to a travel agency with the thought of seeing California or the Grand Canyon. Instead, she returned with tickets for a journey through Mexico and the Yucatán Peninsula. The timing turned out to be essential. The year before, my father had suffered a massive heart attack but now had the okay from his doctors to travel; the following year, she'd be diagnosed with terminal cancer. But in December of '79, we flew to Mexico City for our only overseas vacation.

Although a moody teenager who probably veiled emotions, I became overwhelmed with sensory thrills: scarlet tapestries in Oaxaca, majestic Teotihuacan, sharks swimming beneath our glass-bottomed boat. But, far more than anything else, I remember Palenque for its hypnotic, lush surroundings. (Our guide said that if workers didn't mow and machete the grounds each day, everything would disappear in weeks.) The intense foliage made the temples seem all the more ancient, and I'll never forget splaying my hands to feel the increasing moisture on wet walls along the stairway from the Temple of Inscription to the tomb of K'inich Janaab Pakal. The other tourists descended slowly, too, carefully navigating the stone steps as though reaching the bottom constituted a grand achievement. We were so focused on footing, I don't think any of us contemplated how the crew directed by Alberto Ruz struggled to release those steps, the years of heavy removal.

The nature of a package tour evades the identity of a Third World country, with the realities of poverty walled out by luxurious hotels. Apart from our guide, I don't recall even speaking to a single local in Palenque. But we had not landed in this country to witness its socio-economic structures; we were there to bathe in the eternal artifice of art. Our adventure was as beautiful and surreal as being in balmy Mérida and, in my case, celebrating Christmas with a midnight dive into a warm outdoor pool.

After my mother died, my father and I approached celebrations somewhat timidly. For that first Thanksgiving, he suggested we go out for Chinese food and, afterwards, hear the pianist Dave McKenna. Both venues, I now realize, had been chosen exclusively for my pleasure: my father didn't want me to cook an elaborate meal, and he knew my love of jazz. Maybe, too, he wanted to crush any sense of tradition, sidestepping the emotional triggers of the holiday. In any case, we had a good meal at Chun Cha Fu (now defunct and, that night, understandably vacant), and then we rode the crosstown bus to Hanratty's, where McKenna had already swung himself into a "Home" med-ley: "Back Home Again in Indiana," "Walkin' My Baby Back Home," "You'd Be So Nice to Come Home To," "The House I Live In."

A couple of months later, in February, I felt inspired to throw him a sur-prise birthday party, the first of his life. When I say I "threw" the party what I really mean is I made the invitations. I informed his students and old friends, and told them to congregate at the bar around the corner, Wilby's, so they could arrive en masse. But moments before their appointed entrance, my fa-ther decided to take out the trash, and although I tried to grab the can from him, he brushed me off as though responding to an automated telephone sur-vey. Garbage was *his* world. And that's why his sixty-fifth celebration began on the streets of New York, my father at the trash cans with scores of people suddenly surrounding him, nudging him back into the house, his whole sense of the night reduced to a half-stammered and unfinished question. "Happy birthday!" I said, and the party began.

The few Polaroids that remain from that evening capture much of the spirit, from dramatic gestures that punctuated conversation to a portrait of my father with two of his young female students leaning into him, left and right. (He's grinning as if to say, "How can I help my animal magnetism?") I remember feeling ridiculously proud of myself, much like the fathers of brides in Philip Larkin's "The Whitsun Weddings," who "had never known / Success so huge and wholly farcical." But the evening, once it whittled down to the youngest crowd, ended in argument. One of his students, who'd left by that point, had accepted a marriage proposal to a man about whom, frankly, everyone had doubts. Still, her friends—including the two women who had posed flirtatiously by my father's side—felt we needed to support the decision. My father refused. And when they challenged the depth of his knowledge about her character, he spoke with the confidence of Picasso: "I know her from her art."

It silenced the room in a way that only a room of artists could be silenced. Were they afraid to challenge the notion that their identity might *not* be fully exposed in their work? How much truth lay in his proclamation? Even what we carve into tombs or write on paintings can only provide an inexact narrative. In a portfolio of work created by my mother a year or two before her diagnosis, before any of the signs, she added captions to a series of medium-sized works, and I remember my father cringing as we pulled them out, each of us reading in silence: "Anger," "Confused & Agonized," "Death Wish," "Deceived," "Grief," "Groping for Roots," "Lost," "Desperate, Deceived & Destroyed," "Stabbed in the Gut," "The Dance that Swept Away." He put them back in the binder, gave it to me, and didn't say a word.

When I released *Celebrant* and two other companion paintings from the dusty rafters in Philadelphia, an image of them hanging in the Cape house— a kind of holy trilogy—burned into my mind as though remembering the future. (The sensation paralleled my experience with the mixed-media piece found beneath the bed in the Cape attic.) *Celebrant* paired perfectly with an untitled canvas from the same period in the very early '50s; a third, probably painted a few years later, spoke to them like a seasoned elder. Sunny and buoyant, they belonged on the Cape, and they belonged together. And after the Cape renovation, I hung them exactly in their imagined locations. I felt almost as though the house had been built precisely to highlight individual paintings. In fact, it's difficult even for those who knew the home during my father's lifetime to imagine the panoply of objects that used to obscure the walls. For the first time in half a century, these paintings can be celebrated appropriately. I suppose, like Ruz and his crew, I will forever be a celebrant of art and not the rubble that entombs it.

As for the dismantled stone foundation around our house and the cause of that destruction, we know nothing more than we did on the day of the accident. A couple of months later, the doctor sold her house and moved away. The police still call the investigation "ongoing," and I guess it's fair to say that my skepticism extends beyond academic targets. Like the mysterious obliteration of Maya civilization, the cause for this accident may never be revealed. But our comfort resides in the home itself. We hired a young sculptor who, like our friend Jon Bogle, also restores houses. He spent the summer purchasing stone from local quarries and repointing the blocks around the perimeter. He shored up the porch and repainted the spindles, recreating every facet of the initial effort in 1893, fully reclaiming the historic dignity of architecture.

CHAPTER TWELVE

~

Vegetable Chow Mein Pizza

Let me not postpone this title's promise: The vegetable chow mein pizza existed. It was a one-hit wonder, or at least a wonder, and I cooked it as per my father's instructions.

I *had* to cook it. He knew only how to make tea. After my mother died, I became the house chef by necessity, and I wasn't bad, though I certainly wasn't great. (I know the difference; I'm now married to a culinary genius.) The largest limitation—and this was true for all his wives as well—had to do with dietary preferences: He refused to eat onions or garlic. The cause for his objection concerned not only his digestive tract but psychological scarring. The story goes that the rabbi who coached him for his bar mitzvah in 1928 used to eat raw onions and had savage breath. He'd bark corrective pronunciation, fumigating the room with Hebrew. Not long after the ceremony, my father abandoned both Judaism and onions.

So I improvised with other spices. I also had a cook's widest safety net: Although I never forgot about dishes on the stove or set anything aflame, my father *preferred* food to be not just blackened but burned. We're not talking Cajun cuisine; we're talking the aftermath of an Australian brush fire. In my childhood, when roasted marshmallows accidentally touched flame so that heavenly white turned to hellish crust, he devoured every failure. Bread stuck in toasters transformed from problem to treat. He even claimed that, during drawing classes in art school, he nibbled on charcoal.

Similarly, he loved just about anything that crunched like a twig. Burnt food worked, but so did toasted multigrain bread, hard crackers, and many bran products. At the end of a meal, he'd sweep his hand across the kitchen table to round up crumbs, then thrust them into his mouth like a dog chomping on a biscuit. Hard pretzels. Ginger snaps. Were it humanly possible to crunch and digest, the shell of a lobster would have been far superior to its flesh; in his case, he liked most of all the marshy cartilage in the crustacean's head and upper body. The ends of bones, the earthy marrow, the bones themselves. My father was part Rembrandt, part carpenter ant.

In terms of his own efforts to cook, the one dish he claimed to make more than once was surprisingly soft in texture—a prune omelet—and I witnessed that creation one afternoon. (He served it to the man whose wife he'd later steal. Revenge may be a dish best served cold, but attacks, apparently, can involve warm prunes.) But his best-known cooking story involved spaghetti. He had company arriving and figured pasta would be hard to screw up. In the process, he tasted the ready-made sauce and found it bland. So he opened up cabinets and took out spices.

"Cloves," he thought. "That sounds healthy."

But they were whole cloves, and he poured from the large opening, not the perforated end.

"Half the damn bottle came out," he explained, "but there was plenty of sauce, so I just stirred it in, and pretty soon you couldn't see them."

Guests arrived, and, around the table, each first bite went pretty well.

"Sam! This is pretty— Hey, I think I just ate—"

They went out for Chinese that night.

Such stories became part of his legend; he prided himself in his culinary hopelessness. So after my mother died—from the end of my junior year in high school until I left for college—I cooked, and while I didn't burn food, and liked things saucier than he did, and longed for the day when I could cook with onions and garlic, we did okay. Roasts. Pork chops with applesauce. Pineapple chicken.

I worried a great deal about him when I left for college in 1981, but I've saved all his letters and still laugh at this note sent to me that fall: "Don't worry. I'm eating, I'm eating. People make stuff for me to have around and I'm picking up a few pointers along the way. The other day I unfrosted some giblets and fried them up all by myself. Delish! And Kasha and jello, yum."

The vegetable chow mein pizza made its stunning debut the summer before I left for college. His friend Harry Holl had become, for that period of time, a vegetarian. My father wanted to host him for dinner and, somehow, arrived at this cockamamie vision, a dish with plenty of substance—or at least calories—and no meat.

At first, I refused. Steadfastly. I wasn't a great cook, but I had my teenaged pride. I suggested a stir-fry, or pasta, or even a nice egg dish.

"Look," my father said, already pissed off. "I want you to make this thing."

"I don't know how."

"I'll tell you how."

"I don't want to be responsible for this," I said. "I don't want anything to do with this."

"*Look*," he said again. "Just cook the goddamn thing."

"I'm not gonna eat it."

"You don't have to eat it."

"*Fine.*"

I suspect he was particularly adamant about the selection and irritated with me because he had already purchased the ingredients. There was no going back: You bought it, you eat it. So now, for the first time, let me unveil the infamous recipe for vegetable chow mein pizza:

1. Place large frozen cheese pizza in oven and cook for ¾ of the time listed on the box
2. Remove from oven and obscure the pizza with an avalanche of grated Parmesan cheese
3. Add a thick layer of dried Chinese noodles
4. Over the crunchy swamp, pour (after slightly heating) a full can of vegetable chow mein
5. Add another opaque layer of Parmesan cheese
6. Add another layer of dried Chinese noodles
7. Place in oven until, well, "done"

I don't know what inspired this calamitous entrée, although I suspect it had to do with the hard noodles—the idea of making a pizza more crunchy—as well as his general philosophy that adding layers to something necessarily made the product more satisfying. Why have one rug, for example, when you can have two or three on top of one another? (In New York, this multicarpet approach eventually led to months of torment after he rescued an abandoned rug infested with larvae. Week after week, I heard his punished spirit report on swarming moths, each single birth an insult to his advocacy of mothballs—a smell that eventually permeated both the houses and its occupants).

When applied to art, however, his seasoned awareness of layers, especially under-painting, created great radiance from the outermost layer, the color that reaches the eyes. "Cézanne's major innovation," he wrote, "was the result of his shift from contained form to projected form. In nature, form grows from within, whereas we have been trying to imprison it from without." He spoke similarly about Hans Hofmann's best works: "What comes through is what André Malraux called 'density,' a layered buildup of spirit emanating from the painting, which is more than builtup layers of paint as such." He credited his predecessors, but his work rivaled Cézanne's and, in my opinion, exceeded Hofmann's. From plastic—the essence of acrylic paint—he created phenomenal luminosity through a layering of color. In terms of density, it seems as miraculous as Louis Kahn creating spaciousness out of forms of poured cement, or Clarence Laughlin enticing our eyes and mythic imaginations by superimposing unrelated images.

After the allusion to Malraux, he added, "This kind of painting might be compared to a city such as Rome that has been built up over and over again and attains that quality," but I'm not sure the analogy to Rome really works in this case. An indiscriminate use of layers simply invites destruction: multiple rugs lead to moths; old wood hosts termites. What's buried in Italy remains out of sight and, for those without an archeological knowledge of particular areas, out of mind. I believe, in other words, that the majesty of the Colosseum or the Pantheon (just to select obvious choices) has to do with their own presence and history and not the energy beneath ground. Ironically, a stronger analogy would be with food, such as Indian cuisine, in which the myriad of spices needs time to coalesce; the resonance of a curry or vindaloo depends on a layering of flavors that become integral. For obvious reasons, that comparison would never have emerged in his contemplations about art.

Yet his relatively tasteless culinary sensibilities also allowed for tremendous graciousness when served disastrous meals, ruined either by execution or concept. I'm thinking now of his final years when he chewed and swallowed platefuls of horror. One of his wife's go-to meals presented slices of squash awash in an orange sauce so breathtakingly bright it rivaled a highway cone. Shellfish meals often contained enough grit to crack molars. One evening, Marleni and I were told to wait at the table while the chef went outside to the grill. Then we heard screaming.

"Oh, craaaap," my father said before standing to investigate. "Look: Just sit here."

Turns out, she had forgotten to soak the wooden satay sticks, and both the skewers and the speared scallops erupted into a charring blaze. Later, he spoke of her weeping and whimpering about never being as good a cook as my wife. In the end, we crunched out effusive compliments—but the lines from my father were *sincere*. He couldn't get enough of burned food. A different night, more screaming ensued because a loaf of bread had been placed under the broiler and caught fire, causing his wife to smash at it with a flapping kitchen towel until flames turned to smoke. He just beamed and said, "Alright!"

The one meal that tested even my father's patience had been created for a potluck event on the Cape, one hosted at our house. His students brought outstanding dishes, from lavish salads to hand-rolled sushi. His wife's contribution, one that she claimed had always been a huge hit, combined tuna fish with lime Jell-O. The perfect green ring began to soften in the summer sun, and when she saw the untouched creation, she muttered maniacally about people not knowing what was inside. So she macheted the mold, slashing out slices and slapping them on their sides to expose the tuna fish. This did not help. It took my father a full week to spoon it down. "I finally finished this damn thing," he said like an out-of-shape marathon runner.

Half a century earlier, during his period in the army, he began a letter to Barbara Crawford with this enthusiastic, one-sentence paragraph: "O, how well fed I am!!" Here's what had filled his belly:

Tomato juice, potato soup (almost as good as yours darlingest), liver and bacon, peas, string beans, carrots and a sauce, and whole wheat rolls (4) with jelly and butter and chocolate ice cream and coffee—for 45¢ (forty five cents!) We are allowed 50¢ by the G.I. I think I shall go buy a hotdog. . . .

Hey, do you detect a giddy note in this one? You should eat good food always, honey, and you will be just as happy as I.

Was his giddiness really about the "good food," or the price?

Great chefs can stun their audiences by providing the unexpected; cooks often delight in a critic's comment that he or she had never imagined such ingredients working together in the same dish. Speaking more personally, I recall my wonder and sensual overload when I experienced the combination of chocolate ice cream with sea salt: I felt like a city boy witnessing a hemisphere of stars for the first time. There's often a fine line between incongruity and brilliance.

"We all know that what Sam was able to do with transforming junk into a still life was amazing," wrote a student, Joyce Barrow, who studied with my father for decades:

The collections of stuff that he put together in the cellar were always interesting to me and an endless jumping off place for paintings. I was incredulous, at first, unable to see how this thing or that formed some sort of animated body—a person, a bird, an animal, etc. But then, as Sam talked about it, I began to see how various things could come together in that way. And they always did.

Given his genius for finding organic relationships among the planet's incongruous ingredients, his recipe for vegetable chow mein pizza (or his willingness to consume tuna-infused Jell-O, for that matter) seems somewhat less absurd.

The great majority of his class's work focused on these wraparound still lifes, which, to a layman's eyes, merely appeared to be a conglomeration of incongruous junk. But my father spent considerable time positioning objects for shape and color and movement, and he insisted that if students could see the elastic connections in a display that eschewed narrative, then they would be all the more prepared for investigating aesthetic relationships in the natural world. His students dutifully reconsidered the energetic drive of form itself, distancing themselves from the practicality of objects and focusing instead on the patterned dance of contours and the startling vitality of color. A "useless" ribbed section of ventilation tubing suddenly became as mobile as ridged sand flats, directing our eyes not merely *toward* other objects but dancing *with* them. Ripped construction paper, broken vases, tree limbs, fake flowers, abandoned children's toys—the world of shattered forms functioned, through the artists' transformative vision, as a collective, unified expression in much the same way that utterly diverse instruments can be orchestrated to form symphonic brilliance.

But just as innovative cooking requires tremendous knowledge of the culinary arts, so does transforming junk into beauty require great technical skill and vision. Nor do such skills necessarily overlap, and it's a blessing that my father rarely crossed those lines. His refreshments for his students were simple and satisfying: a pot of tea and ginger snaps. Sometimes, especially in childhood, I'd happily bring in the tray because the class inevitably greeted me with gratitude. Most memorably, I recall the very last time I offered to prepare the tea. This was in August, the end of the summer season, only a couple of years before his death. The kettle whistled, and I opened the tea-pot's lid expecting an empty chamber. Instead I saw a mass of used tea bags. My father caught my stare.

"Take two out," he instructed, "and then put two fresh ones in."

"You're kidding."

"No—I've been doing that the entire summer, and the class says this is the *best* tea I've ever made."

He had no boundaries for his collections. And I could be wrong, but I suspect some weeks he didn't even add a single fresh leaf.

CHAPTER THIRTEEN

~

Sacred Ground

We hadn't expected to discover anything in particular, and certainly nothing life-changing, nor did the history of America matter to us a great deal. We were just a bunch of sweaty boys, riding bikes on a day dreary enough to rule out the beach but warm enough to keep us outside. Two of the kids, brothers, lived at the start of a cul-de-sac just around the corner from my Cape house, and so we cruised slowly, talking about the usual—which is to say, not much. When we reached the turnaround, I noticed a patch of ground that seemed a bit worn, and we decided to follow it on foot.

Today that trail's a good three feet wide and very well marked. There's even a plaque on a boulder that announces the entryway and tells the history of what's to be found a mere fifty feet into the woods. The area's built up, too. But on that gray day, we weren't even sure we'd found a path as we stutter-stepped over clumps of poison ivy. So when the mossy stone wall caught our eyes, we moved faster. Then we saw the tombstones and ran to the iron gate, and, to our amazement and delight, found it unlocked. The Dennis Howes Cemetery. Although the grounds looked cared for—the patchy grass cut— we felt as though we'd uncovered a ruin worthy of Palenque.

The deeper we explored, the older the stones, and the ornamental carv-ings fascinated us: winged skulls, some baring large square teeth, others surre-ally wrinkling their brows. We all agreed this was the coolest place we'd ever seen, and we kept shouting death dates to find the oldest stone. I wasn't the winner, but that mattered not at all. And I remembered how we crouched before the marker for Thomas Howes, who died in 1665 at the age of 75.

Born 1590. The Mayflower, we knew, had landed when he was thirty, a mere forty miles from where we stood. Were these second- or third-generation Americans?

History aside, our thrill derived from the gravitas of age. Stones that had chipped and flaked beyond readability seemed all the more remarkable because of their *possible* antiquity. And what was with those winged skulls? Who would want such a frightening visage for an eternal marker? Even the hybrid of orange and green moss, a brilliant union of opposing colors, blossomed like a gesture from the heavens to tell us that we had uncovered a place both captivating and bizarre, sacred and frightening. The level gray of that afternoon only intensified the slate markers in their forested sanctuary. When we ran our fingers across the teeth of grimacing skulls, we felt empowered.

The names, too, delighted our tongues. Ebenezer Howes. Thankful Howes. Temperance Howes. Experience Howes. Dorcas, wife of Prince Howes. A younger Thankful Howes. (He had a winged, smiling head—not a skull—that looked not only less cool but a bit dorky. *He* should have been Dorcas.) Drusilla. Hepsy.

The graves nearest to the iron gates were more recent, and after 1750 few engravers chiseled those weird and fabulous flying skulls, so we dismissed them. In fact, I recall feeling not quite betrayed but most certainly disappointed in their height, thickness, and clarity. They looked too standard, and their disproportionate size made those below ground seem pompous. So I rejected and tried not even to glance at the tall, fat markers for Abraham and Huldah Howes. I didn't want their relative modernity to sully the experience.

This was not a passing resentment. Each summer, I'd return to the Howes Cemetery as a pilgrimage of sorts. When friends from out of town visited, I'd take them there—as I still do. But I'd glare at those comparably massive headstones. And then there was the wife's name: Huldah. Who does that to a girl? In high school, when I encountered for the first time Flannery O'Connor's "Good County People," I laughed out loud when I read how the protagonist changed her name from Joy to Hulga. That experience colored this one as well: different consonants, same effect. Huldah. Of German and Hebrew origin, it means both "loved one" and "mole." In Swedish: lovable. Hebrew: weasel.

The Howes family populated a great deal of Dennis, thanks to a Puritan delight in large families. Thomas came first, arriving from England in 1637 and soon settling in Nobscussett (the part of Yarmouth now known as Dennis). He fathered three sons—Joseph, Thomas, and Jeremiah—and their

American family tree quickly became a forest of Howes. The Halls and Sears families got thrown into the mix by marriage, adding a bit of variety to this orchard. The 1880 Atlas for Barnstable County, which includes Dennis, maps out our street; of the twenty houses, eight are owned by Hall family members, ten by Howes. In that year, our home was owned by Warren Hall. And who sold it to him in 1861? Unbeknownst to me in childhood: Abraham and Huldah. And they're the ones who had the house built.

It is, I'm aware, unflattering and perhaps inappropriate to admit that I searched Abraham and Huldah's genealogy largely because I suspected inbreeding and wanted to locate those tangled branches in the family tree. And, indeed, both Abraham and Huldah are direct descendants of Joseph, son of the patriarch, Thomas. Huldah had a paternal link. Her father was named Joseph, whose father was also Joseph, whose father was Joseph, whose father was Joseph, whose father was—wait for it—Samuel (one of the few in the Howes genealogy whose wife remains unknown). And Samuel's father was the Joseph brought by his father, Thomas, from England. More interesting, perhaps, is the fact that the marriage of Abraham's parents connected a circle arcing back to Thomas through his sons Joseph and Jeremiah: Abraham's father, Micah, descended from the Joseph branch, and his mother, Hepsy, descended from Jeremiah's. It may well have been a genetic blessing that Abraham and Huldah never had children.

I don't disbelieve in ghosts—in spirits, for example, that linger in beloved properties—but I do think they leave if they're fed up, and I suspect Huldah and Abraham left our Cape house long ago. And yet, my chair at this moment rests on wide pine boards cut and pegged into the floor joists 150 years ago, when this house had two internal chimneys and no insulation. With the walls now bedazzled with bright abstract art, the air charged with high-end speakers pumping jazz—both art forms nonexistent in the nineteenth century—it's almost impossible to imagine the original owners in their stiff, dark outfits. Were the Howes time travelers, we wouldn't know what to do with one another. What would they make of such sound and color? How could I pretend to enjoy their Puritan conservatism? Assuming a spirit world exists, what will my ghost-self encounter a century or more from now?

In this now-modern home, it's easy to dismiss the presence of early Americans; it's more interesting for me to wonder what spiritual presence exists with my parents. I suspect my father disapproves of and perhaps resents the dramatic changes on the house and grounds. But with still more conviction, I know my mother adores them. During her lifetime, she made strides liberating the house from clutter, throwing out bags full of refuse on the sly, and she would have loved the Scandinavian purity of display, the walls clean and well lit, the art beaming from earned respect. As one old friend said after the renovation: "You must know Anita's dancing."

Even those who never met my mother, like my friend G.W., sense her presence. When I took him for a trip in May, not long after the finished renovation, he felt her spirit to such a profound, tangible degree that, to this day when I leave for the Cape, he never fails to say, "Send my best to Anita." I have sensed my father, as well, though the sensations have not been positive. The summer of his death, I walked through the tormented house with the contractor we'd hired. He knew we'd have to start from the studs and beams, a virtual demolition, and spoke about tearing everything out. When we walked from the central dining area to the hall, I sensed something terribly wrong, dark gray, gravitational. For no rational reason, I turned back into the dining room, at which point my father's largest and best-known canvas, *Summer*, fell off the wall. Points on a chair's back would have punctured the painting had I not grabbed it.

Only once during my father's lifetime did I voice my vision for making some improvements to the house. It was the summer he told me he'd changed his mind, that he wanted my stepmother to have the Cape property as well as the brownstone in New York. We stood on the front lawn beside the willow tree that he'd failed to transform into a bush.

"She told me this is the only place she ever considered to be home," he said to me, "and I want her to have it."

That summer visit was supposed to be one of pure celebration. My wife and I arrived for just a few days, along with our only child at that time, Kiran, age two. I'd landed my first tenure-track position, and we were ready to start a new life in Pennsylvania. And perhaps all that youthful energy—wife, child, career—made my father feel as though I didn't need any of my childhood roots. Perhaps there were other factors, but, whatever the cause, his pronouncement gutted me.

Although in no position to tell my father about his moral obligations to a son who'd been promised this inheritance, or the fact that this home had belonged to my mother, too, I tried to articulate my passion for the property. That's when I mentioned a couple of fantasies about the future: having a washer and dryer, for example, and perhaps pumping in heat. For this, I suffered. My father raised his voice into a snarl I knew well. It meant there would be no discussion.

"I looked into that *years* ago," he began. "I've tried to get estimates ever since you were a baby." He pronounced words like "washer" and "heat" as though spitting out chew. "It's *impossible*," he said. "You don't have your head screwed on right."

He had already made arrangements for the three of us to meet with a real estate lawyer. I was instructed to be attentive and silent.

"If you speak about that house with the kind of passion that you've expressed today, I'll leave you *nothing*, understand?"

So I joined them like a good dog. And a day or so later, I woke my wife and child before sunrise so we could get the hell out of there. My father and his wife heard our footsteps and groggily met us downstairs.

"We're taking off early," I said. "Thanks for everything."

During the eight-hour drive, I neither seethed nor cried. I felt deadened, buried alive. And when we arrived at our new home, I wasted no time in writing a lengthy letter. I spoke passionately, ready, in fact, for him to sever ties with me forever. "My interest in that house," I explained,

> has absolutely nothing to do with its market value and everything to do with nostalgia, sentimentality, and a sense of family history. It's where I was conceived and raised for every childhood summer of my life. It is, I think, an ideal summer location for children. And it is, most important, a spiritual embodiment of my mother, whose presence radiates in that house and on that property.

The letter, apparently, stunned him, and he telephoned to say that the house would go to me, that I should "relax," and that his will would remain unchanged.

We fall in love with properties for so many different reasons—sentimental, practical, territorial. We identify with land because it reflects our nature and connects us to history, even if our own history differs wildly from that of our predecessors. And those connections make our proprietary nature swell, from room to house, house to town, town to state, even country. People on the Cape who search for Native American artifacts delight in imagining the Indians forging their weaponry. The experience broadens their sense of time by pulling them *out* of time.

In July of 2012, the Scargo Stoneware Pottery celebrated the sixtieth year since its founder, Harry Holl, opened the gallery. The night before the party, his eldest daughter, Kim, called to ask if I would say a few words of welcome, and I found myself telling a story about Harry taking me into the woods behind the pottery. He'd discovered a mound of antique bottles, and he thought I might like to join him to dig in the pile. I was a kid, and I adored Harry. If he had said, "Let's go to the high school to scrape peanut butter off food trays," I would have cheerfully said, "Sure!" But this *really* had my interest.

In those days, it was really wild back there—the kind of "Cape wild" where you walk for seven minutes and suddenly can't see anything but green—so, after a bit, I asked Harry how he could possibly find this bottle pile, and he became something of a Sherpa, pointing out the location of the sun, showing me trees with broken limbs to use as markers, and so on. I found this incredibly cool. And sure enough, we eventually came across the sought-after mound. He handed me a trowel and told me to dig carefully so as not to break anything. He told me to take my time—to engage in the experience fully—because some of the best ones might be buried deep. And then he *left* me!

My whole being wanted to chase after him, but I had a sense of pride, and I really did want to check out those bottles. (I am, after all, my father's son.) So I dug for a while, but eventually a sense of panic took hold and I thought, Boy, I'd better head back. I started to walk—and I recognized exactly *nothing*. Brush, trees. So I calmed myself and tried to remember Harry's lessons about the position of the sun and the various markers in the forest.

I'm pretty sure that's when I started to scream for help.

Meanwhile, Harry was back at the pottery, no doubt throwing one masterpiece after another from the wheel—vases, decanters with swan-shaped necks, turrets for castles—and of course he couldn't hear me because of the distance and the classical music, probably Mozart or Bach, that commonly filled the gallery space. He may well have been flirting, too, entertaining the usual flock of admirers while I was running through the woods, bottles clanking at my side, yelling for someone to save me.

In my welcoming speech, I then turned to metaphor: How Harry had invited countless people to join him at this astonishing pottery, an oasis in the midst of the woods, so they could find their own treasures—unique statements of great beauty and artistry. He'd also mentored many students, offering creative guidance and practical philosophy. And like all the best art mentors, including my father, he understood that, ultimately, people need to do their own digging, and they need to find their own way home.

The amusing anecdote about the woods had been fresh in my mind because, just a couple of years earlier, I'd been digging in the back of my own Cape property for antique bottles. The last area to be cleared of poison ivy included an inexplicable mound of earth, its features totally incongruous with the land. I felt certain it had been manmade; I also knew that many families had used their woods as a dumping ground for bottles and abandoned glassware (as well as incalculable types of metal and cloth objects). This *had* to be a bottle mound, and the anticipation captivated me the same way *Treasure Island* consumed my boyhood spirit.

The initial dig coincided with a visit from my brother-in-law, Pravin, with whom I'd traveled to the hill tribes of northern Thailand and the ancient architecture of Cambodia. Together, we had witnessed ruins encased in tree roots the way Melville describes a giant squid: "innumerable long arms radiating from its centre, and curling and twisting like a nest of anacondas, as if blindly to clutch at any hapless object within reach." We had navigated rivers on rafts primitively constructed with thatched bamboo. I knew he'd share my enthusiasm, and I was spot on. Although the mound wasn't completely clear of poison ivy, we decided to risk it. Hell, I think we would have risked landmines.

The sandy earth gave way easily to our shovels, and in no time we created significant holes. Nothing. We poked around a bit, but sand merely begat sand. I couldn't believe our absolute failure. Beyond that, the mound became all the more puzzling. Why bury nothing? And then it occurred to me that the mound may have been the remains of an excavation *around* the unusual formation. Could it be that a bottle pile existed just a few feet away, in the lower areas?

The answer had to be postponed because of more poison ivy, which had carpeted the ground, consumed trees, and risen within a miasma of honeysuckle. After decades of reigning on earth, poison ivy must be killed in stages; as a summer resident, I needed two more years. But in June of 2011, I sprayed myself with bug killer and marched to the back of the property. Thick gloves carried a Razorback shovel, a metal rake, and some loppers for extraneous dead branches and brush.

The first hole once again yielded nothing, and I dug fairly deep—a little over four feet. This had indeed become Sascha's Folly, and I felt a wind of relief that no one had seen me approach the woods, nor did anyone know that day of my focused goal. My family, especially my fourteen-year-old daughter, enjoyed teasing me about unsuccessful projects. That summer, for example, I'd seeded grass in the backyard, and it took, but a couple of storms spread the seed, so green blades emerged in patches. Then the new lawn got fungus. For many mornings in a row, my daughter took great pleasure in saying, "Hi, Dad—how's the fungus?"

From my vacant post hole, I dropped back roughly ten feet to an indentation and gently sank my spade into the dirt, and damned if I didn't hit glass. It was merely a brown shard, and I'd be lying if I said my heart raced like a gold prospector. Still, the buzz drove my shovel back into the ground.

This was late morning, about 10:30, on a day that would become unnaturally humid for the Cape. I'd already soaked myself digging that first hole, even though I dug slowly; searching for glass means gentle excavation, so I picked and nudged at the soil as much as I removed dirt. I continued to find broken glass, including a shard with the Pepsi logo, the largest remnant from a vintage soda bottle. And that's when I came across the undergarment.

At first, I thought I'd encountered a mass of soft roots, but then the skin-colored mesh unraveled from its burial. It's possible they belonged to Mrs. Warren Hall, or the Aunt Sarah in the sepia photo of this house at the turn of the twentieth century, or even (I say this to Patricia) to your great-aunt, Alice F. Walker. All had lived on the property. To the appropriate spirit, I apologize for inadvertently exhuming your bloomers.

Out of respect for the dead, I'll say no more—but it shocked me enough that I decided to take a break and rehydrate myself. From the porch, my wife peered up from her mystery novel and smiled.

"Killing poison ivy?" she asked.

"No, I've been digging for bottles." I could tell she was stifling laughter.

"Find anything?"

"Mainly shards," I said, "although I do believe I've found where my father buried his compassion."

We laughed, and then I went inside to down some Gatorade.

The tattered remains of clothing disturbed me enough to dig in a new area, about three feet away. Nothing. But a couple more feet in that same direction I hit glass almost immediately, and the bottle was whole. Then small jars began to emerge, most with semi-rounded bottoms. Two coffee cups, one blue and one pink, both with broken handles. Suddenly, I was teleported to seventh grade, when I laboriously worked my way through the hundreds of pages of James Michener's *The Source*: "You start what looks like a simple dig. Historical fragments hiding in earth. And before you've filled the first basket you find yourself digging into your own understanding of the civilization involved." I even unearthed a clock—although, frankly, this disappointed me because it stamped the remains with modernity. I found bottles for pectin and perfume, bottles with rubber stoppers barely intact, and small drinking glasses. A man's razor. Two broken combs. To quote Michener again:

> And then in quick succession, some distance inside the inner wall, the diggers at Trench A came up with three finds, none so spectacular as the remnants of the castle but all of a nature that sent the history of Makor rocketing backwards, so that after these items were appraised by the scholars the balance between the trenches was restored, and the hidden secrets of the mound began to unfold in an orderly pattern.

The strangest artifact from my dig was a large broken jar filled with what at first appeared to be some kind of black larvae. I'd discovered the glop two or three feet below ground, so its wet, organic presence shocked me. My father had purchased this land in 1960; these artifacts were unquestionably older than half a century. How could this not have rotted? Was it destined to be unearthed? To quote the epitaph from Abraham Howes's gravestone: "Heaven's immortal spring will soon arrive, / and man's majestic beauty bloom again."

Inspecting the contents more closely, I guessed canned currents, but later my wife and I decided they were wild blueberries, possibly picked on this very property. Someone must have knocked or dropped the jar, then tossed the whole mess into the glass pile. Beneath ground, it had been preserved for decades; exposed to air, the berries lasted less than a week.

On that first day of digging, I discovered two appealing pieces of glassware, including a quart-sized green soda bottle of Moxie, with the brand name boldly raised on the front. (According to one Internet source, the bottle was probably manufactured between 1905 and 1916.) I liked even more a brown post-Prohibition bottle for Ancient Age bourbon. The embossed glass doesn't spell out the brand, and the Kentucky distillery would have had no idea how entertaining their AA logo would become decades later.

As for the overall project, I might add, no one in my family cared about this archeological site. In my three days of shoveling, neither my wife nor my children ventured to the back of the property to cheer me on or simply witness the excavation. I would bring back little gems besides the bottles—an ornately filigreed silver spoon, a shimmering gold compact with the mirror intact—but I didn't get much more than "Hmmm."

I'd become a bit obsessed, but I had to postpone the dig to finish a dirty job on the north side of the house where bamboo marked the property. The protective liner needed my attention—roots had jumped the top and launched into the lawn—and parts of the exposed liner needed to be dug out and straightened. I also wanted to reposition an ornamental rock of substantial size (it had only been moved before with a Bobcat) because it had now become obscured by our raspberry bushes. My neighbor, Ruth, spotted me just after I'd finished, and she crossed the street to say hello.

"Want to see my latest folly?" I asked. "Let me show you the bottles I've been digging up from the back."

Ruth looked very pleased—not so much because of the items themselves, I think, but because she imagined her deceased husband sharing in my escapades.

"Allan would have loved this," she said.

"Is that right?"

"Oh yes." Then she added, "You can sell them, you know."

Bolstered by her enthusiasm and my own treasure-hunting verve, I returned to the woods, already drenched in sweat but high with a bring-it-on attitude.

The third day turned out to be a winner, I felt. In addition to the compact, I'd found antique test tubes, a vintage Pepsi bottle, a half-gallon hooch growler, a whisky pint, and much more. But the day's big catch appeared in one of my final shovelfuls: a cognac bottle with an embossed portrait of our first president; above his profile, arcing like a rainbow, the glass read *1732 George Washington 1932*. Hadn't Prohibition ended in 1933? This was pretty cool.

The metal screw-top for this bottle had rusted solidly onto the glass, but the bottle itself wasn't scratched or cracked. Eager to amass my fortune, I went online to price its equivalent, partly to satisfy my curiosity and partly to counter my wife's crushing research: she'd found a Pepsi bottle in better condition than mine on sale for 99 cents.

"Damn," I said out loud, half to me and half to my wife who peered at my computer search. "Here's a pristine bottle, with the cap, for $29.95." I scrolled down. "Here's another for $14.95."

My wife tried to look earnest and understanding. "Maybe," Marleni said, "it's time for you to let sleeping jars lie." Then she added, "You've spent a lot of time throwing away bottles"—meaning, of course, the pounds and pounds of glass that my father had squirreled away. Bottles, bowls, plates, windows, doors, skylights. How many tons of glass had I removed? Why on earth was I looking for more?

I kept quiet and skulked off to the outdoor shower. In the cedar trees, a catbird began to call, perhaps to a mate, though it sure sounded like mockery. I later walked back to the site, cleansed of sweat and soaked in irony. Near my feet, a child's armless, plastic doll stared into my eyes, and I turned her over with my shoe. I began to focus on artifacts of identity, things people had used, touched, maybe cherished. Suddenly, I felt overwhelmed by the morality of excavation. With thrill and whimsy, I had probed what I had labeled merely a garbage pile, but had I betrayed the ceremony of burial? How, I wondered, can we ever know if we've insulted the dignity of spirits?

And at that exact moment, I heard something—not a person, not a squirrel—coming quickly in my direction, and then revealing itself: a dog I'd never seen, with a full, perfectly white coat. He sniffed my hand and leg, circled the excavation, and then disappeared into the pines.

CHAPTER FOURTEEN

~

Urushiol

"You can trust him," my mother said about Charlie Johnson, the man selling them the Cape property. She based her faith on nationalistic pride: Both Johnson and my mother hailed from Sweden, and she felt confident that they wouldn't be cheated (or "sheeted," as she would have pronounced the word). My father assumed anyone selling anything shouldn't be trusted, but, in fairness, exchanges of property inevitably include wariness and questions of honesty. What has not been disclosed? Where are the hidden horrors beneath seemingly perfect exteriors?

Although my father merely chuckled at her Swedish pride, the home appealed to him because it included a barn (he needed a separate area for his teaching), as well as a shack in the woods that he spotted and knew would make a fine painting studio for himself. When he asked how much more he'd have to pay for that shack, Johnson said he'd have to buy a whole extra acre. "He thought he was sticking it to me," my father would say in his innumerable retellings of the story. He'd also note that, unbeknownst to them all, the cost of Cape land would rocket just a few months later with Kennedy's election. He bought that extra acre, with the studio, for about a grand.

The back half of the property had once been used to cultivate asparagus, with the shack no doubt used to house tools and farm equipment. Now it was empty, of course, and the land reclaimed its wild nature. The structure itself had been consumed by vines, and my father's first step in transforming it into a painting studio required clearing its exterior. My mother told me she worked on the house while he disappeared into the woods, and around

127

lunchtime he returned triumphantly, the studio free of entanglement, a kind of rebirth.

Having spent a decade clearing this same land, I now appreciate his macho satisfaction. There's the job itself, of course, one with an immediately noticeable (and therefore satisfying) result. There's a pride in the body when we've struggled and reduced ourselves to our sweatiest, physical core. There's even a sense of spirituality, as though, by saving a section of strangulated wilderness, you've participated in the human condition at its most positive. But, to speak less dramatically, and to be true to mankind's desire for acknowledgment, this triumph is never complete without a witness, especially a loving wife. It's elemental: "I am man. I clear woods. Later, we make fire."

And so my father, bare-chested and in shorts, brought my mother out back to view the released cedar shingles and the enormous piles of raked-up foliage. I'm sure she told him everything looked great—and then she gasped. Unlike her proud husband, she recognized the vines as poison ivy. And although they ran to the house and scrubbed him with a fury, the rich oils had permeated his skin. Within days, he swelled and blistered as though exposed to radiation.

Was this karmic? Almost thirty years earlier, in August of 1932 when my father was seventeen, he received a letter from a girl named Dorothy. "Hello Haircut," she begins: "So after all I told you about my ivy poison [sic] you still consider it a 'mild case.' If this is a mild case, I wouldn't want a severe one, or you would have occasion to send me flowers again and it wouldn't be a prom either." (In a subsequent letter, she would write, "I cannot call you a rat. I shudder to think how insulted the poor little rodents would be." And she is probably the author of this unsigned note that had also been stored for seventy years: "Dear Rat! You are a viper! Take it from one who knows— You are also a cockroach. PS: Happy birthday.") But now he most certainly knew the difference between mild and severe rashes, agonizing for two weeks.

Once he healed, however, the studio became an oasis for him, and although he maintained a poison-ivy-free path to and around the structure, he allowed nature to rule that extra acre so that the studio became a hut in the middle of a jungle, a pool table in the middle of bamboo. True, he reduced the interior space considerably with hoarded junk and wood, but he concealed much of the rotting messes with tall Homasote boards, on which he pinned massive canvases. He'd work on several at a time, as well as smaller drawings and paintings that he placed on a long, low-standing table. This shack that had been so dangerously guarded by infectious growth became his private palace for creative freedom.

After his death, I learned that a number of the local boys thought him to be "the crazy artist in the woods," and one summer a kid named Michael accepted a dare to spy on the madman. Somehow, Michael scratched his way through rich brush and crept around the studio to peer into the open door. My father had seen his agile figure from the small window and instinctively assessed the situation as harmless, but he also wanted to teach the boy a lesson. When Michael reached the doorjamb, the crazed painter leapt into view and growled like a bear, sending the boy screaming into the woods. My father walked down to the house, laughing and eager to talk about how he'd scared the crap out of some kid. Many years later, ironically, Michael would join the final group of painting students—but my father never made the connection, and Michael never confessed.

My favorite story about the studio, however, took place during a wickedly hot August afternoon. On such sweltering days he often removed his shorts and painted in the nude. (Michael trespassed on a cooler day; his scare could have been exponentially greater.) He felt lost in the combination of heat and artistic endeavor, staring at one of his canvases, his palette knife poised.

"Suddenly," my father would say as he retold the story to guests, "I felt a presence behind me, and I turned around, stark naked, to face this old Cape Codder. His jaw has dropped. My jaw then dropped. We're just staring at each other. Finally, the guy says to me, 'Have you seen a swa'm of bees go by?'"

The beekeeper had been following their migratory path, waiting for the queen to settle on a location. I suppose he had planned to capture them. I have no idea if he succeeded, but you can be sure that the hunt itself was among his most memorable. How did *he* tell that story?

Not long ago in my Pennsylvania home, we had to open a wall so a beekeeper could retrieve the hive of honeybees. He carefully carved out and preserved their combs for transport. My daughter and I helped, and none of us wore protective gear. We stood in a bedroom with thousands of bees clustered together, only a few in flight or crawling across windows. We all got stung, but only when they'd get trapped beneath shirts, and the stings didn't hurt much. It felt thrilling and surreal to be surrounded by danger—or at least what one assumes will be dangerous.

Tackling poison ivy elicits a similar rush. In an eight-by-ten portrait taken, developed, and printed by my mother, my father's wearing his vine-warfare ensemble: baggy, rubberized fishing waders cinched at his waist. No head protection, though his long-sleeved flannel shirt disappears within black rubber gloves that cover most of his forearms. He's holding a mass of poison ivy vines in front of the barn door; against the expanse of black, the leaves become still more lively in their oil sheen. The ivy drops as low as his knees and towers four or five feet over his head. There's easily three feet of growth tangling outward in front of his body.

The cause for the portrait? Sheer machismo. Though photographed on our front lawn, the vines would have been extracted an acre away. He must have yelled for my mother to grab her Nikkormat and preserve his triumph. With the poisonous entanglement now severed, the snapshot comes across as a contemporary depiction of Perseus gripping Medusa's head.

Poison ivy is to the Cape what roaches are to Manhattan: vile and primordial, infiltrating available empty spaces with alarming ease and staggering replication. Their purpose on this planet confounds me. (A friend once said that because mosquitos exist she could never believe in God.) Companies that manufacture combative poisons make billions of dollars worldwide—but my father refused to buy sprays. He noted that insecticide caused leaves to shrivel but left the stems and mature vines, which channeled the poison to the ivy. He insisted the only way to eradicate the foliage was to work by hand, ripping it out by its roots.

The rubber gloves and fishing waders worked well, but he still got tagged with some frequency. And he would have spread an ocean of calamine lotion had he believed in standard drugstore curatives, but, of course, he opted instead for his own medication: Noxema skin cream. He insisted that this beauty cream included the active ingredient found in healing lotions. He also said that Noxema, if you glopped it on, wouldn't dry out, therefore releasing the aid for a longer time. Like Louis Armstrong proselytizing the invaluable qualities of Swiss Kriss laxatives, my father preached as though he had stock in the company.

It half kills me to say that the old man may have been on to something. I've since queried a former student, Tanzina Fazal, who's become a genius in the field of biomedical research, and she wrote:

> I can tell you there is no reason why Noxzema wouldn't have cleaned up the irritants from poison ivy. I looked up the chemical structure of the substance that bites in poison ivy—it's called urushiol, and it is a phenol. Noxzema's ingredients list phenols, catechol, and other oils. You can definitely wash away phenols with other phenols (i.e., the phenol from poison ivy can be dissolved in the phenols from Noxzema, and thus washed with water). I also looked up a few poison ivy treatments, and all of them have "active ingredients" that are alcohols and phenols. Basically Tecnu [the most popular treatment for outbreaks] is made of alcohols. So yes, it makes total sense to me that you can treat poison ivy with Noxzema; in fact, I would have used Noxzema over Tecnu because Noxzema has phenols while Tecnu has other alcohols . . .
>
> I am curious to find out why your dad came to the same conclusion.

He would have answered, "Pure brilliance." The note would have been read aloud in all his classes, and at social gatherings. He would have been *insufferable*. Still: impressive.

Although I've made a conscious effort to educate myself about local flora and fauna, I'm still embarrassingly naïve about many things that grow on our property. That said, I can spot poison ivy with bloodhound-like expertise, and it's partly because my father educated me early on, instilling Boy Scout knowledge with the subtlety of a drill sergeant. He explained how its color might change from verdant green to scarlet, but it always sprouted in groups of three shiny leaves, slick edged (not serrated). Even a single plant was to be considered a three-headed monster, the Cerberus of the plant world.

We had no poison ivy battles around the house and few around the barn; between those structures and his studio, he monitored the grounds vigilantly during my childhood. Behind his studio, however, the vines took hold like something post-Apocalyptic, a full acre gleaming with tropical toxicity. As he grew older, that wilderness encroached on the space between the house and studio. By the time I inherited the property, most of the land seemed hopelessly strangled.

Hans Hofmann once said, "To create, one must first destroy." He was talking about canvases, of course, and how the first dab of paint in some respects destroys the absolute purity of white gesso. Although the Cape landscape does not equate to an untouched rectangle, the concept shares similarities: to save the damaged cedars and white pines, to infuse the forest with dynamic hydrangeas—to simply make the ground habitable—the poisoned soil required a purging.

In fact, I became obsessively drawn to the challenge of clearing away the dangerous growth, releasing beautiful hardwoods and creating airy spaces where we could enjoy those trees. I had saved a number of wooden planks from the barn and dragged them along the clear path to the studio. From there, I dropped the boards onto ground completely carpeted by poison ivy, creating a treacherous walkway from which I could spray powerful herbicide. I felt like a tightrope walker balancing over a tank of piranhas.

I worked my way toward towering dead oaks, some easily forty feet tall with massive trunks. They needed to be removed for the sake of healthy trees (cedars and white pines being my favorite), but I also knew that their length could be used in lieu of boards. The planks, ultimately, could not be placed over the nearly ubiquitous brush, but a felled tree pummeled anything in its way. The oaks hit the ground with a force worthy of Kali, each primordial *boom* ringing like a cosmic gong announcing the emergence of life on Earth.

After significant spraying and seasonal decay, the ground remains as brown as fallen leaves, and the brittle honeysuckle stalks begin to splinter.

Pine needles, now dispersed freely by Atlantic winds, luxuriate across and texture the soil. Slowly, vegetation returns in patches: wild grasses, daisies, nubs of cedar saplings, and many varieties of dreaded, invasive vines. Some locals insist that it takes three seasons to fully eradicate poison ivy, and even then you'll still find occasional sprigs prickling the needled ground, often camouflaged within English ivy and Virginia creeper. Each summer, I walk the property with the cautionary steps of a Cambodian farmer, where thousands of landmines still lurk within jungle grasses and rice fields. I'd look ridiculous on camera. But on my own, devoid of spectators, I tend to feel like 007 with his PPK and silencer, targeting fresh ivy sprouts and generously soaking them with brush killer. In a way, this noxious, primordial plant has created a strange bond between father and son, like people from disparate sensibilities united by war.

In the movie *Aliens*, the crew gets too used to frontal attacks by monsters; when they realize the creatures have infiltrated the venting overhead, it's too late, at least for most, but no viewer of the film faults them for expectations that leave them emotionally disarmed and physically vulnerable. The secret of deep horror—whether in film or in life—often lies in our failure to imagine the unexpected malleability of danger.

For me, the most daunting and frightening moment during the Great Clearing arrived in the first summer when, like the bewildered crew in *Aliens*, I gazed overhead, slowly, without intent, and found myself on the verge of being enveloped by poison ivy. I'd been so focused on the completely green ground and wrapped bushes that I registered hanging leaves simply as tree leaves. In actuality, I stood beneath an entire canopy of poison ivy. I could not move and became all too aware of my breathing.

And while I continue to eradicate unwanted growth—a challenge as perpetual as the Atlantic's tidal drive—I luxuriate in a pasture liberated for the first time in nearly a century. I've kept some sections wild for privacy and, in the center, for Eastern box turtles that return to lay eggs. I've witnessed and photographed red tailed hawks sunning themselves with such proximity they seem tamed. On summer mornings, after starting the coffee maker, that part of the land calls to me, mellowing my psyche and focusing my thoughts before I return to the porch with coffee, a writing pad, and a pen.

During the winter, a painter requires a studio; a writer requires a study. And my study in Pennsylvania includes some assorted trinkets. The open hutch above my computer, for example, displays my father's high-school portrait, a set of Russian matryoshka dolls (Gorbachev to Lenin), two awards I received as a kid for good sportsmanship, a tiny Maya face carved in the Yucatán, a Thelonious Monk postage stamp, and an African stone sculpture of embracing abstract figures given to me in gratitude for a free reading. I've also placed some Chinese souvenirs from Singapore, such as a wax letter sealer (with a symbol that marginally represents the sound of my name) and a rose-red snuff bottle that I purchased simply for its ornamental qualities. It's made from lacquer, the surface carved into intricate florets and curling vines. Hard to imagine that someone had to tap a lacquer tree for its dangerous sap—urushiol, the same toxin in poison ivy—before transforming the malleable substance into something resilient and shimmering, and then transforming it yet again into art.

CHAPTER FIFTEEN

~

Validating Rhyme

In 1950, the poet Robert Creeley wrote one of many letters to his mentor, Charles Olson, in which he advocated the magnificence of Charlie Parker and jazz. "There is nothing being put down," Creeley insisted, "that can match/ that timing: Bird's." Given Olson's liberating use of space on the page, and his pioneering theory of projective verse, one would have assumed a warm reception. But Olson called music—*all* music—"a bug in my ear," and would not bend. Similarly, I know a marvelous fiction writer who doesn't care at all about music and who finds abstract expressionism virtually unapproachable. For some, aesthetic comprehension and delight does not cross into other arts.

In my father's case, his entrenched philosophies and expertise in the field of abstract painting never carried through to free verse; for years, he asked why poetry written without absolute meter and rhyme could not simply be presented in paragraph form. Abstraction—or at least form without traditional contours created by realistic depiction—did not translate to poetry. And for years I responded with references to his own teaching: Just as the edges of a canvas amplify the power of the touching colors, so do words at the ends of lines (and, more so, at the conclusion of stanzas) resonate all the more in the reader's mind, whether consciously or unconsciously. Every line, like every brush stroke, embodies its own lyricism; poetry, painting, and music are by no means limited to set rhythms.

He'd nod respectfully, but I knew we'd have the very same conversation at our next visit. I felt more confounded than irritated, although he certainly could irritate me. Once, for example, I telephoned to share good news: My work had been solicited for an important anthology published by Penguin and covering five hundred years of sonnet writing. Shakespeare, Donne, Wordsworth, Yeats, Auden, Plath, Heaney, Dove—no poet could ask for greater company.

"What's the name of this book again?" he asked.

"*The Penguin Book of the Sonnet.*"

"Oh," he said, "I thought you said '*The Penguin Book of the Gannet*,' and I was going to say I thought it was for the birds."

I laughed—but that's *all* he had to say on the topic, and I'd long since grown bored by his miserly praise. It hardened me. But it is also true, as I learned from others, that when I sent him a copy of that anthology, he made sure every student arriving for his classes saw it.

Somewhat ironically, my father enjoyed writing light verse, and he mailed rhymed invitations to his students each season announcing the commencement date for painting classes. Usually, the poems consisted of two couplets, handwritten with thick black strokes and splashy red ink for emphasis. Here's an example, quoted from memory (and therefore inexact but true in spirit):

> June 12th! That's the day—
> We start to paint. Hip hip, hooray!
> Leave the shore! Forego the tennis!
> Brighten up the town of Dennis.

Obviously, he intended to make cute jingles, not high art, but it's interesting to me that he desired rhyme and meter for something as mundane as a start-up date.

My uncle Al, I might add, also tried his hand at poetry, and his effort had been more intensive and serious. The manuscript for his first book, *Clinical Judgment* (1967), began with a multipage poem about the importance of commitment and care between doctor and patient. It concluded, "I sit by his side, / I take his tired hand, / and lead him into night." Al had sent the poem to my father and Thorpe, who lived on the fourth floor of the brownstone at that time; Thorpe had befriended Charles Olson and many other poets, and he also founded a couple of short-lived literary magazines. Al's editor wanted the poem to be significantly tighter, if not cut entirely. Both Thorpe and my father agreed, and they worked for a long time, cutting passages, even pages. Finally, my father said, "I've *got* it. The whole poem will be just three lines: 'I sit by his side, / I take his tired hand— / He won't need it where he's going.'"

No version of the poem appeared with the book, which became a classic in the medical field of epidemiology, although decades later, my uncle still insisted that the poem "wasn't bad."

Of my formal poetry readings, the one my father attended took place in lower Manhattan at the National Arts Club in 1995. I'd received the Writers Exchange Program Award for poetry, sponsored by Poets & Writers, and it included a lavish half-week in Manhattan where I and the fiction winner were fêted at upscale restaurants, the kinds of places my family never imagined dining in. We were joined at those meals by a range of writers—Cornelius Eady, William Matthews, Molly Peacock, Calvin Trillin—as well as editors and publishers. I felt launched into literary society.

The second half of that week, I might add, they flew us to South Carolina, the location of the subsequent Writers Exchange Program Award. Our guide there, Quitman Marshall, made arrangements for us to meet James Dickey, whose poetry I greatly admired, although I'd heard more than a few stories about his drinking and womanizing. Quitman had studied with Dickey, and he knew, as we did not, that the poet was dying. In fact, when Quitman called to make the request, Dickey picked up the phone and, in a deep drawl, said, "Death's door."

Quitman tried to explain a bit about the program, but Dickey interrupted him:

"Are they smart?"

"Well, yeah. I mean—"

"They'd better be smart."

We were greeted at Death's door by a helper or friend and brought to a large room with a grand piano, the top closed and covered with pictures of the author in his prime. James Dickey sat in the center of the room, surrounded by stalagmites of books that, apparently, he'd read and then pile up. A sofa faced his chair, and after he greeted us politely, he asked us to sit before him. He apologized for not getting up, then took a slurp of some chalky fluid prepared, no doubt, to calm his ulcerated body. Judging from famous PR photos, I could tell he'd lost an enormous amount of weight, an evaporating man surrounded by artifacts to remind him of robust years.

"Now," he began, "if one were to select the five most important poets from the twentieth century, who would they be?"

The fiction winner, my companion on the hot seat, said, "That's a question for the poet," meaning, "I think you're screwed, buddy." I'm sure I swallowed hard. It felt like a trap. I knew enough about egomaniacs to realize that Dickey didn't want *a* list; he wanted to hear *his* list. And I knew his list would only include white men. Still, I figured I could offer an unassailable first choice that would please us both.

"The list would have to include Yeats," I said.

Dickey came alive and almost rose from his chair.

"Yes, yes," he replied. "The list would *have* to include Yeats."

"And I suppose, if only for the impact of 'The Waste Land,' the list would include Eliot."

"Absolutely," he said with just as much conviction although with slightly less enthusiasm.

At this point, I suppose I'd proven to be if not smart then at least smart enough, and Dickey took charge, expanding his list with Auden; contemplating other candidates (including Pound, Rilke, and Valéry); and then going backwards to rank *the* most important poet of the twentieth century: Yeats. I realized, then, how fortunate I'd been with my initial answer.

He agreed to sign some books, speaking while he inscribed them and writing so slowly that I battled my great desire to read the inscription in his company. (Back in the car, I learned that he'd merely written, "To Sascha, from James Dickey," and that the time expenditure resulted from floral script and his flamboyantly underlined name, the ink curling like elegant vines.) We left his home feeling happy and unscathed, and then drove for miles along a highway engulfed on either side with irrepressible kudzu. As Dickey writes in a poem named after that invasive plant:

> You open your windows,
>
> With the lightning restored to the sky
> And no leaves rising to bury
>
> You alive inside your frail house,
> And you think, in the opened cold
> Of the surface of things and its terrors,
> And of the mistaken, mortal
> Arrogance of the snakes
> As the vines, growing insanely, sent
> Great powers into their bodies

With its eerie plantations, South Carolina seemed like another country. Manhattan, however, still felt like home, and I felt both nervous and charged to be reading at the musty yet distinguished National Arts Club. My father and his wife arrived early, as did my uncle Al, who had driven from Connecticut. I read from a manuscript that would eventually be published as

Misterioso, and, when I'd finished, I spotted my father as he left the room during the applause.

He returned, fortunately, and he smiled as he shook my hand. But mainly he wanted to talk about a personal struggle that took place during my reading, one that I hadn't noticed because of my focus on the poems. Eighty at that time, he battled common disorders with his prostate, experiencing frequent and acute impulses to urinate but with very little result. He knew he wouldn't last the reading without extreme discomfort, so he improvised a solution: He'd bring condoms and slip one on if faced with a desperate urge.

Although a mere footnote to this bizarre story, it's interesting to note that he still *owned* condoms. He'd been married for ten years and had no need for contraception; these rubbers would have been remainders from his dating craze in the early '80s, right after my mother died. Now, finally, they had a use.

Never one to sidestep a good joke, he said he was doing very well until I read a jazz poem and reached the phrase "Monk's pissed," at which point he pulled a condom from his pocket and ripped open the packaging. The problem then, of course, was getting it on. Surrounded by strangers (not that friends would have made this any less ridiculous and weird), he stuffed his hands down his pants and began to fumble. His wife, taking note, thrust the program over his lap in order to conceal what must have looked purely perverse, and later I couldn't help but wonder if a person from the Writers Exchange Program, someone whom I'd introduced to my father, noticed him with his hands inside his slacks, squirming for the angle of salvation while I delivered my poems.

And yet, had he been caught, I'm convinced he would have come up with some magical line that transformed mortification into triumph. (Harry Holl's son, José, once pointed in my father's direction and jokingly warned a friend, "Watch out for this guy. He's got a fast mouth.") The combination of linguistic cleverness and an insistence on never being wrong deflected almost any strange or offensive action he committed. The results could be hilarious or infuriating.

He also had a fairly healthy contempt for mankind's intelligence, and he enjoyed thinking the worst of the world because every now and then, when something bad occurred, he'd take cosmic credit for predicting the misfortune. Never mind the other 98 percent of the time, when the world orbited just fine without his proclamations. He'd point to the ground—terra firma as sacred witness—and proclaim in a tone that seemed to validate his presence on earth, "And people call me *paranoid!*"

This also meant it was difficult to get away with pranks; he suspected foul play before anyone had a notion. In his younger days, he himself hoodwinked scores of friends and acquaintances. Frankly, I loved those stories, and one way to keep my father's attention was to ask to hear them again. I even replicated some of the pranks, especially the Page 2 letter, a particularly effective zinger for sluggish friends who have failed to correspond: Simply mail a sheet of paper with "2" typed at the top of the page and begin in mid-sentence with something enticing, for example, "but fortunately I'm insured, and most of the burns will be scar-less. Anyway, enough of that! Let me tell you about . . ."

Another favorite: During his years with Barbara, he set up two people on a blind date. But he told both parties, individually, that the other person was terribly hard of hearing, and not to be alarmed or dismayed if their date spoke very loudly. The couple met at a restaurant and screamed at each other before somehow uncovering the truth. I don't know if their relationship lasted; they never spoke to my father again.

He'd come from a tradition of good-spirited chiding. I'm thinking now of my grandfather in the early twentieth century. He was on the docks in Philly and had given a man a hotfoot. (I've never seen this done, but apparently you place a match, head first, into the sole of someone's shoe. Then you light the stick like a fuse burning toward the phosphorus end.) The victim claimed that his pants had been singed and demanded ten dollars—a lot of money at that time. He was paid on the spot.

"Now," my grandfather said, "I want your pants."

"What do you mean?"

"I paid for your pants. Now I want them."

He refused, but several guys on the dock grabbed his arms and fleeced him of his slacks. I don't know how he got home.

Over the years, several people tried to pull one over on my father, but nothing ever panned out. Again, it's a tremendous challenge to fool someone who's paranoid. My best effort took place in February of 1982, during my first year of college. The previous year had been strange at best, with my father leaping into bed with anyone who accepted his bold overtures. They had been conquests more than love interests, a collection of willing women who stoked his ego, and he wanted me to know of his prowess. (Once, he held up a pair of dainty panties and said, "I can narrow it down to three possibilities.") In one instance, however, a former student now living in another state appeared in Manhattan for a visit and, according to him, made undesired advances.

"She just grabbed my arm," he said. "In *public*."

I found this entertaining, and I knew I could set the hook. I enlisted the help of his third-floor tenant: I'd mail a postcard to her in an envelope, and she would just slip it in with the rest of the mail so that a postmark wouldn't give me away. It would be a Valentine's Day proposition—passionate, obvious, and filthy—and it would be in the form of a limerick. Also, I had letters from this person that included her rather telling signature; I would type the poem on the card, trace her signature lightly on carbon paper, and then ink it in.

The limerick itself spoke of her desire for his firm, hairy body. It said she lusted for his "sweet tush," and it concluded with a marriage proposal. I typed in everything (poem and addresses), perfectly forged her signature, and then, cherry on the sundae, added some hearts with a red felt pen. Then I mailed the card to our tenant and waited, somewhat impatiently, for his response. Three or four days later, I got the call.

"You will not *believe* this," my father said. "You absolutely will not believe this."

In the spirit of Othello requiring ocular proof, he promised to make a Xerox copy for me. He could not get over the brazen language.

"She wrote this on a *postcard*," he said. "Everyone could see it. The postman now looks at me funny." (And people called him paranoid . . .) Then he decided he couldn't wait for me to receive it by mail and read the Valentine's limerick over the phone.

I was dying on the other end, but he interpreted my laughter as indignation, not celebration. Then, as promised, he copied the card and posted it to my campus address. The following day, as usual, he left for his weekly classes in Philadelphia and Princeton, where he entertained those students with the news of this outrageous former friend.

On February 16, he mailed the Xerox, along with a parenthetical note on the bottom: "Just one of my groupies." But somewhere along the line—perhaps literally along the line from Princeton to New York—he started to suspect the scam. He pored over the card with a magnifying glass. Why was there no postmark? Why was this typed? Was there some hesitation in the signature, and, beyond that, would she *really* be so reckless and aggressive? No.

In retaliation, he sent me a note that told me to have a Xerox made of the Xerox sent, claiming that he'd "sent the original back to her, marked 'MOVED—ADDRESS UNKNOWN.'" But on the 22nd, realizing the shallowness of that comeback, he scratched out a far better reply, one comprised of four limericks. All are pretty clever, but the first still slays me, almost to the point of calling it a draw:

Oh Sascha, my heretofore solace
I'd not thought that such vicious malice
was part of your makeup.
But now I must wake up
to fact: I have fathered a phallus!

CHAPTER SIXTEEN

~

Boats and Starships

In August of 1988, I went fishing with my father for the first time. I initiated the outing because I had news that required coaxing and, I thought, deserved a bit of ceremony. Marleni and I had gotten engaged that winter; we'd now set a date for the following summer, and I wanted to invite him to attend. It would be a traditional Indian wedding, held in her home country (Singapore). He was my only living parent, and a snub would be culturally shameful. But how would I convince him to travel?

I decided to break the news during a father-and-son outing, one unlike anything we'd experienced. In retrospect, I realize the absurdity of this idea, one that forced an idealized American scenario onto a decidedly unusual family dynamic. But during my undergraduate years (1981–1985), I became completely enamored of a Hemingwayesque professor, Jim Spenko, who idealized what "real men" should do. In that spirit, I decided we would bond, man to man, talking love, marriage, and futures. I would clean our canoe, revitalize a couple of old rods, and we would fish the mill ponds in Brewster.

A grand, New England fishing trip. Call me Imbecile.

The canoe had been purchased in the summer of '77 at a store, not a yard sale. (I mention this to emphasize the fact that it was a big deal.) That year, my eighth-grade class had divided into large groups intended to bring classmates together—various summer-camp programs that began in the spring. The most popular, as I recall, was Outward Bound, for which I held a Woody Allen–like contempt. Of the choices, the canoe trip appealed to me the most, but I had little interest in joining a group, despite my mother's prodding. She eagerly nudged me to make more friends, but I was content to be a loner. Finally, my father interceded: "Look, with the money I'd be spending on this trip, we can *buy* our own canoe." If he had to spend this kind of cash, he could at least save some money in the process and, much more important, end up owning something of value.

That June, we left the Goose Hummock shop in Orleans with a bright yellow Merrimack strapped to the roof of our '58 Volvo. It was a beaut, wider than traditional canoes—almost forty inches—with an interior luxuriously lined with mahogany. The yellow body was fiberglass, not meant for rapids, and so attention had been paid to detail and design, including the attractively caned seats. One could immediately respect the craftsmanship, whether or not one had any inclination for water sports.

My mother and I launched the canoe a number of times in nearby Scargo Lake as well as the mill ponds in Brewster. We never fished from it; we simply paddled out to enjoy gliding by the waterscapes. Our excursions took place that first summer and the next. In '79, her last summer, she suffered back pains—the undiagnosed cancer taking hold—and I don't recall any trips to the ponds. In fact, the canoe probably remained dry until 1988, when I invited my father to fish.

We drove to the Grist Mill in Brewster on a morning so clear and crisp, so ideal for my naïve intentions, that I considered the day sun-blessed. I know my father felt perplexed by the experience because in uncomfortable situations he rattled off bad jokes and one-liners. Nothing I said or observed could get him into the spirit of camaraderie. When I pointed to a perfect arrow of geese overhead, he responded, "Listen to them—they're laughing at us." When I noticed the tip of a largely submerged boat, its shattered remains reminiscent of a storybook pirate scene, he said, "Yeah—those are the last people who tried to fish here."

His insistence that we wouldn't catch anything locked into a general philosophy, if not his modus operandi: Preach failure, and failure won't disappoint.

But I remained an idealistic fool. I wanted our first fishing experience to feel somewhat spiritual, primal. Father and son. Mysterious water. I wanted a vibe worthy of a serious discussion before I brought up the forthcoming nuptials. I wanted something joyously quiet. I wanted respectful solemnity, and a sense of shared experience.

"Jesus Christ!" my father shouted.

"What?"

"Jesus *Christ*—I've caught a whale!"

The tip of his rod had plunged into the water, and now he had it in the air while he reeled maniacally, the freshwater rod arced with such strain I feared it might snap.

"Could be a bass," I said, grinning in shared victory. "I think you've hooked a bass, Dad."

A catch not only disproved his insistent pessimism; it transformed the experience into something, well, more macho. "We are men. We hunt food." And I felt no competition. In fact, I badly wanted him to catch something, and a bass was ideal. In the Mill Ponds, they grew to ten or twelve pounds.

I grabbed the net as the fish's shadow edged toward us. By now, it seemed aware of its captivity; the fight had concluded and its body moved with my father's steady reeling. I leaned a bit over the side, cautious not to create too much of a shift so that we didn't tip. Then I netted the prize.

This was no bass. Apart from monkfish that sometimes washed ashore along the bay, it was the ugliest sea creature I'd ever seen, as homely and brown as Elizabeth Bishop's famous catch in her poem "The Fish," except I saw no heroic features here.

"What the hell is that?" my father asked.

"Catfish," I said. "We don't want to keep it."

"I should hope not."

The morning sun eventually heated the water and sent the fish away from their feeding grounds near the shore, so we paddled back. As I recall, I didn't broach the wedding topic until we'd reached Land Amen, the canoe strapped to the car, the failed experiment blessedly over. When I told him of our plans, he said everything sounded fine, but he would not be attending—not a chance, end of story. His abrupt, determined negation stunned and saddened me, although I tried not to show emotion or suggest judgment. And then, in a relatively short time, I began to feel liberated in a number of ways. I did not have to concern myself, for example, with his happiness or comfort, and both would be challenged. Singapore is known for its astonishing cuisine, which would not have interested him in the slightest, and its museums focused primarily on Southeast Asian culture; in 1989, at least, the country didn't own any paintings by Western masters. Humidity drenches your body as soon as you step outside the airport. He would have been bored and steamed.

Still, it's entertaining to envision him in the temple among the small oil fires and tossed rose petals, following the gestures of our hefty priest who spoke only in Sanskrit. I also suspect he would have been baffled by the architecture of Indian temples, as I was initially. The entrance to the Sri Veeramakaliamman Temple where we got married, for example, features the requisite tiled walls with vertical red-and-white stripes, colors as subtle as an emergency exit. Above the doorway itself rises a masterfully carved pagoda of three-dimensional reliefs in celebration of Kali, who's depicted astride a lion on the lowest, largest tier. But the color choices for these reliefs—treasured gold, blood red, sky blue—make the narratives almost overwhelming for the eyes. And then, above the golden minarets at the pagoda's crest, aesthetically as incongruous as a chunk of Kryptonite, the builders affixed a glowing, neon Om sign.

My own bewilderment at this mélange of architecture caused me to query Marleni's uncle, Kanaga, a renowned art historian in Singapore.

"What is the thinking behind these choices?" I asked, trying to sound sincere and not critical.

"It means," he said, grinning both at my question and his impending answer, "'We want everything. We want it all.'"

The Indian architects had united the incongruity of tile, sculpture, and neon through tradition and theme. The incongruity of forms in my father's still lifes, on the other hand, united because of color and movement. One was based on narrative; the other resisted narrative. Both, of course, strove for something spiritual.

Kali herself fascinated me because of her oxymoronic nature: healing humanity by ingesting evil. In my favorite wedding photo, we're smiling on a wooden settee beneath her four outstretched arms that each held a golden weapon. The pupils within her huge eyes target the world beneath her, as though ready to scorch the ground with laser vision. Elsewhere in the temple, she's presented with a regal crown and decorated with immense garlands of jasmine, roses, and lush limes, all the while balancing across her lap a corpse with its torso splayed open. Her fangs and wide tongue secure the demon's intestines that hang from her mouth like dead wisteria.

My father's absence from the ceremony ended up being far less embarrassing than I had feared. People were told the edited truth: that he was seventy-four and had a heart condition. They were not told, of course, that neither played a factor in his decision. The day of our canoe trip, he explained with passion how he and his wife had visited Italy earlier that summer, and the trip had totally interfered with his painting schedule, from the planning, to the time away, to the jet lag upon return. (This did not surprise me. As a tourist, he replicated a Travelator. He bragged about seeing fourteen cities in thirteen days, including Assisi to witness the basilica with work by Giotto and Cimabue, and I'm told he'd spend much of each night pinpointing the itinerary for the next excursion. In a way, he preferred to collect cities rather than experience them.) So he insisted that he would not attend my wedding in Singapore. He'd learned his lesson: Italy had ruined his rhythm.

What does that mean, exactly—to have one's rhythm ruined? In *Rhythms of Vision: The Changing Patterns of Myth and Consciousness*, a book my father admired, Lawrence Blair discusses the expansive topic by providing a Whitmanesque embrace of the world. "The difference between blue and orange, F sharp and E flat, even between a circle and a square," he explains, "are differences only in wave motion." To break that wave motion would mean organic collapse—but doesn't his statement imply that we should move *with* the world?

Before reading *Rhythms of Vision*, I had encountered Lawrence Blair through a TV series called *Ring of Fire: An Indonesian Odyssey*. He and his brother Lorne set out in 1972 "looking for a little adventure." They spent ten years traveling, much of the time battling conditions unimaginable even to seasoned travelers. When they made their initial launch from Singapore, for example, they spent weeks living in a cramped cabin on a Bugis pirate ship—a space barely large enough for them to sleep in—and shared it, as Lawrence explains in the film's narration, with five varieties of ants, plus many unidentifiable creatures, "all of them seeming to bite." To make us squirm just a bit more, he adds, "But the most active are the cockroaches, which at night come out in vast hordes."

That's one of the few moments in the series when the brothers highlight hardship. Like so many nature documentaries, *Ring of Fire* makes us fantasize about firsthand experiences without dwelling on the necessary personal sacrifice. We hear transient lines about "a wet and windless week going nowhere," and easily cast-off introductory phrases such as "seven weeks later," but who among us has the time for that kind of travel, and, if we did, the patience?

The Blairs eventually reach the Indonesian island of Sulawesi, where the rooftops arc toward the heavens. For many years, it was believed that this architecture paid homage to the starships that first brought the Torajans to their land. "Your anthropologists laugh at us for saying we came from the stars," a high priest explains to the Blair brothers, before modifying the oral history.

> They do not think we may mean the "inner stars." The old Tominahs say that this crescent-moon shape means the bottom arc of a great vertical circle of our lives—the section at which we are all most deeply plunged into matter. It's to remind us that we sweep down from the upper world, slide round the bottom of the circle, and sweep up again, no trouble, if we have any sense.

By the time I visited Tana Toraja in 1998, the influence of Christianity had caused a less imaginative interpretation of their architecture: My guide explained that the starships were merely ships, boats that had landed on the shores of Sulawesi, then known as Celebes. I tried to smile approvingly, to be respectful, despite the loss of magic and the disintegration of myth.

My disappointment connected to personal pleasure and sentimentality: myth, albeit Scandinavian myth, inspired many of my mother's artworks, especially her tapestries. The weavings did not depict realistic portraiture as much as their godly presences. She titled a dark, brooding piece *Odin*, father of Thor; a more animated work, with sea blues and a variety of grays that frame a warmed, red center, bore the title *Loki*, after the trickster figure. Much more dramatically red was *Sleipnir*, named after Thor's enormous horse. With or without the mythic story—and I suppose this holds true as well for Torajan architecture—the works exude a penetrating dignity.

In the summer of 2001, we held a large retrospective of my mother's work at the Cape Museum of Fine Arts, and, oh boy, what a show! Weavings and paintings and fabric appliqués. Woven dresses, exquisite line drawings, carved wooden blocks and textile designs, even children's books under glass. What she accomplished by forty-seven excited and challenged us all.

Equally bewildering for me, however, was a gesture by my father so unexpected I didn't trust his sincerity: He said I could take the show's contents, and any other works of hers that we didn't display, back with me to Pennsylvania.

Let me put this overture in perspective: The year before, my family and I moved to a large Victorian house with high ceilings, large rooms, and unpainted woodwork. It dwarfed our previous home, and suddenly we needed to think about filling spaces. That's when I remembered a large bentwood rocker from my childhood. It had been stored in New York after a houseguest broke through the caned seat, and it remained hidden for decades.

"I'd like to have it polished and re-caned," I explained to my father. "Can I take it back to Pennsylvania?" He didn't pause even momentarily before shutting down the idea. I tried again, smiling at the absurdity: "It's been stored away—unseen, broken—for *years*."

"No," he repeated. "That's an expensive rocker."

So relinquishing the legacy of my mother's art could hardly have astounded me more. Did he know he only had two years to live? Having taken most of the work from New York City, did he decide the extra space could be better filled with more junk? I'll never know.

I returned to the Cape that fall when the show closed, having borrowed from our friends Jon and Deb their Jeep named Moe. And because most of the work could be rolled, I managed to stuff it all in, leaving nothing behind. I also decided to take the canoe, which hadn't felt water since my father landed the catfish. Once again thinking unrealistically, I imagined family trips along the mighty Susquehanna, our nation's longest unnavigable river. Had the canoe strapped to the Jeep been inverted, tips to the sky, the silhouette would have resembled a Torajan house.

My father played no games with the deal. He applauded my packing skills, and we had a loving goodbye; ironically, what had caused the greatest amount of anxiety turned out to be the easiest part of the journey. Fifteen minutes into the trip, while on the highway, the roof strapping began to fail, and the canoe began to swish from side to side. I pulled over and tightened the straps, but two minutes later the canoe once again shifted diagonally in front of my windshield.

I followed an off ramp, found a hardware store, and properly secured the canoe to Moe's roof, and while the worst possibilities seemed over (shattered yellow fiberglass, car crashes, manslaughter), the weather darkened considerably just twenty minutes later, and I found myself in near-blinding lightning storms. Also, the new straps, while tight, vibrated intensely from the vicious winds; between their merciless buzz and the tormenting rain, the Jeep resounded more loudly than the interior of a prop plane. At times, the noise died down as I joined a stream of brake lights, cars inching through negligible visibility. At all speeds, I leaned into and over the steering wheel to eye patches of road while trying simultaneously to mark the exact position of the canoe's tip, still fearful that the new straps might fail. Lightning flashes. The rain, the rain, the rain.

Over four hours later, I pulled over when my tank neared empty and the skies, too, had finally run dry. I remember closing my eyes at the gas pump, almost napping until the handle clicked. I wanted something warm to eat and staggered into a small pizza joint. A gal with freckled milky skin and big teeth smiled from behind the register. From the highway, I hadn't noticed the name of the town. I didn't even know the state.

"Where am I?"

The gal beamed still wider. "Pizza Phil!"

"No, I mean, what town is this?"

"Oh," she said, slowly. "You're not from around here, are ya?"

I'd landed in Fishkill, New York, just three hours from home, and the rest of the drive was comparably easy, although I almost collapsed in our driveway. Still, I wanted to empty the Jeep right away, partly so I could return Moe to Jon and Deb, but mainly from a need of closure. I used the new straps to create hanging harnesses inside the carriage house, loops that cradled the canoe's yellow belly, its shape now appropriately righted. From a distance, it seemed to float in air.

And after I had unpacked the wealth of my mother's art and my own few personal belongings, I indeed felt a sense of triumph and a huge swell of relief. I had survived the toughest drive of my life; now was the time for contemplation. As Lawrence Blair said when returning to Bantu after the death of his brother, a trip that culminated in a ceremonial encounter with the royal family and a descent down a slope of loose stone: "It is these fragile communities that teach us that we must visit with care, and they remind us, in turn, that the pathway's both sacred and treacherous, and that it is worth paying attention to the now, and to the rhythms of the present."

Although my college had been in session for two weeks that fall, I had not truly found my teaching legs. My thoughts had kept returning to the forthcoming roundtrip, disbelieving my father's release of my mother's work, and fretting about the mere practicalities of bringing it home. (Would everything fit? Would work get damaged?) I felt only partly focused on the now; my rhythms of the present had been shaken. Do we say "closure" when we mean "focused rhythm"?

That night in bed, I thought, "Now I can start fresh. Tomorrow, in the classroom, they'll have *all* of me."

The following morning, I enjoyed the sunlight through my office windows, drank strong coffee, thought about locations for the newly returned art, and then turned to the poetry of William Carlos Williams and Langston Hughes, to be discussed in the morning class. I felt focused and serene. But I'd fallen into the trap of thinking of time as merely cyclic, with the Wheel of Fortune turning in either one direction or another, rather than thinking of fate as a constant flux of fortune. I'd forgotten that Kali translates to both Time and Black.

An hour later, two starships, one from each of the states where I was raised—New York and Massachusetts—blasted into Manhattan's skyline and brought the world to prayer.

CHAPTER SEVENTEEN

~

Fallen Basilica

The crack is moving down the wall.
Defective plaster isn't all the cause.
We must remain until the roof falls in.

—Weldon Kees, "Five Villanelles"

In the same way that betrayal by a loved one can feel as though the ground has shifted, so can the literal shifting of ground betray the land we love.

In this case, I'm talking of the sacred ground in Assisi where they built the basilica of San Francesco, later deemed a UNESCO World Heritage Site. Normally in museums, I share the guards' attentive concern, watching to see if anyone's too close to the art (not that I'd say anything), but I must confess to breaking museum law in Italy by snapping a photograph: the nave of the Upper Basilica, with its lapis vaults sun-struck with gold stars. Nor was I terribly clever (the guard caught me), but he simply waved a finger. I cherish that slide, whether illicit or not. What I had photographed—what I felt I simply could not leave without capturing even on a minute scale—would be shaken to ruin eleven years later, on September 26, 1997, by a devastating quake and its aftershocks.

In Luciano Bellosi's lavish study, *Cimabue*, an expert describes the wreckage like this:

The most serious damage—irreparable or only partially reparable—involves the frescoes in the Upper Basilica, which crumbled following the partial collapse of the vaults and half of the arch of the rear wall. . . . The area comprises more than 120 square meters of original paintings (made by the workshop of the young Giotto and Cimabue), today reduced to about fifty thousand colored shards.

After the first quake, friars and art inspectors congregated to assess the disaster. Some were inside the structure when the next wave hit, brutalizing the art and architecture, and killing four people, including two Franciscan friars.

I know where my father died, how he looked, approximately what he saw. But I don't know what the friars witnessed before their deaths. The irrecoverable frescos by Cimabue? The rattled but tenacious work of Giotto? The starry hemisphere from the upper nave? I cannot even tell you their names, although I know they entered the basilica to assess the future of art, and the sacredness of this holy landscape. Bless them. May they be witness to some semblance of Mark Doty's poem, "A Green Crab's Shell," the interior "open to reveal / a shocking, Giotto blue." In the poet's words: "Not so bad, to die, / if we could be opened / into *this*."

In the winter of 2005, during the most intense renovations on the Cape property, I thought again of those painted stars falling to the ground and shattering. I had stored many belongings in the barn so carpenters and painters could reconstruct the now-empty house, but work stalled completely for many weeks because record-setting snowstorms suffocated the region. (Months later, in the summer, the locals only wanted to talk about the winter.) Nature had smothered the inhabitants as the landscape swelled like muffin tops. Snowplows created impenetrable banks and sealed off the entrance to the property. Meanwhile, snow accumulated on the rooftops of the house and barn, despite the steep pitch, and that's when my father's makeshift skylight in the barn—an inserted sheet of safety glass two-and-a-half feet wide and six feet long—bowed enough to crack into thousands of glistening shards.

Snow continued to fall through the roof's hole, and no one noticed (much less repaired) the opening because no one could access the property. By the time workers boarded up and shingled the area, enough snow had accumulated to soak through the joists and flooring, thus destroying many of the items I had worked diligently to salvage. The sides of a wooden chest now warped beyond any function, and the circular top to a charming pedestal table split and opened like the mouth of a dying fish. Objects had fallen, and I found a ceramic lioness, given to me in childhood, cracked into thirds. I had stored a 1924, multivolume edition of *The Outline of Knowledge* with packets to absorb humidity, but they could not compete with such a soaking. Although by that point I had become increasingly able and willing to abandon things, the ruined settee, elegantly carved and brightly upholstered by my mother, depressed me with a heaviness more than equal to the wet snow that destroyed it.

Ultimately, though, I felt grateful that the schoolmaster's desk and the blanket chest, the two pieces of furniture that mattered most to me, remained unharmed. And the damage could have been far more extensive since the second skylight, also a large sheet of safety glass, had withstood the weight. In fact, with the damage long out of sight, it now feels almost like a Buddhist blessing to have been relieved of still more material possessions.

I also understood the limitations of my misfortune, especially when compared to genuine tragedy. At the time of the earthquake in Assisi, the photographer Ghigo Roli had been documenting the international treasure. His final images appear in Giorgio Bonsanti's *The Basilica of St. Francis of Assisi: Glory and Destruction*, a visual and visceral exploration of the book's subtitle. Forever damaged himself, Roli writes with poetic prose about the collapse:

> Every night I see those same images of chaos, superimposed and very clear: the scaffolding banging against the façade; the darkness inside the basilica from which, around the piles of rubble, confused white phantoms appear; the large key on the floor, and then the great door that won't open, with people calling and running and weeping, the great, immobile church trembling, the rents in the vaulting, the rubble lined up on the lawn outside, the work of the firemen, the dogs and the nurses, and then the great cloud of ocher dust, filmed live as it snuffs out, without distinction, the lives of four people, the symbol of a faith, and a treasury of art.

During my father's lifetime, other ceilings had collapsed. On the Cape, for example, the upstairs shower began to leak through porous grout between the tub tiles. He had stopped further leakage by duct-taping huge sheets of thick plastic on the interior. (In the shower, one felt like a sandwich in a wet baggie.) For the downstairs, where that portion of the ceiling had saturated, stained, and collapsed, he simply stapled a sheet of thick but flimsy white paper. In New York, he retiled the second-floor bathroom wall with his own exciting mosaic, but it never withstood the water pressure, so he covered his mosaic with plastic, effectively obscuring his artwork—but not before water ruined much of the architecture beneath.

The damaged area below, I might add, had been my room until I turned sixteen. Yes, I grew up in a room the size of a bathroom—and, quite likely, given the layout of the second and third floors, it had once been a bath-room—but I adored it. The story goes like this: we moved into the brown-stone on the Upper West Side of Manhattan when I was two. My mother walked me through the house toward the back, where this tiny, windowless room jutted out into a courtyard. She called it my bedroom and then moved on for what she figured would be the highlight of this first-floor tour. "Now," she said, like a magician unveiling the show's *dénouement*, "look at what we have here." And she opened the French doors onto the courtyard. But I no longer stood near her heels, and she turned her head to my slamming bed-room door: "It's mice!" I yelled, apparently unable to say "mine" but able to claim space. I slept there for the next thirteen years.

Initially, my parents placed a crib in there, and later replaced it with a bed that my father constructed. I remember the switch because one of their friends entertained me with a new Beatles album, *A Hard Day's Night*, and tried to mesmerize me into digging my new digs, but I didn't need coaxing. I loved the bed. As long as the room remained my room, nothing else mattered.

Dressers and bureaus that my father brought in from the street eventually became the foundation for yet a new bed placed above those drawers. (He built a ladder and painted it deep blue. The thought of a "bunk" bed thrilled me, as he knew it would.) The L-shaped base had a gap just wide enough for a child to slide through, creating a hiding space, which, of course, I also loved. I became much like a mouse who repositions its environment into tunnels leading to nests. I felt a primitive if not primal satisfaction. It was mice.

One of my favorite essayists, Bernard Cooper, speaks of his urgent desire in childhood to enter the world of abstract expressionism, changing not merely individual objects but his entire environment:

> Soon I was scavenging trash cans for material with which to make mock Rauschenbergs. Junkyards provided the small, twisted scraps of metal I epox-ied into a tortured jumble, just as John Chamberlain had welded together the shrapnel of crashed cars. I bolted an actual terrycloth towel to a painted rack, homage to the bathroom interiors of Tom Wesselmann. My room became a gallery in which I showed derivative work and brooded on what it meant to be modern.

I find that description so charming. And in many ways, his artistic soul-searching makes me feel all the more grateful for the domestic "galleries" in which I lived.

Whatever toys I brought out of the room would, at the end of the day, have to be returned—fair enough—and this meant selective material joy because the room could only hold so much. I say that in admiration of my early ideals: I never felt deprived, ever, but what I kept, I used. As I grew older, in fact, this became a problem for others; I didn't *want* more stuff. One summer, I spent the entire afternoon shopping with my uncle Al, who offered me *anything*. We went from store to store, and he tried so persistently to spark my interest, but I judged everything by long-term value: How many times would I play with X? Could Y possibly be worth that much money? The next day, my aunt told me that her husband came home exhausted from the experience, took a nap, and almost slept to the next morning. I felt guilty, despite my uncompromising beliefs.

After I moved away, my father requested that I empty my old room in New York so he could create a small library, an idea that fully appealed to me. I ended up keeping very little. I saved my massive Lego collection, my baseball cards, and (I admit rather sheepishly) some plastic dolls: Action Jackson—the diminutive version of G.I. Joe—and the comparably-sized *Planet of the Apes* figures. I had never seen any movies from the *Planet of the Apes* series, but I loved the concept: the world's sensibility turned inside-out. I thought my children, when I had them, might especially enjoy the Legos and cards.

The library never materialized. Although he moved a number of books into that limited space, he primarily crammed it with his usual accumulation of broken artifacts—which I can't specify because, by my next visit, I could only see the impenetrable façade. It was almost solid within.

"Nice library," I said, to absolutely no effect.

Fantasies about my own children rekindling my passions also largely failed, through no fault of their own. Neither followed baseball (and, in fairness, I had stopped following the sport long before their births), so the cards were a bust. My son became briefly hooked on elaborate Lego sets but, understandably, found my thirty-year-old collection rather primitive, even fragile. (Plastic, apparently, isn't indestructible.) And the poor Action Jacksons and *Planet of the Apes* figures got savagely eaten by squirrels that invaded our Pennsylvania attic when we were summering on the Cape. Apparently, one good bite to the interior elastic and the entire body collapses. Had Charlton Heston been at my side, he would have hollered, "They chewed it all to Hell!"

During my teenage years, squirrels entered and died in the Cape house during the winter, a kind of animalistic reenactment of Géricault's *The Raft of the Medusa*. The metal mesh that my father had secured over the chimney top had given way from the weather or animals or both, and when we entered our home that spring, the acrid smell of rotting flesh overwhelmed us. Then the body count began—five or six in total, as I recall. Unable to go back up the chimney, or unable to recall their entry point, the squirrels frantically gnawed at the window sills, often leveling wood and caulk to the glass but never breaking through. Until our huge renovation decades later, in which we replaced all sashes, the windows remained raw and splintery, constant reminders of creatures mortally betrayed by their shelter.

By the time of my father's death, both the Philadelphia and New York properties had leaking roofs. (This would have been true in Dennis, too, except that, to his profound consternation, he had been forced to replace the shingles.) And, once again, I'm reminded of *The Gleaners and I*, when director Agnès Varda returns to her home after filming out of town and meditates, with both mind and camera, on her ceiling's spreading stain: "Then I look at the leak in the ceiling and the mold, I got used to it. I like it in the end. [The camera pans over a flaking crust.] It's like a landscape, an abstract painting. [Framed image:] a Tápies. [New frame:] a Guo Qiang. [New frame:] a Borderie." She and my father found stains more fascinating than threatening.

This sensibility carried over to cracks in the plaster caused from stored weight that the original builders would never have imagined. (How did Yeats put it in "Lapis Lazuli"? "Every discoloration of the stone, / Every accidental crack or dent, / Seems a water-course or an avalanche. / Or lofty slope where it still snows.") For my father, architecture became a sculptural aesthetic, virtually removed from physics. On the Cape, his bold extraction of interior walls caused the seller, Charlie Johnson, to warn him about the house collapsing, so my father built an ornamental post to the right of the front door-jamb. It was his own little joke: Not only was its position inconsequential, but the purely ornamental post had been raised six inches off the floor.

Can a painting's roof fall in? I'm not talking about literal depiction, like those my father made of the burning house, but more generally about aesthetics, particularly tonality. A painting, my father explained during our conversations about Hans Hofmann, ought to have a "kind of rhythmic consistency":

> You can have close intervals, very close, if they're consistent; you can have intervals that offer great contrast, if they're consistent. You might even have contrasting and close intervals together, providing you lead into them gently enough. For example, you can ride on a road with huge potholes, but if there are ramps—blendings into and out of the holes—you would get in and out of them and hardly feel it. If they were sudden, of course, you would get a jolt. And that's what the eye experiences in the suddenness of such contrasts.

This strikes me as absolutely right, and the rhythmic vitality of his work bore out his philosophy almost without fail. I just wish the "potholes" in the houses had been repaired with equal care.

In the last fall of his life, I drove to see him in New York. That same day, I took the subway downtown to stoke my own collections (jazz CDs and books), but also to find something appealing as a gift. That's when I spotted Lucianno Bellosi's *Cimabue*, a well-researched, coffee-table book with luminous illustrations worthy both of the artist and the artist's goal. History had not treated Cimabue with the appropriate number of publications. I'd never seen this book's equal, and I knew he'd appreciate it.

According to the book's Postscript, the manuscript "was in its final stages" when the earthquake rocked Assisi, and two pages later, a full-bleed photo depicts the devastation. It contrasts with tragic vividness the two-page spread in the center of the monograph: the lapis vaults unharmed, resplendent. "It almost seems that a curse is attached to Cimabue and his works," Bellosi explains. "There came a time when he was in danger of disappearing from art history altogether. Almost all of his surviving paintings are in deplorable conditions." As we see even in the reproductions of work untouched by quakes and floods, much of Cimabue's art appears to have been painted on crumbling sponge cake.

Must an artist's legacy be determined by artifact? More and more I lean toward Yeats's "Lapis Lazuli," where the ingenious work of Callimachus, the fifth-century Greek sculptor, has been obliterated by time. Isn't it enough, the poem asks us, to celebrate the act over the product, to believe in the *spirit* of creativity rather than the materialistic "proof"? Ultimately, I'd like to think so—but I'm also so grateful to witness genius, both to be humbled and inspired.

Back at the house after giving my father his present, my wife and I did much of the talking to spare his energy. We tried to be upbeat, telling humorous anecdotes about the children, and we made him chuckle a few times. Then he stood and pointed to a stack of relatively small paintings that he'd been creating—in essence, his final works.

"I'd like you to choose one," he said. "If you want."

At first, language escaped me. I already owned some of his paintings, but I had *begged* for them (failing in my efforts more often than not). Now, for the first time, he had made the overture. He *wanted* me to have a painting. I couldn't believe it. The only situation to rival this gesture had been on the day when he released my mother's artwork.

I accepted with as much loving gratitude as I could express, and slowly sifted through the pile. Frankly, and no surprise given the conditions and the circumstance, they were wildly uneven, and many seemed more like thin starts. Then I came across a dramatically horizontal acrylic (one foot by two feet) that demonstrated the kind of organic, rhythmic consistency he advocated. And in that extraordinary moment, I talked a bit about those qualities, just to let him know, I suppose, that I had actually learned something over the years, that his teaching had deeply influenced me, and that the painting would be loved.

Then he shook his head and said, quite sincerely, "No—I don't think you can have that one."

The ground seemed to shift. "Are you serious?"

"Yeah, I might want to have that one shown."

So I laughed and said, "Okay!" and took off without selecting an alternative.

Outside, my wife said she was sorry. As usual, she was wise enough not to push too hard, and not to psychoanalyze the situation. She just offered tight, consoling smiles as I sputtered.

"Why do this to your only son when you're *dying?*" I asked, rhetorically. "Why make the offer in the first place?"

"I don't know," she said.

"Did I talk myself out of it? What kind of power play is this?"

"I don't know."

That night, like every night in Manhattan, the bright architecture obscured the stars. I probably should have gone to a jazz club, but sometimes the blues overshadow the blues. Let him keep the damn painting, I thought. Let it stay by his bedside while he passes into the spirit world, a glowing reminder of what he can't take with him, and what he's left behind.

The following morning, with no prompting, he said he'd changed his mind. "I've decided to give you that painting," he said, "because you gave me such a nice book on Cimabue."

Maybe I should have told him to stuff it, but I accepted gracefully. It's framed, now, and displayed so that I see it every morning of the academic year. A strange gift, yes, but a gift nonetheless, and, devoid of context, it represents the best aspect of his legacy. As Weldon Kees wrote in "A Salvo for Hans Hofmann":

> Out of the summer's heat, the winter's cold,
> The look of harbors and the trees,
>
> The slashed world traced and traced again,
> Enriched, enlarged, caught in a burning scrutiny

Like fog-lamps on a rotten night. The scraps
Of living shift and change. Because of you,

The light burns sharper in how many rooms,
Shaped to a new identity; the dark hall

Finds a door; the wind comes in;
A rainbow sleeps and wakes against the wall.

Slashed with cadmium yellows and springtime green, my father's last important painting excites the wall in my study, much like a lightning strike that you know will be followed by thunder loud enough to threaten your rafters.

CHAPTER EIGHTEEN

~

Patterns of Organic Energy

The pair of branches, which had probably snapped from a large fallen cedar, rose over six feet in the air and, side by side, seemed to have been momentarily stopped, mid-march, across the patchy crabgrass. Quite consciously inverted and positioned, the grounded ends triangulated toward the thickest part that had once connected to the cedar's trunk. Coupled with "the willow bush," which had now lost all its bushiness and assumed a stunted tree identity, they consumed a fair amount of lawn. The branches presented a sculptural presence that asked viewers to reconsider the energy of abandoned objects, and my father named the pair after Gary Zukov's book, *The Dancing Wu Li Masters*.

I knew at some point they'd be removed (I didn't want to live with them; I wanted to live on the lawn) but I still felt the weight of my father's legacy. Should the branches be considered works of art—albeit readymades—and, if so, would throwing them out be akin to smashing a sculpture? Where is the line between celebrating abandoned forms in nature and attributing that celebration to an act of creation? And if all forms should be acknowledged for their energy and movement, should we throw out or even adjust *anything* in nature?

I realize the absurdity of two branches generating such immense issues, but, as I said, I felt the weight of those questions. So when renovations began, I told our contractor to make sure that the branches remained untouched, a quite-specific request since they were not the only chunks of wood on the lawn: In my excavation of the barn, I had unearthed entire tree trunks, some with substantial girth, that had been completely obscured for decades by the northwest corner of the still life. (Presumably, my father once had big plans for the trunks, but, like the abandoned barbeque pit and stone table, plans changed.) With wagons and dollies, I unloaded the dead trees and stacked them in a pile across the lawn from the "walking" branches. There could be no confusing the piles; still, I made a point of repeating my rather urgent desire not to move or damage the branches. My contractor, Guy Coletti, had known my father. He understood.

Guy's wife had studied painting with my father for many years, and I'd always found him to be unfailingly amiable. He had tight curls and cherubic, Gerber cheeks, so when he smiled, his whole face rounded into an emblem of happiness. We'd chosen him for his expertise—a legacy of beautifully constructed houses throughout Cape Cod—but his demeanor and our personal history provided an incalculable solace.

We returned several months later—after the winter season, which had badly delayed work on the house—and found all the wood, including the branches, removed from the lawn. I shouldn't have been surprised. And I felt no sadness; by then, I'd let go of so much that I simply couldn't embrace the responsibility of maintaining dead wood as art. Still, I dreaded my next encounter with my stepmother.

Guy arrived the following morning to walk us through recent developments and future plans. Despite delays, the workers had actually accomplished a great deal, and I felt not merely encouraged but excited. Before he left, however, I quietly inquired about the branches. I wanted him to know about the mistake, but I didn't want to make a big deal out of it, either.

Guy looked puzzled. "Didn't you hear?" he asked.

"No. Hear what?"

"She didn't tell you?"

"No," I said, realizing immediately that he must have been referring to my stepmother. "We arrived yesterday, and the branches were gone. That's all I know."

"Oh my God," he said, smiling widely. "I thought you knew. It's quite a story."

Guy had subcontracted a man to remove the trees from the lawn and, of course, this fellow assumed the branches needed to go as well. (The brush sites have a pretty good racket going. You pay them to offload, and then they turn everything into mulch, which people purchase in bulk. It's as clever as a barber who manages to sell cut hair.) Perhaps Guy had arrived late; perhaps the worker had come early. In any case, Guy wasn't there to stop him and arrived to find a completely clean expanse.

Not long afterward, Guy returned for another inspection, and my stepmother, according to him, threw herself at his vehicle, stopping him from leaving while screaming, *"The Dancing Wu Li Masters! The Dancing Wu Li Masters!"*

"At first," Guy said, "she was incomprehensible. Then she said the branches were gone."

At this point, he said, she began to beat the roof of his silver VW. She became apoplectic, screaming that he had thrown away sculpture and, beyond that, had absolutely *ruined* the house with his restoration.

"I wanted to calm her down," Guy explained, "and when I couldn't, when she kept banging harder on my roof, I thought, 'Well, I've got a hammer in the front seat . . .'"

She demanded to know where the branches had been taken, and he told her the man he'd hired lived in Sandwich, roughly forty minutes away. That's when she strapped her fury into her hatchback and gunned it down-Cape in search of *The Dancing Wu Li Masters.*

When she entered Sandwich, she saw a truck with brush and asked for the nearest dumpsite. And, astonishingly—the odds are just about impossible to calculate—the man she asked happened to be the same man who had cleared our lawn. At this point, she ordered him to lead the way to the brush pile and point in the general area where he had dumped a mix of loads, including the cedar branches. She explained all this to Guy in what he generously described as an apologetic phone call.

Sometimes I imagine her picking through the brush piles, upending tree limbs while workers paused to witness the frenzied search. I imagine, too, the branches dragged and shoved into the back of her Honda, the hatch raised to accommodate their length. Ropes. The cautious drive home. And what about the brush hauler who got flagged, harangued, and virtually hijacked? What would a crusty Cape Codder make of a middle-aged woman with a New York license plate as she tore through rubbish to find two specific broken branches? Like my father and the wandering beekeeper, they had no hope of connecting on any level.

In the years that have passed, I've never discussed the branches with her. I'm sure she just assumes their removal demonstrated yet another lack of respect on my part, although I can't begin to express how little that means to me now. But I'm fascinated by the psychology of loss and recovery, and, still more, by the relationships between the organic and inorganic elements of our world. The cover of Gary Zukov's book, *The Dancing Wu Li Masters,* suggests this union: Sixteen human legs encircling a sun. Sunflower pattern. Star-shaped gear. And the book itself eloquently speaks to this complexity:

> When we talk of physics as patterns of organic energy, the word that catches our attention is "organic." Organic means living. Most people think that

physics is about things that are not living, such as pendulums and billiard balls. This is a common point of view, even among physicists, but it is not as evident as it may seem. . . .

The distinction between organic and inorganic is a conceptual prejudice. It becomes even harder to maintain as we advance into quantum mechanics. Something is organic, according to our definition, if it can respond to processed information. The astounding discovery awaiting newcomers to physics is that the evidence gathered in the development of quantum mechanics indicates that subatomic "particles" constantly appear to be making decisions!

If all nature has an implicit order, and if the driving force of nature also applies to inorganic material, it follows that someone like my father, who painted and preached the fluid movement between all forms, would be incapable of seeing (or making) a mess. In fact, neatening the world—interiors to gardens—sterilized it to some degree. Beauty arrived with the seemingly arbitrary thrust of forces tangling the landscape.

So in the '70s, when Cape neighbors ripped out half an acre of their brush, he insisted they had "ruined" the land. What had been utterly impenetrable—thickets of honeysuckle, poison ivy, fallen branches, Virginia creeper, thorny brambles, and so much more—now highlighted an elegant stand of hardwoods across cut grass. The original wilderness created the illusion of privacy because nothing could be seen beyond the first two or three feet. Cleared and open to the street, the plot suddenly gleamed with sunlight. My father insisted that this exposure had been a disastrous mistake. Allow the world to see your life, and you've damaged your life. You become vulnerable.

And yet, despite his insistence that taming the wilds meant ruining its natural vitality, he believed passionately in art organizing chaos; he may have been an abstract expressionist, but he by no means abandoned rules for aesthetics. Far from it. "If there were no rules for painting," he frequently said, "then all paintings would have equal merit." Amen to that.

The four corners of a canvas represent (to some degree) a defined plot of land. With that, one needs to create a vibrant, balanced expression that in its gestures toward the eye makes it expand far beyond those four corners. About his own work, he wrote:

These paintings are conceived to project their own expression. Each is a body of color-forms shaped to gesture emotive pantomime: to radiate a specific presence whose pictorial stance can engage the viewer subjectively to draw forth direct feeling-response. They are optical structures composed to touch human spirit, to turn a rectangle into an evocation.

The painting thus becomes its own self-expression, liberated from its maker. From the subatomic particles that create hues, to the manipulated use of color and form, what we usually consider inorganic comes alive. No wonder he responded to Wu Li—"Patterns of Organic Energy"—and titled his lively branches after the book.

My clearing of the Cape property was immeasurably aided by our longtime friend, Paul Fitzgerald, whose wife, Bunny, had studied with my father for decades. Paul delivered his macho brush mower on permanent loan; with the poison ivy under control, I now had the capability of maintaining the grounds without the use of poison. Hiring people to clear the land was more than a little costly. Before Paul's gift, I'd hired on-the-cheap a kid with a brush mower, and both kept breaking down—the machine from neglect, the young man from dehydration. (We heard operatic retching from the woods and dubbed him Barfy Boy.) But now I could do the work on my own, and Paul loved what he saw. "This is great," he said, smiling widely. "Now you can make *sense* of the land."

An oral surgeon, he had manicured his own property with the precision required for his field and the elegance of his greatest artistic passion, pottery. From fruit trees to Monet-rich gardens, his property burst from within its carefully composed structure. He even planted bamboo at one point, but ripped it out when it proved to be ungovernable.

While Paul helped to save my property, he had, years earlier, literally saved my father's life. In June of '84, knowing we'd recently returned to the Cape, he stopped by to greet us. What he didn't know—what no one on the Cape knew because my father made me vow to say *nothing*—was that my father had undergone heart surgery that spring. He said people on the Cape lived for gossip, and that news would gush faster than the tide, all the while skirting the truth: that he feared vulnerability and refused to display weakness.

The surgery had not followed another heart attack; it was preventative but essential (a quadruple bypass). This took place at the end of my junior year at the University of Rochester, and I refused to be in Upstate New York during his surgery, but it meant completing the academic year two weeks early. I accelerated my library work and cranked out term papers on James Joyce and James Baldwin. I don't recall my third course, but I remember the fourth, Writing about Music, because I cheated: One of our final assignments required us to attend a concert off campus and write a review. With only a few days left before my departure, I fictionalized a visit to a club outside of Boston, pirating tidbits that Thorpe had reported, being sure to offer specific details (the tiny plastic cups, the cheap Italian tablecloth) for "accuracy." I'm sorry, Professor Schildkret. I meant no disrespect.

The surgery went well enough to release him for the Cape journey just a few weeks later, but then his skin began to blotch with blood spots, primarily in his mouth and legs. Fearing that the hemorrhaging would give him away, he consciously tanned himself on our porch—the only time in my life I can recall him sunbathing—and refused to seek medical help, insisting this was just the body's way of naturally healing itself. But when Paul arrived that day, my father decided to trust the Hippocratic Oath.

"What do you make of this?" my father asked, rolling up his pant legs.

Paul took a look, then asked to see the inside of his mouth. "We're going to the hospital," he said, "and we're going right now."

We'd later learn an allergy to one of the post-operative prescription drugs, Quinidine, had decimated his platelet count from the hundreds of thousands to almost nothing. Without the body's natural coagulant, blood vessels turned to sieves. And his drug allergy persisted, eviscerating platelets as fast as they could be pumped into his body.

"I'll be straight with you," the doctor in charge said to me. "He could be fine in a week, or he could die in five minutes."

I was alone on the Cape and felt simultaneously numb and panic-stricken. At twenty, I had no secure vision of my future, unsure how my passions for writing and jazz would merge into a viable profession. I didn't even know how to drive, having relied on public transport in Manhattan and my bicycle on the Cape. But my friend Patricia—the niece of Danny Walker, who kept our Volvo alive—sprang into action, calming me down with one-step-at-a-time philosophies. (She'd grown into that role of an older sister: When my mother died, she made sure I didn't remain idle for too long.) And then Thorpe drove down from the North Shore of Massachusetts. What can I say? Their love and guidance was invaluable.

I've often wondered how my life would have turned out had my father died that week. For one, my image of him would have myopically portrayed him as an untarnished genius, a master painter and revered teacher. Period. Suddenly responsible for two significant properties, would I have finished college? And would I have changed the architecture of those houses? The thought fascinates me because I believe my sentimental attachments to those homes, coupled with parental reverence and a fear of still more change, would have turned my environment into a massive time capsule worthy of *The Twilight Zone*. I suspect I would have lived among the clutter, as I always had, not seeing anything bizarre in the chaos, not fearing mold and decay. I believe I would have survived in my father's world exactly the way he dreamed I would.

Eventually, the bags of spun platelets outlasted the diminishing effects of Quinidine, and he left the hospital with the specific instructions to lie low and rest. "Spend some time on the beach," his doctor said. At sixty-nine, my father should have felt reborn, and I thought the near-death experience might soften his crusty nature, kindling a sentimentality for family that he had eschewed. Instead, he became crazed, completely unapproachable. Determined to start teaching as soon as possible, he charged into the barn's mayhem, repositioning objects *far* heavier than anything the doctors would have approved him to lift. The entire summer, in fact, he remained like Jupiter: huge and commanding, dictatorial—and as silent as the farthest recesses of space.

Nobody at that time knew that his eventual death would lead back to that summer. In the early '80s, hospitals tested for hepatitis A and B, but not for C. (They didn't even have a name for it and referred to the disease as "non-A non-B.") He contracted hepatitis C from the platelet infusions; the same treatment that saved his life would help kill him nineteen years later.

Given my father's great thirst to be on Cape Cod in the summer months, two things remain somewhat bewildering: that he never returned to the property between fall and spring, and that he spent minimal time enjoying the natural landscapes of the Cape, most obviously the beaches. (His doctor's advice was laughably incongruous with his personality.) For me, no activity makes me feel more free and focused than shore walks during the pre-tourist hours, when the riveting patterns across sand flats expose only the organic patterns of the tide and the imprints of creatures from the sea and sky.

In fact, the backgrounds of my computer screens tend to be photographs from Dennis, including a crab shell discovered one morning at Crowes Pasture. With an interior long-since eaten by gulls and washed clean by the bay, it stood upright on its edge, allowing the sun to gleam through the underside so that the elemental qualities of the shell, intensified by the purity of salt, bedazzled the camera lens with a decorative dance of tiny leopard spots. Like Torajan architecture, a series of sharp ridges curve skyward. And in its center, from the sun's ascent and the windblown angle of the shell, a ghostly figure burns with a luminosity neither the crab nor an observer could have experienced during its lifetime, when the opaque abdomen secured the light-deadening flesh.

CHAPTER NINETEEN

~

Still Life with Raccoon

The word *unrecoverable* kept coming up when different contractors assessed the barn, but I had a feeling—call it blind faith, call it something elemental—that told me otherwise. And, now that I think about it, the first person I asked to inspect the building supported my desire to save the barn. I wanted to hire him because he was an artist, a sculptor. He poked around and thought he could salvage the structure, but I learned two things that ultimately nixed the deal: He wanted twice his usual hourly wage, and he only had full use of one hand. We left on good terms, in part because I let him keep some raccoon skulls that he'd unearthed from the perimeter. He cheerfully explained how he enjoyed studying animal skulls.

I don't know how many skulls he owned, but I'm certain his examples were dwarfed by Alan Dudley in the UK, who amassed over two thousand, from tiny reptiles to giant mammals. In *Skulls: An Exploration of Alan Dudley's Curious Collection*, Simon Winchester explains Dudley's tedious process of purifying the bones, one that included weeks or months of soaking in water that became so noxious the collector's wife threatened to leave him. Strange and systematic, the multitude of skulls transformed from sensory horror to scientific beauty, a fascinating museum of death that comments on our lives. As Winchester explains:

> The difference between unorganized acquiring and hoarding on the one hand, and systematized acquisition and classification on the other, is often a pathological need to win psychological security through the domination of inanimate entities. But in most cases—stamp collecting, coin collecting,

matchbox- and antique- and beermat- and vintage car-collecting—collecting is entirely harmless.

The skulls found alongside our barn did not surprise me because I knew that, for decades, raccoons wintered and bred in its second floor, and yet they never seemed to die there. Without heat, the barn wasn't the Hilton, but it was dry and, for a raccoon, quite practical, with all sorts of objects that could be used for additional housing. I realize now that my father had no way of keeping the animals out because the floorboards and foundation had rotted, creating various openings that remained out of reach largely because of the ever-expanding still life. (After his death, when friends replaced the floorboards, they evicted a ground-floor possum who stared in disbelief like a squatter who feels legally entitled to the land.) The barn door itself left gaping entrances for critters of significant size. We should have charged rent.

At the start of every summer, before my father could fully excavate areas in the barn to prepare it for his classes, he spent mornings howling and growling—the kind of primal screaming described in Robert Bly's *Iron John*—in order to let the raccoons know it was time to leave their winter residence on the second floor. *Raaaaah! Greeeeeeow!* The great and mighty Sam has returned!

In truth, we rather feared the raccoons because of a story repeated by Harry Holl. In the late '60s or very early '70s, the story goes, Harry had a pet raccoon that used to walk with him on the pottery grounds. One day, a prospective customer arrived with a Great Dane that started to bark, and the coon crouched low.

"You'd better get your dog out of here," Harry said, "or at least pull him back."

The dog owner chuckled, first looking at the midsized furry creature, and then at his majestic Dane. The dog continued to bark.

"I'm serious," Harry said. "Put a leash on him."

The dog pressed forward, and then the raccoon leapt beneath the Dane's belly, and scooped his guts out.

The story stuck—and as far as I know, it's true. What I know with absolute certainty, however, is that the *impact* of this narrative lasted. Raccoons commanded utmost respect, if not fear. I thought about them on summer nights when I'd take out the trash to a somewhat difficult location behind the barn. I had to step over my father's stone wall, angle down into a pit to pull out the garbage cans from under his makeshift enclosure, then remove the cinder blocks balanced on the lids so the raccoons wouldn't pry them open. Were they near, watching, poised? Depositing garbage wasn't merely a stinky chore, it was a treacherous obstacle course.

In the early '70s (which is to say, pre-bamboo and unchecked hoarding mania), one could still find a path or two on the barn's second level, and my father's favorite story took place one summer when he had growled long enough to force the annual evacuation. Still, he needed to check, so he carefully ascended and started to tiptoe around the strewn contents. Suddenly, he sensed a presence and looked behind him. He'd woken a large raccoon that now sluggishly followed his clockwise motion, careful to match pace and maintain distance.

"It was like a pantomime," he said, laughing. "There we were, circling around each other in a kind of dance."

A different year, midsummer, the painting class was quietly focused on their canvases when one of the students said, "Hey—is that a raccoon in the still life?" And, yes, she saw correctly. It had been injured and seemed disoriented. Perhaps it had returned prematurely to the barn in search of a reasonable place to die.

For the students, and for my father, this was a fascinating happenstance. But as I think of that afternoon, I'm also fascinated by the convergence of purpose and chance: Here was a barn filled with people diligently trying to make a still life *become* life, trying in other words to consider the forces of contour and color so that the movement between inorganic form became an organic entity. And interposed in this endeavor, crawling from the recesses in the second floor madness, was something that could not be studied for weeks and that, without any artistic manipulation, attained mobility. In some respects, the scenario might be interpreted as the opposite of Wallace Stevens's "Anecdote of the Jar," where manmade order challenges and changes the natural world. Here was a wild animal out of nature, and out of its own nature, making its presence both marvelously strange and memorable. (One student tried but ultimately failed to paint him into her work.) It became an event, life no longer stilled, bringing a kind of eternality to this dying creature's spirit.

In size, the area of that second floor paled compared to the rest of the barn (the floor was twenty by twenty, with the roof peaking at ten feet in the center) and one could only access it from a small opening pierced by a ladder. But even here my father had managed to store a prodigious amount. Trying to photograph the mysterious contents, I climbed the steep rungs and raised my camera overhead, aiming indiscriminately, relying on autofocus and flash. What emerged was little more than chaos, indecipherable to the human eye.

I postponed cleaning that second floor until I felt confident the structure could be saved. Then, in 2007, I cut a hole in the floor and built a chute out of plywood so things could be dropped and slid, usually with help, onto the lawn. As the clearing took place, however, I separated the contents into six major piles: two for wood (everything from splintered planks to shapely pillars); one for windows and glass; one for screens and solid doors; one for dried stalks of bamboo, which he had intended to braid into a fence; and one for metal, including bed springs, stove piping, broken lobster traps, flashing, sink basins, folding-table bases, and many rolls of chicken wire. Some of the largest objects, like the remains of an antique plough and a shattered spinning wheel, were shunted to the side. On a circular piece of cardboard ply, someone had painted in large letters "HI SAM" (possibly as a greeting for our return to the Cape); I placed the board on top of the largest woodpile. Then I went inside the house and, from above, photographed the eclipsed front yard. The barn, at long last, had been emptied.

The final significant excavation on the Cape property took place in 2012, when I decided to tackle my father's studio, now in condemnable condition. Unlike my positive intuition about the barn's restoration, I knew that structural repairs would be futile. Still, I wanted to be sure—to actually see the walls and assess the foundation—and so, once again, I found myself clawing through a staggering allotment of artifacts that arrived from inspiration and now caused absolute destruction. Because I felt confident that the structure could not be saved, I had no desire to spend hundreds of dollars removing the rubble. Fortunately, pickers seem abundant on the Cape, and I contacted someone willing to haul away, gratis, all the metal and most everything else.

At sixteen-and-a-half by twenty-four feet, and with only one level, the structure couldn't house nearly the amount of salvaged "goods" as the barn. And, of course, my father had left room to paint in the center. But the contents for such a shack would still stifle the uninitiated. In addition to painting equipment and still life material, the studio housed a kitchen table; a large, low wooden table; many wooden doors; scores of window frames, most with glass; several glass shower doors; four brutally heavy panels of safety glass (some double-paned); eight enormous Homasote boards and others of smaller dimension; various plaster boards; floor and wall boards; broken and usable chairs of various types; boxes of roofing shingles; boxes of cedar shingles; jugs, bottles, jars, and other glass containers; coffee cans filled with rusted nails; a television console (without the tube, which, perhaps, I previously found beneath the rhododendron); infested tree limbs; and several storage cabinets, one with a complete squirrel skeleton.

An assortment of furniture supported a tabletop along the widest window, including a metal rolling cart and two sets of wooden drawers (possibly ends to a worktable) with broken legs. Over the years, the drawers themselves ceased functioning as storage for art supplies, and two had been stuffed almost to the brim with cushion contents from a long-lost area in the studio. And on top of this nest of heavenly stuffing lay the soft body of a gray field mouse, which had not yet begun to decompose.

The squirrel skeleton entranced me, a dramatic *memento mori* that remained freakishly aggressive even in death. The sharp incisors, far longer than one might expect, proved what we know but usually don't consider: that squirrels must continue to gnaw on hard substances to stave their relentlessly elongating teeth from puncturing their jaws. (I wondered, briefly, if the teeth kept enlarging after death, like the corpse's fingernails in George Orwell's "A Hanging.") Tiny leg bones remained poised in their unending support, and scraps of preserved skin stuck to its prickly vertebrae. I became overwhelmed with the same bizarre attraction that led me to purchase Marco Lanza's *The Living Dead*, an arresting coffee-table book on the mummies from Palermo's crypts. What is it about mummification that so captivates the living? Is it partly the exposure of our elemental physicality and the raw expression of air sockets and gumless teeth? Do we covet terror?

My attraction to Tana Toraja, in addition to the Indonesian belief that the island's original inhabitants had descended from the stars, had to do with bones and the ceremony of death. My colorful guidebook reproduced basalt monoliths checkered with graves and lined with effigies—*Tau taus*—representing those who had passed, protectors of both the deceased and the living. Elsewhere, in caves and accessible sites, children played with the bones of their ancestors, and while I did not witness that bizarre circumstance, I walked freely among scattered skulls, and carefully beneath overhanging coffins with limbs dangling from the rotting wood.

Funeral ceremonies included animal sacrifices, from chickens and pigs to the majestic water buffalo. My guide, much like a Spaniard enamored of matadors, spoke with great enthusiasm about the swiftness and grace of blade-work, and my guidebook prominently displayed an exhalation of blood from a water buffalo's neck. But I had been photographing these regal animals—including a series of one immersed in cool mud, then rising into the textures of Giacometti and the boldness of Rodin—so I insisted we leave before the *dénouement*. I couldn't watch the slaughter. At that same funeral ceremony, I had accidentally witnessed a blade thrust into a pig's heart. That was more than enough.

And yet, walking around human bones and a plethora of skulls fascinated me. Removed from human suffering and identity, the skeletal remains in this foreign setting became more sculptural than anything else. I understood how children could treat bones as shapes; they were Torajan Legos. For similar reasons, I kept the large bones my father collected, including a whale's rib and vertebrae. No wonder the squirrel's skeleton mesmerized me.

But the dead field mouse, still supple and furry, evoked instead a strange tenderness. If the squirrel skeleton looked twice its size because of its dramatic form, the mouse appeared charmingly diminutive. I extracted the drawer and dug a hole near the studio to bury the mouse in its created tomb. Wasn't this exactly how my father wanted to die—adrift within his nest of refuse, having reconfigured the world's stuffing into a place of serenity, if not sacred respect? To some degree, he achieved exactly that, dying within a house disintegrating around him.

In the studio, the scrap metal included hernia-inducing, eight-foot iron bars and other anchor-heavy fragments. He had stored a refrigerator and roughly a ton of cast iron, including all the parts to a cast-iron stove. Two snow plows. The remains of my childhood swing set. Stove piping. Unidentifiable chunks of iron and brass slag. A tiny bit of copper, barely worth the gas money to sell it.

All the metal went to a local sculptor who built castles and landscapes for fairies and sprites. Even with me and his friend helping out, it took him a number of truckloads to move all the metal, but I must say I enjoyed the experience. Beneath a cap, he sported a gray Van Dyke and reminded me a bit of Thorpe. But this artist suffered from Tourette's, and he whooped a great deal as we sorted the wreckage.

"What're these?" I asked, grunting to upend one of the long, arcing metal bars. I had interrupted the man's focused gaze as he evaluated the weight of his truck's load.

"*Whoop!* Springs from a truck. *Whoop! Whoop!* Like the ones I'm lookin' at on mine."

The refrigerator made me laugh. I knew it from childhood, and I remembered my father talking about its arrival: How Dicky Buck, one of the town's well-known characters, carried it into the house on his back. (Buck did not work for an appliance company; who knows where he got it.) The box conked out during my teenage years, and if I helped my father move it to the studio, I've forgotten that memory. But there it was, on its side, the door off and resting elsewhere. The fridge itself was packed full, of course, primarily with two large containers—boxes or crates (I couldn't tell in the shadow). I got on my knees, gripped the edge of one, and pulled back, *hard*.

Nothing. Then I pulled using my body weight as well and slowly inched it out.

"Jesus," I said, out loud but to myself, "this is like a box of rocks!"

Turned out, it *was* a box of rocks. So was the other. The purpose? Perhaps my father envisioned a stone path. Maybe a tabletop. Whatever the concept, it was postponed—though not necessarily abandoned; in his mind, no project was ever considered hopeless. I laboriously dragged the crates outside and poured their contents near the studio, creating a mound that looked like a small memorial in a poverty-stricken country.

From the studio wreckage, I kept about five things: two star-shaped iron cogs; an antique fire extinguisher that I recall being part of his still life; an antique clothes mangle made in Erie, Pennsylvania; and a hefty blown-glass jug with a rusted spring-pressed top (originally used, I'm told, for insecticide). Tomb of K'inich Janaab Pakal this was not. Still, the artifacts were cool.

And although I initially placed it on the scrap metal heap, I ended up keeping a circular piece of iron, shaped like the top of a boiler with a two-inch lip. I have no use for it—but it's the centerpiece to the greatest still life my father ever created in that studio. The vertical painting's forty-seven by sixty-seven inches—about four by five and a half feet—with the painted objects scaled down by roughly a third. As he did in New York with the realistic rendering of the burned-out house, he'd unearth this realistic work for visitors who felt uneasy about abstraction, as though proving the merits of his craft. ("Now *that* I like," many would say.) But because the painting never hung inside the house, the image remained primarily in my memory: a still life centered on that radiant, circular piece of iron, glowing from its center to the edges of the canvas with sun-like fury.

So it's startling now, with the canvas prominently displayed and well lit, to accept that easily 40 percent of the still life—most of the bottom half and all of the top four inches—accurately depicts the studio's gray wood. Gray. What creates the feeling of uniformly explosive radiance? Four dramatic conclaves of warmth that, in color and gesture, stretch the canvas's shoulders and arms.

The eye almost immediately turns to the window on the upper-right edge; its pane, Vermeer-like, orchestrates both the lighting and the viewer's attention. Beside it, my father roughed in a painting start that had been pinned to the back wall, an abstraction undeniably warm in its expression (red, orange, summer). On the left edge, he's reproduced a drapery that bleeds with the intensity of a beheaded bull.

The centerpiece is that circular piece of iron. Flaking and therefore receptive to the magic of light, it recasts shadow and reflection. But at its center, my father bejeweled the object with a fiery treasure of glowing metal, as though the iron were being forged anew, and this burst of encrusted orange pulls the warmth from the reproduced cloth, and the pinned-up painting start, and the window emanating July, so that the energy surging left and right in this decidedly vertical canvas coalesces in the center like the riveting eye of Kali.

And one can speak of so much more! A wooden, ladder-like object angles to counter the traditional geometry of the window; a serpentine hose dances from the center, off the edge, and back in; a two-pronged firebrand pierces the iron's flaming center; cleverly positioned streaks of green drive against flame-like orange to generate new drama. It's a painting that celebrates the extraordinary driving forces in the mundane, and it's so fully charged that the grayish areas—which he gave texture and substance, geometry and depth—balance and govern like an ideal rhythm section for a host of sizzling soloists.

But I want to talk to you about the window in this painting, because, for me, it acts as a tutelary guide for appreciating abstract expressionism. As I noted, those who felt uneasy confronting abstraction received comfort from this painting's recognizable shapes: the table and stovepipe, the window and frame, the forked prong. This painting elicits *Ah*'s even from the most reticent audiences. So why has no one ever questioned the spirit of July *beyond* the window—four glass panes of vibrant, fully abstract imagery? Why is it accepted once the window itself has been fully established but not without the context of those frames?

I think much of this has to do with our need for narrative: It is easier, and therefore more comforting, to be told a story rather than imagine the context. With the visual arts, many demand absolute meaning. They desire tamed wilderness, appreciating the patterned gardens of Versailles more than the majesty of wildflower fields in an unknown country. Without a narrative context, the abstraction fails them. Philip Ball's *Bright Earth*, a book with a cover that leaps into vision because it reproduces Hans Hofmann's *The Lark*, speaks to this matter:

> Kandinsky's fruitless search for the emotional language of color, like the tangles of color linguistics, reminds us that it is futile to be dogmatic about color. There can be no consensus about what colors "mean" or how to use them "truthfully." Color theories can assist the construction of good art, but they do not define it. In the end, the modern artist's struggle to find form for color is an individual quest.

José Argüelles's fascinating *Transformative Vision* includes this similarly flawed assessment:

> Hence fine art in the twentieth century is the marriage of anarchic avant-garde subjectivism and the academic pretense at being aesthetically significant. This accounts for the predominance of abstract art as the major fine-arts expressive mode in the twentieth century. The pity is that, feeling driven into unphotographable realms, artists at the same time felt ill-prepared to deal with the psychic splendors of the imagination. Thus abstract art unfortunately tended more and more to be purely aesthetic, pertaining to no reality at all, except that of pure sensation.

The problem with these stands, despite their intellectual integrity, has to do with the assumption that "pure sensation" (that is, without "meaning") cannot represent art in its most spiritual and satisfying forms. Put another way: These arguments collapse when they're compared to instrumental music, such as Beethoven's symphonies, Ravi Shankar's ragas, or John Coltrane's improvisations. As Theodore Roethke succinctly put it in "The Waking," "We think by feeling. What is there to know?"

Supporters of the marginalized arts strain to sway the conservative world. Still, the power of art can inspire utterly unexpected epiphanies. I'm recalling another moment of childhood, when a woman from Russia came to visit our friends, Ria and Lazar (who, years later, gave us the cypress tree to honor my mother). It had taken them years to secure a visa for her, nor was her introduction to American society a smooth one; she suffered vertigo, for example, when she entered a supermarket, so overwhelmed by opulence. Her exposure to art had only consisted of dark, dour portraiture—grim visages that nevertheless had "meaning."

Ria had been begging my father to show this woman his art, but he refused. He understood that she had no avenue into this world, and that it would only cause a pronounced awkwardness for them all. But on the woman's final day, he acquiesced and took her inside the house to see his only well-lit painting: *Summer*, a completely abstract celebration. The woman exhaled, said something in Russian, pulled out a chair, and sat down.

"'The sky, the sea—'" Ria translated, tearing up. "'I'm staying.'"

When damp Cape weather seeps into the house, some paintings still release a moldy odor, despite my annual efforts to kill whatever remains in the stained canvases, and the most consistent culprit has been the large still life with the fiery iron centerpiece. For years, my father stored this painting, and others, in the unheated barn where the acrylic froze and thawed. He'd pin them to the giant Homasote boards, packing them tight, but plenty of things shifted over the winter, and we never returned until June. Yes, this was an art restorer's nightmare, but my father never would have considered his actions neglectful. After switching from oils to acrylics, he preached the enduring nature of plastic. I think he considered his canvases impervious to harm.

At the start of each summer season, even before the raccoons had been screamed away, I'd help him unbury the paintings and haul them up to his studio, clearing the center of the barn for his teaching space. And one year, as we pulled protective boards away from the canvases, I spotted a black blotch on the still life that caused my hand to cover my mouth. From the second floor, a raccoon had wiggled its butt over the edge and defecated. Enough room had been left between the paintings so that the dropping fell midway down the canvas, hardened, and stuck. I knew all too well my father's anger, but this time, to my amazement, the episode concluded in laughter.

"Goddamn critics," he snapped. Then he snatched the offending turd with his bare hand and threw it across the barn, where it shattered into the still life.

CHAPTER TWENTY

~

Punishment

Queequeg in his own proper person was a riddle to unfold; a wondrous work in one volume; but whose mysteries not even himself could read, though his own live heart beat against them.

—Herman Melville, *Moby-Dick*

At the end of *The Savage Is Loose*, a '70s sexploitation film about parents and their child surviving on an uninhabited island, the son binds his father between two trees and leaves him to burn like a boar on a spit. The late-adolescent son—who begins the movie at age twelve, a year older than I was when my parents brought me to the screening—then stalks his voluptuous mother. (George C. Scott titled the film after the novel, although *Oedipus Shipwrecks* may have been more accurate.) Guilt overwhelms the boy, and he falls to his knees, sobbing in his mother's cleavage. Then the camera shifts to his abandoned spear, suddenly gripped by charred hands. Unbeknownst to the blubbering son, the father has survived and points his weapon, only to lower it when his wife raises her hand. The lens focuses on her outstretched palm, which the burned husband clings to for a moment before she releases his hold. The vanquished elder, roasted and flaking, glares. Then the woman grasps their son's face with both of her hands as though teaching him how to focus passion, and opens her mouth to his. We're left with the sky, then credits, as well as the assumption that the father returns to the forest to die.

The movie bombed. In the *New York Times*, Vincent Canby accurately noted that it "works neither as an adventure film, as a psychological exploration, nor, heaven help us, as a family melodrama." On the uneasy topic of incest, Canby adds, "[T]he subject is so genteelly handled that I can't imagine children seeing the film would be anything but confused and probably bored." And that's where his criticism may have puzzled readers: How many children actually saw this R-rated movie? Certainly none besides me for that particular viewing.

And yet, as a child who did indeed witness the film, I felt anything but bored—emotionally confused, yes, but not bored. Sitting between my parents, I wanted to assure my father that I could never hurt him, and I couldn't even *look* at my mother. I'd not yet read Sophocles, nor the story of Seth from the Bible, and therefore could not mask my awkward feelings with intellectual knowledge.

And then, arriving like springtime, a second film began: a screening of the boxing match between Muhammad Ali and George Foreman, which had taken place a month earlier on October 30, 1974. The Rumble in the Jungle! (It's possible my parents told me of the double feature, but the trauma of the first film pushed that out of my consciousness.) I didn't have to look at anything except the screen, and a kind of nausea gave way to excitement: The Heavyweight Champion of the World would now perform his genius, and his already-celebrated victory meant a complete release of anxiety.

In *The Fight*, Norman Mailer's book on the Ali/Foreman match (and one of Mailer's greatest works, largely because he pursues an ego even greater than his own), he begins by acknowledging the physical majesty of Muhammad Ali: "There is always a shock in seeing him again. Not *live* as in television but standing before you, looking his best. Then the World's Greatest Athlete is in danger of being our most beautiful man." And this screening gave me a glimmer into such hyperbolic claims. In color, larger than life, the drama in the ring unfolded almost as though we had seats in Zaïre. Even the camera flashes onscreen seemed to be generated by people in the back of the theater.

The anticipation for the Ali/Foreman fight had excited the boys in my sixth-grade class. My favorite teacher, Bo Farson, loved boxing and revered Ali. In the days before the match, he spoke with more and more confidence about "The Dancing Master," with the same wacky confidence that Ali himself exuded. I, like most of the world, thought Foreman would brutalize him. I had followed heavyweight boxing because my father enjoyed it. I knew, for example, that Foreman had recently fought Joe Frazier and Ken Norton, the only two men who had beaten Ali, and he dismantled them both within two rounds. I imagined Foreman much the way Mailer would later describe him during his training sessions:

> Each of these blows was enough to smash an average athlete's ribs; anybody with poor stomach muscles would have a broken spine. Foreman hit the heavy bag with the confidence of a man who can pick up a sledgehammer and knock down a tree. The bag developed a hollow as deep as his head. . . . Sooner or later, there must come a time in the fight when Ali would be so tired he could not move, could only use his arms to protect himself. Then he would be like a heavy bag.

In the dressing room before the match, Archie Moore, a former champion who helped to train and coach Foreman, found his mind drifting into a kind of foreboding compassion for his man's opponent: "I was praying, and in great sincerity, that George wouldn't *kill* Ali. I really felt that was a possibility."

Four decades later, watching on a far smaller screen, I remain daunted by George Foreman's stare and meaty physique. I wince each time he strikes Ali, especially the body blows. And as the fight progresses, I'm still astonished at Foreman's withering strength, and Ali's flurry at the end of the eighth round, and the final combo that finishes him off. Foreman's body descends almost in slow motion, like a massive Cape Cod oak cut at its base until it leans, shatters internally, and finally punishes the ground.

The following year, 1975, Ali disposed of two white hopes—Chuck Wepner (the "real" Rocky) and the dogged Joe Bugner—as well as a more substantial opponent, Ron Lyle. Then, on October 1, only eleven months after capturing the championship from Foreman in what might be the most mythic boxing match in history, he took on Joe Frazier for the third time, winning by TKO in a fight that epitomized heavyweight drama. Of all the bouts I've ever seen, I can think of no footage more exhausting.

And that's where Ali's career should have ended. Instead, he fought four more times in 1976, and twice in '77, including a match against Earnie Shavers ("The Black Destroyer"), who lost on points but not before cracking Ali's head with devastating blows. The champ lost the belt in February of '78 to Leon Spinks, and though he won the rematch that September, he should not have been allowed back in the ring. In fact, Dr. Ferdie Pacheco, Ali's doctor for sixteen years, begged him to quit after the Frazier fight, knowing too well that his beloved fighter could not control his machismo. He expected the worst, and he got it: a fight against Larry Holmes on October 2, 1980. Pacheco would later call the fight "an abomination" and "a crime": "All of the people involved in this fight should have been arrested."

Ironically, Larry Holmes had been one of Ali's sparring partners in preparation for the Foreman fight, and Holmes had showed real promise even then. As Mailer states in the movie *When We Were Kings*, "He dominated Ali," though he adds,

> That wasn't uncommon. Ali very often would not show his best stuff with his sparring partners but, in fact, would work on his weaknesses. He'd go against the ropes, and he'd let people pummel him—very heavy hitters who were sort of clumsy. He'd let them bang away at him. It was as if he wanted to train his body to receive these messages of punishment.

I probably knew about the Holmes fight, but Ali's egotistical return didn't concern me in the slightest: My father and I had spent that day in Columbia Presbyterian Hospital with my mother for her forty-seventh and final birthday. They'd scheduled the first round of chemo for the following day, although we spoke instead about the gifts we'd brought, mainly art books. Later that evening at the house with just my father, I did not turn on the radio to hear the announcements of Holmes hitting so hard that Ali howled. I went to bed desperately believing that the cancer could be fought, and that my mother would not die.

I later learned she knew instinctively that the appearance of cancer, minute at that point, translated to a death sentence, despite the doctors' initial reports. She knew her body well and accepted, in ways that most men do not, physical vulnerability. But whether or not we acknowledge our mortality, almost everyone must face a turn in health that marks an unrecoverable decline.

For my father, the event occurred late in his life. When I received a call alerting me to his hospitalization, the cause for blood vessels exploding in his neck had not been diagnosed. One possibility, his wife told me, concerned food in their fridge that "may have been a bit old." But she also spoke of several doors—solid wood, tall, extremely heavy—that he had hauled from the New York streets. He told her some boys from the neighborhood had helped him with the transport, but I knew he had lied; he never would have allowed strange kids into the house. No, he moved them on his own, and now he lay in the hospital having savaged his body irreparably—and ironically: his treasures had mortally betrayed him.

The hospital staff moved swiftly, and by the time I was notified, they had stopped the bleeding and stabilized his condition. Still, I sped along I-80 in the middle of the night, a panic-stricken drive but one, at least, more direct and faster than my previous medical-emergency journey: A few years earlier, while in Singapore, I got a call informing me that he'd been hospitalized on Cape Cod. I rebooked my return for that evening and flew from Singapore to Tokyo, Tokyo to Detroit, Detroit to Boston, Boston to Nantucket, and finally Hyannis. I left my suitcase at the front desk and tried to greet him with the energy of a comedian walking onstage. Pennsylvania to New York? Cakewalk.

But this attack, unlike the one on the Cape, had done significant damage, and it seemed to trigger other failing parts of his body, including the liver eroding away from hepatitis C. He was eighty-seven and would live another year, but from then on, he would mark time. As Ferdie Pacheco said of the Ali/Holmes fiasco: "All the other fights pushed him to the edge. This one buried him."

I stayed in New York over three weeks, mainly monitoring his situation in the hospital, and then helping at home. And the day before I left, I sat by his bedside and asked about the heavy doors in the courtyard. It was easy—all too easy—to imagine him tilting them individually, right bottom point to left bottom point, walking the massive weight down the block, through the house, and out to the courtyard. Repeat. During his lifetime, he'd moved so many tons this way, never imagining a physical collapse.

But deep into his eighties, the strain proved too much. Yes, the "old food" probably didn't help, but even with his "walking" method, he would have had to lift each door down the three steps from the sidewalk, and angle them through the smaller door jambs. He would have strained his whole body, including the vessels in his neck.

"Dad," I said, smiling, pointing to the courtyard, "what really happened with those doors?"

He paused, searching for something clever, something evasive, but he didn't even have the strength to change his expressionless face. "Shut up," he said, and that was that. He had no intention of admitting that his delight for the world's junk had just about killed him.

In his final year, I experienced a range of bewildering behavior, in keeping with the story I've already told about his offer to give me a painting, followed by his retraction. Part of the tensions arose because of a long-standing sensibility: Even at his healthiest he seemed overtly burdened by houseguests. With his health profoundly compromised, my wife and I felt it much more sensitive and sensible to stay with friends and visit in the afternoons, between meals, thereby avoiding all pressures to host or entertain. But this led to passive-aggressive hostility. One day, after making the trip into New York exclusively to see him, I telephoned to say that I had arrived and to ask when it might be most convenient to stop over.

"Maybe another time," he said.

"You mean, not right now, or not at all?"

"Maybe another time," he repeated.

There wouldn't be many other times. We both knew it, but some kind of conversation with his wife had taken place in his house. My best guess? Since we were staying in a friend's apartment—ironically, a decision made in order not to be a burden—we probably had been accused of judging my father's home as being unworthy. Something like that. Whatever the cause, he didn't want to see me.

My next trip to Manhattan occurred during record-breaking cold, and maybe he agreed to have me visit because he needed me to represent him at City Hall. A former tenant had filed a small claims suit (as I recall, she wanted a little over a hundred bucks) and he wasn't about to pay it. I found out what I could about the case, and, downtown, argued to the best of my ability. When I left, I knew the suit would either be dismissed or the amount greatly reduced.

Back at the house, I reported the event in detail, and with pleasure, actually, because I knew I'd done well. Although not a lawyer, I'd logged years teaching the art of the argument, as well as presenting lectures and readings, and it gave me great satisfaction to recount the conversation. I did not expect my father to thank me—he never thanked me—but I didn't anticipate his bizarre response, either.

"Okay, fine," he said, slowly. "Now, tomorrow, I want you to go to my cardiologist and get me a prescription for testosterone."

I looked in his eyes to gauge the joke, but he continued to explain how he felt compromised by his current medications, and he needed a boost. He wouldn't let go of the idea; he demanded I obey, but I made no promises because I knew this would not happen. He was just shy of eighty-eight. His body had begun to swell, both from a massive hernia and edema. He had cancer, a bad heart, and poisoned blood. And he wanted testosterone, to die in the saddle, to fight Larry Holmes.

The visits in his final months *should* have been times of loving connectedness: my only father, his only child. But the disrespect and, yes, insanity wore me down. Why travel only to be told, "Maybe next time"? So I stayed in touch by phone and stopped pressuring myself to drive into Manhattan. This worked out well, actually: We had very pleasant weekend chats devoid of all the mania and stress.

I also faced unexpected difficulties with our home in Pennsylvania. With the spring thaw, we noticed black, pungent oil bubbling into a thin stream along our property, as well as through a crack in our basement floor. This did not translate into a million-dollar geyser; it meant a previous owner had buried a huge heating-oil receptacle and failed to empty the contents. I imagined kids playing with matches, or even someone dropping a cigarette. Once again, I found myself plagued by the burial of an enormous object, and once again I would have to unearth it.

The process took longer than expected. We knew the oil connected to our house because our pal, Jon, hammered open a cement crack to expose a leaking pipe that led to and through the exterior wall. But we needed the exact location of the tank itself, and the first crew got it wrong. (They felt "fairly confident" and planned a major excavation, but I needed more proof before ripping open the property.) Fortunately, the next fellow had better gear, and he located the huge container: half beneath our property's edge, and half into the street. They brought in a backhoe and dug up the lawn to pull out all the pipe, then drained the oil. Filling the tank with cement, they said, was far more cost-efficient than removal and disposal. I concurred—making me culpable, to some degree, of burial worthy of my father's handiwork.

At that point, I decided I should try to see my father again, even if I arrived and was told, "Maybe another time." I left for New York with the innate knowledge that this would be my final visit. I shared stories about my children, and he smiled. I told him my promotion to full professor had been confirmed, and that pleased him as well. When I left, we expressed our love for each other; that final exchange seemed as good as it could get.

Although virtually marooned in a reclining chair at that point, my father insisted on traveling to the Cape, and somehow his wife and two helpers managed to transport his weak, bloated body. But I didn't join him there. Although he only survived about a week, I didn't know whether he'd live for the whole summer. For the first time, I chose not to have my life ruled by his mortality. After his first heart attack in 1977, I fought anxiety throughout the rest of high school and college. I was just a kid when we almost lost him again. *Enough*, I thought.

But I had requested a call if his condition turned dire, and when the call came, I left at five in the morning and drove the eight hours to Massachusetts. Twenty minutes before arriving, my wife telephoned my cell to say that my father had died.

"Do you want to pull over?" she asked.

"No," I said, having crossed the bridge and turned onto Route 6. "I'm fine."

"You sure?"

"Absolutely."

"Call me when you get there, okay?"

"Of course."

I found out later that my father's wife had given him some extra morphine that guided him into the next life; I had no chance of seeing him alive. And while a number of friends expressed their sadness over that fact, I never felt cheated of any final-moment experience. He didn't want me there. He had never wanted me to see him vulnerable—ever. Better to have him surrounded by women: the one he chose to marry, and a nurse who met me on the lawn and assured me that the transition had been serene.

That afternoon, a chubby undertaker arrived brimming with cultivated empathy, a polyester man who seemed to have leapt from a Flannery O'Connor story. When my stepmother told him to leave my father's Greek fisherman's cap on, the man clasped his hands in front of his bulging suit: "Let me tell you a story that's near and dear to my heart." I knew, of course, it had to do with another dead person wearing a cap, but we dutifully stayed silent. And while my eyes meandered, I felt the powerful presence of my father's painting, *Summer*. It seemed to illuminate all the physical and emotional wreckage in that house.

And, oh, how the house needed light. After the men drove off to the funeral home to prepare my father's body for cremation, I called my wife and a few friends. Then I started to take off wooden, handmade window coverings. A quarter of a century earlier, a kid had broken into the house; to deter other incidents during the offseason, my father fashioned heavy, opaque structures that covered the panes and latched from within. Some became increasingly difficult to remove and simply remained during the summer, sealing the house with all its mold and rot.

I began the removal somewhat tentatively, hoping for a relatively easy transition, but soon I found myself smashing the wood, splintering the protective armor into useless piles. In some places, sunlight touched the floor for the first time in years. As the rooms brightened, so did my resolve to resurrect the property.

I stayed a few days to help with arrangements, then headed back to Pennsylvania through kind, early June weather—nothing remotely like the exhausting trip with my mother's work and the poorly strapped canoe. I'd never felt more loving urgency to be home. My son, ten at the time, had been stoic, having understood his grandfather's steady decline, but my daughter, only six, had been overcome by her first encounter with death. I needed to be with them.

During the eight-hour trip, my mind naturally replayed the fresh experience of seeing my father's body, holding his hands, nodding. I thought a bit about the Cape property and the vast challenges that confronted me. Tired but tranquil, I focused on the purity of weather and the comforting glide of cruise control, with jazz CDs played just loud enough to drown out the road noise.

And I realized the obvious: that I would never again be waiting for the telephone call announcing dramatic news about my father's health. For how many years, especially during my young adulthood, had his mortality governed my life? Every single week during my undergraduate years, I expected a dreadful notification of some sort; when the college nominated me for a Rhodes Scholarship (a laughable concept, since I was not an athlete, nor remotely bright enough), I told the committee I had no intention of going to England because I feared being too far away from my father. The sudden flights from Southeast Asia, the midnight runs into Manhattan—that anxiety would no longer be part of my life, nor would I have to concern myself with pleasing him, or just being welcomed.

Along with the miles, my mind unspooled reflections of my father's mortality, including the first dramatic heart attack, from which he recovered as decisively as Muhammad Ali after his defeats to Joe Frazier and Ken Norton. But the essence of that bravado also required blame, and he pointed a finger at a televised light-heavyweight bout between the champ Víctor Galíndez and young but formidable Eddie Mustafa Muhammad (then known as Eddie Gregory). The TV commentators kept calling the fifteen-round thriller "a war," and, yes, my father had been an active viewer, yelling advice and scolding boxers for what he deemed crucial mistakes. He'd gotten too excited, he said.

That was Saturday night, November 19, 1977. He then left for Philly on Sunday and taught all his classes, although he felt "off." When he returned on Tuesday, just two days before Thanksgiving, the attack leveled him. But he refused to stay down, refused to believe that his heart had betrayed him. He lay in bed, groaning occasionally. At one point, he sprang to his feet and pounded his upper torso with both fists as though he could beat the pain out of his chest.

My mother finally convinced him to go to the hospital, and though he eventually acquiesced, he insisted on taking the subway (six blocks away) rather than call an ambulance. His mother, Bubba, had been visiting for the forthcoming holidays. I had been told the reality of the situation, but I'd also been instructed not to say anything to my grandmother. It could be nothing; why worry her? My parents simply said they were "going out for a while." My grandmother told my father to wear a hat.

Strange hours passed. Bubba and I played gin rummy for round after round. Eventually, my mother returned by herself. When she explained that my father had suffered a heart attack and had to remain in the hospital, my grandmother, the funniest non-comedic person I've ever known, said, "I *told* him he should ver a het."

If we can believe my father's account of his first night in the ICU, we must also believe in astonishing negligence: He claimed they overdosed him with morphine, and that he began to hallucinate, imagining himself, he said, as Jack Nicholson in *One Flew Over the Cuckoo's Nest*. He had to escape. Somehow he managed to lower the metal bed guard, but then he realized he'd been harpooned by IV drips, so he ripped out the tubing.

"Blood completely splattered the sheets," he said, "and I thought to myself, 'Gee, this is exactly like a Jackson Pollock—and in color!'"

Nurses found him walking half-naked in the hallway, and then a team of people scrambled to change the bedding, settle him down, and hook him back up.

At fourteen, I never doubted the story. I needed to believe in his invincibility, and in the following weeks of recovery, I tried to convince myself that the entire experience had been little more than an aberration. But my wise Bubba knew better, and during her next visit, she warned him not to test the physical limits of his body. "Don' voik too hard," she said. "Remember: You're just a cracked piece of junk."

CHAPTER TWENTY-ONE

~

Fire Dance

[T]he winter house fell with the summer house,
and the houses, Egypt, the great houses, had an end.

—Howard Nemerov, "The Icehouse in Summer"

At the start of 1944, my father remained in Carlyle, Pennsylvania, while the world burned. In his barracks, they pinned up weekly, poster-sized NEWSMAPs—forty inches wide by thirty-five inches high—and he saved large clippings from the January 24, 1944, edition, which covered the period from January 13 through 20, or, as the subheading tells us, the "228th Week of the War—110th Week of U.S. Participation." An article titled "The War Fronts" addresses German occupation in areas that include the USSR: "Some of the week's most bitter fighting has occurred near enemy-held Vinnitsa," a Russian city near the meandering Dniester River. Throughout, turquoise arrows point to areas of attack, as though to say, "These landscapes change by the day." Jeffrey Veidlinger's *In the Shadow of the Shtetl* notes, "In Vinnytsya Province, a total of about 150,000 Jews were killed between 1941 and 1943." In calculated stages, the Nazis excavated deep ditches, lined up the locals, and opened fire.

The *NEWSMAP* reference to Vinnitsa and its surrounding towns captivated my father because he knew the region. His parents had lived in Voronovitsa (they spelled it Voronovitza, one of several alternate spellings), a *shtetl* just a few kilometers southeast of the city. Though no photos exist of my grandparents' house, we know it had been offered as part of my grand-mother's dowry, and that my father, born in 1915, spent his first four years there. And in my childhood, I frequently asked if he ever wanted to return to Voronovitsa, but he would remind me of a story that he told countless others: He had seen his town mentioned on an army map just once during the war, and that, afterward, it disappeared forever.

The large reproduction in *NEWSMAP* covered too much ground to in-clude his birthplace, but this army poster covered that region and allowed my father, then twenty-eight, to transform the threatening universality of war into something far more personalized. In fact, the sight of that province inspired more love than loss. He marked the location of his birthplace with a dot resembling an Indian caste mark, and elegantly inked *Voronovitza* in an undulating script so that it flowed like the Dniester. Above it, he painted an intricate miniature, very roughly two-and-a-half inches wide by three-and-a-half inches tall. For some of the details, he may have used the head of a pin.

Created during his marriage to Barbara, the illustration turns army map into love note. In an idealized sky, a portrait of Barbara as a child floats into view from within the clouds. She clutches an American flag but gazes toward a tree filled with yellow apples, a vision, perhaps, of peasant orchards. My father stands beneath her on lush, green ground. It's a colorized version of the famous photo he'd later re-create for our friend Bonnie with a Bic pen: a burgundy sash secures his shirt, shadowed with shades of ochre; his green knickers disappear into stockings and shoes colored the same blood-red as the lettering for his town's name. His right hand holds a whip, but his raised left grips onto a white hat—except that the whiteness seems to be made from the clouds, and the shape, while suggesting a hat, also appears to be a valentine. An unwritten caption floats easily into the viewer's imagination: "Destiny. I dreamed of you even in my youth."

Beneath his outstretched arm and to the right of his little legs, he's repro-duced his childhood home, reduced in size, as though several miles away. We see one plaster wall with a window, the angular roof thickened with a type of yellow grass. But he's broken the fourth wall, as they say in theater, removing the exterior to expose what appears to be a single room within that house, a cave-like vision with bricks from a back-wall fireplace ghosted into form. He's painted a wooden table as red as the brightest patches of cedar. What seems to be a yellow boa constrictor squiggles across the floor and then rises to wrap around the center of a table leg. The tabletop holds a yellow vessel and a mysterious spattering of white rocks.

One must strain to make out these details; as he did with his sketch of Josephine the Elephant, he labored over minuscule forms. And what are we to make of these images? Is the boa an obvious metaphor of oppression? Do the white rocks suggest the walls are falling in?

The scene presents itself as an elemental message, the kind my father distrusted. He insisted, for example, that Vermeer's *The Allegory of Faith* had to be a forgery because it relied on symbolism over aesthetics, and certainly no one can deny the bizarre flatness of that canvas as compared to the luminous qualities of, say, *View of Delft* or *The Milkmaid*. But isn't it unfair to suggest that artists don't live for experimentation, often producing inferior or unusual works for the sake of the unknown? To stretch, we must fail. It's part of the process, and to be judged by "failures" is to accept the limitations of those who resign themselves to safety, mediocrity.

The creeping snake could represent Nazis or simply the dictatorial nature of Ukrainian families at that time. The speckles of plaster could therefore range from our crumbling world to his family's vulnerable existence. Many associative guesses would yield informative answers, but the more absolute interpretation arrives from private knowledge, information Barbara would have had and that I grew up knowing from frequent retellings. This is the story:

At the age of three or four, my father came across his family's samovar, freshly cleaned and therefore dry of water or tea. And on that same table, his mother had left a dozen eggs. He lifted one in his hand and dropped it into the cavernous samovar, where, of course, it popped joyously and splatted the inside with color and shattered forms. What happiness! So he took another and dropped it. Again!

One or both of his parents caught him after the sixth Jackson Pollock-like explosion. The situation required scrubbing, but that was utterly secondary to the fact that eggs cost money, money they didn't have. (My Bubba frequently lectured me during childhood: "I told all of my children, 'If you hev a dollar and you spend a penny, then you only hev ninety-nine cents.' Vatch every penny.") Needless to say, this occurred many decades before time-outs and childhood negotiation. His parents relied on swift and immediate punishment, so they roped him under the table and left him there.

In the miniature, therefore, the yellow vase is actually a brass samovar; the white rocks: eggs and eggshells; the snake: a rope after his release. How meticulously he worked to depict that scene within the tiny house. . . . The tabletop's width measures six millimeters. The samovar at its most bulbous: three millimeters. I'm working with a magnifying glass and a ruler. Spare me the eggs.

If we are to trust the psychology of this image, no other childhood memory resonated more. And that intensity reminds me of Nathaniel Kahn's documentary, *My Architect: A Son's Journey*. As a boy who saw his father only sporadically, he'd request stories of his father's youth, appreciating none more than this, which he heard many times:

> He was three years old back in Estonia. There were coals glowing in a stove. He was captivated by the light. He took the coals out and put them in his apron. It caught fire, and the flames seared his face and the backs of his hands. His father thought it would be better if he died, but his mother said he would grow up to be a great man because of it.

In my father's miniature, the only image within the house that does not speak directly to this memory is the unlit fireplace, which would have doubled as a stove. Painted almost as an afterthought, it makes the dark interior less cavernous, thereby giving the illustration more cohesion. Or was my father thinking metaphorically of his father's rage and the firestorm that followed?

To some degree, perhaps, the act of inking *Voronovitza* brought the village back from the ashes, although that would suggest a sentimental attachment to home, and it would be wrong to impose those emotions; he never spoke of the Ukraine with any hint of wistfulness. The world had simply burned away his birthplace like incinerated trash. Still, I grew up assuming that the town required his memory to exist, and I wonder, having learned too late to share the news, if he would have been interested to know that the town never disappeared. Today, it's most commonly spelled Voronovytsya. With or without army maps, or my father's memory, the *shtetl* has survived.

I never served in the military. A child during the Vietnam War, I remember my mother repeatedly saying that she'd take me to Sweden if the war continued when I came of age. I knew her home country because we'd make trips every other winter, although my father, apart from one visit just after my birth, never joined us. My semiliterate letters to him make me laugh. One note speaks of great Christmas presents, including a whoopee cushion and a rubber snake. It begins: "do you like it in new york city? Is it a dum mes? Is new york going to do something? I hope so and I allso wish that someone could stop the war. I hope that you will not have a cold at all."

Decades later, to protest the invasion of Iraq, I contributed to Sam Hamill's anthology, *Poets against the War*. The poem focuses on a female potter, recently divorced, who's avoiding news of the war while awaiting the proper time to open her kiln. "From all-night wood firings," the poem explains,

> Her body smells gray,
> "Seasoned," she likes to say,

Smiling like her porcelain portraits:
Pre-Raphaelite lips, hair spiraling

Into grapevines and honeysuckle.
On a milk pitcher: blue roses
Within a matte ebony finish.
Touching those engraved petals,

I told her of a lagoon in the Yucatán
Where I held my breath to crawl
Down a collage of basalt caverns,
How the walls pulsed and shimmered

As iridescent, indigo fish
Emerged and withdrew
Until I let go and rose,
Desperate as a flame for oxygen.

The potter's imagination then drifts to the inescapable elements of chance and fate: "If the handful of rock salt / Thrown in the ninth hour / Exploded perfectly / Into a nebula of glaze." All potters realize that the kiln fire, to one degree or another, dictates the outcome of art. The elusive nature of fire can produce magnificent surprises, and "failure" often has much to do with our human disposition to consider art in purely logical terms. Take, as an obvious example, one bowl almost smashed by Harry Holl because it lacked perfect symmetry. He knew it could not be sold, and yet it glows to this day in the center of our Cape property, an ever-watchful eye of my father's Monster, mesmerizing visitors almost as much as Harry's masterpieces.

For potters, fire aids in creation; in nature, most fires destroy. For many ceremonies—including my wedding and the blessing of our first child, both in the temple honoring Kali—fire illuminates and purges.

To save the Cape house, we had to destroy it: to bring the structure back to its studs. On my final trip to empty its interior, I rechecked the downstairs bathroom. The fabric floor tiles had grown moldy, and much of the wood felt wet. But inside a cabinet, I found a long-lost bottle of perfume that my mother loved—Maja—featuring a well-dressed Spanish woman waving a fan. One puff of mist brought my mother back, and I found myself walking throughout the empty house and spraying the musty air. I blessed every room, even though the aroma would dissipate long before anyone else entered the home, because private ceremonies matter, too.

I had hoped that equal restorative care would be paid to the New York brownstone, but it was neglected to such a point that rats infested the basement. Once it was sold, the new owners gutted the structure, but their first change occurred outside: extracting the thick English ivy that luxuriated across the entire front. Those vines had defined our property on the block; now the structure stands out only for its boarded-up windows. Soon, I'll recognize nothing. Maybe they'll even renovate the chimneys, fireplaces that could not function during my father's life. Like the entryway to Pakal's tomb, they'd been stuffed solid.

When we renovated the Cape house, the Dennis Historical Society refused to grant us permission for a chimney; more accurately, they said we could position a fireplace anywhere within the structure, but not on the exterior. Given the size of the house, and the space that chimneys demand, we opted to pass on a fireplace. But, like so many events that have transpired since my father's death, disappointment has bred enormous satisfaction: The wall that would have opened to a hearth now flames with a magnificent painting of his, one too large for any other wall in the house. It warms the room in every season.

On either side of that huge canvas, I've placed floor-standing speakers, with wires disappearing beneath the floor and leading to a stereo in a closet beneath the central stairway. To the right stands the schoolmaster's desk and the painting found in the attic. Over the sofa on the adjacent wall, we've centered my mother's painting, *Libra Dance*, a medium-sized acrylic that flames in a whirling dervish of lavish reds—a furnace barely contained by the squared edges.

To the left is an alcove, once impenetrable, highlighting my father's oceanic canvas, *Pool*, as well as his still life with the sparkling iron centerpiece. The third work of art in that area is a black-and-white pen drawing by my mother. Compositionally, it swoops through the dining room and living room, not avoiding perspective, exactly, but compressing the relationships between forms to create a more unified statement. The central table, now stripped and used in the barn, holds a ceramic vase she also made, one stuffed with roses from her garden. On the bottom left, a wooden bowl carved from a single trunk contains a fan of lavender that poofs into a froth. The schoolmaster's desk centers the drawing. A tree limb, with a wooden duck decoy strapped onto the highest bend, rises in front of the chimney.

But I love what's *not* there, too, especially the fairly vacant right side, inked so minimally that the scratches appear almost like an afterthought. The marks define what seems to be a wall of some sort, but only as much as vague contrails define a sky. Yet, that particular flat surface, depicted by marginal wisps, represents my father's painting, *Summer*, the one that caused the Russian visitor to sit down and consider defection. And I cannot help but think of the psychology behind my mother's artistic decision. "Yes, Sam," the drawing says, "you've created magnificent work. But this one is *mine*."

I remember the arrival of the large, arcing branch. My father had spotted it down the road and immediately envisioned its location. He managed to get about half of it into the Volvo, then had a friend, Ashley, grip the protruding end and run with the car until they reached the house. Untreated, the branch eventually coaxed beetles to move in, damaging the floor and some of the furniture. But I liked its position in the house—everyone liked the tree limb—and what's there now pays homage, in part, to that initial vision: a gorgeous sculpture by Jon Bogle. Made of pine, it rises with dramatic verticality before blossoming, Georgia O'Keeffe-like, into a sensual bloom. On a bed of 150-year-old floorboards, also cut from pine, the sculpture causes the interior to recirculate the sheen and warmth of wood like the very arrival of spring air.

The chairs in my mother's drawing, each purchased for twenty-five cents at the town auction, have now been tightened and professionally caned. We renovated the furniture out of respect for its identity, and perhaps with the hope that our children will inherit pure beauty, without the colossal pressures of repair. But am I kidding myself? The man who saved my father's life, when evaluating our house mid-renovation, said to me, "Your children will do the same," and maybe he's right. The overwhelming tonnage of inheritance has certainly made me rethink what I will leave behind.

My children will not be spared the inevitable inheritance of refuse: the poundage of unwanted belongings. What will happen to my thousands of jazz recordings? I imagine, too, a backhoe or Bobcat eradicating the barrier of bamboo, exposing the house, yes, but eliminating a decades-old battle. Perhaps our children will plant trees for their parents; perhaps they will simply sell the property. Whatever happens, I'll die knowing they witnessed the wreckage I inherited, and on their worst days of sorting through artifacts, they'll know in their genes it could have been far worse.

My father claimed I didn't have my head screwed on right for imagining a home with a washer, dryer, and heat—all of which we now have. During the massive restoration, the gas company provided free installation for access to the street's main line, as well as a free water heater. Also running on gas, our professional stove, one worthy of my wife's genius, ignites seasoned woks for dramatically flamed Asian cuisine. Chili peppers and sliced red onions sizzle, and the reliable fridge chills the crisp leeks for garnish.

Frequently, I strap the yellow Merrimack canoe to the top of our car and drive in the early morning to the Brewster ponds where I fish with my daughter. We're excitable amateurs, but we've often returned with largemouth bass that my mother-in-law scales, guts, washes, and salts. She asks only for the head, the Asian prize, and prefers to steam the fish with slices of ginger, black bean paste, plum sauce, soy, sliced mushrooms, and bright red peppers.

We eat at a table surrounded by the paintings discovered in Philadelphia, as well as the presiding canvas, *Summer*, which emanates the nature of that season whether spot lit or glowing in candlelight. As my father once said to me about his mentor, "While Picasso said that Matisse had the sun in his belly, you might say that Hofmann had the whole blazing furnace in his gut and was trying to project that in his work and to his students."

As for the grounds, I doubt I will ever stop unearthing the remains of his abandoned visions. In late June of 2016, for example, I spent time investigating our expanse of privet, puzzled as to why it had such large gaps within its center. I don't recall my father ever fertilizing, or even watering the hedge, but I had been pampering the privet since 2004. Twelve years. The roots should have expanded.

To check the soil, I plunged my shovel's head into a particularly barren area and, about six inches beneath the thick ground cover, hit stone. Then more stone. For two days, I excavated a low wall that my father had built in the 1960s (I vaguely recall it, now that memory has been wrenched into sunlight) but from a combination of neglect and time, it vanished. The stones filled up one wheelbarrow load after another. (In a coincidence that makes me smile, the project coincided with my daughter's first visit to Stonehenge.) Some of the rocks could easily be tossed by hand; some weighed well over one hundred pounds.

What work to uncover the past!—and what a pleasure to take the remains in order to delineate our own desired boundaries, especially around garden beds. The soil now loose, I have transplanted privet, stragglers from around the property, as well as those purchased at a favorite nursery. With luck, sun, and water, the enormous holes will eventually fill with greenery.

This undertaking reminded me, of course, of the impacted rhododendron. And when I described salvaging that compromised plant, I neglected to mention five large objects found in the vicinity of the stone table. Three held little to no interest: a sewage pipe, a large cement opening (probably for a septic system), and, marginally more appealing, a fractured metal base for a potbellied stove, which had some sculptural qualities. The fourth item, however, pleased me quite a bit. My mother had made it: a clay jar of significant size—no doubt her largest work in clay—that she had pinched and molded. It had been fired, too, at which point part of the bottom blew out. But that hole allows it to rest at an engaging angle, the cavernous mouth now greeting the viewer, and the constant drainage avoids mosquito larvae. Had it been "perfect," we could not display it outside.

The fifth item also had a large hole at its bulbous base, as well as chips on the lip's metallic edge, which no doubt explains how my father acquired the object; whole, it would have been priced far higher than he would have paid. At first I didn't recognize it, and my mind drifted to classic literature: a cauldron for the witches in the Scottish play. But I should have turned to a different classic, *Moby-Dick*, for its chapter "The Try-Works": "Give not thyself up, then, to fire, lest it invert thee, deaden thee; as for the time it did me. There is a wisdom that is woe; but there is a woe that is madness. And there is a Catskill eagle in some souls that can alike dive down into the blackest gorges, and soar out of them again and become invisible in the sunny spaces."

Whaling vessels built brick structures to hold and flame iron cauldrons, like this one discovered in my New England jungle. In these try-works, they could boil the vast tonnage of whale carcass and convert it to transportable oil during the voyage. Obviously, the greater the compression of mass, the longer and more lucrative the journey. Marginally skilled workers prepared the whale flesh, stripping it as thinly as possible to produce the maximum extraction of oil. In that sense, the process reminds me of my own cleansing of the property—ridding the land of excess fat and boiling it down to the choice parts. If I could have melted the wreckage for the Dumpsters, I would have.

Each summer, with no care for a perfect lawn, we place the try pot outside the barn for the charred fragrance of hard oak and the incense of cedar. The deadwood on the property seems endless, even if I know it isn't, and my mother-in-law, who lives with us most of the year, enjoys collecting sticks to make the fires blaze. And when we removed the deteriorating second floor of the barn, I burned those powder-posted boards with ceremonial rhythms, each *kerplunk* into the metal belly ringing *goodbye, goodbye, goodbye*.

One summer, when we were visited by my brother-in-law, Pravin, he asked why fire attracted human beings. What is the elemental draw? And, of course, I thought of our most primitive beginnings—where we probably told the first stories, and how we relied on this magical warmth, and how the charred ends of sticks became the tools for artists. (The family of young Louis Kahn could not afford art equipment, so he gleaned twigs from fields and burned their ends.) But I also thought of the other side of the globe—a part of the world I've married into—and the Balinese *kecak* dance, which I've seen performed several times. The dance derives from the *Ramayana*, and the story begins with a vicious, unbalanced stepmother:

Somehow, by manipulating the king, she has banished the son, Rama, and his wife, Sita. The *kecak* dance begins with Rama and his wife accompanied by Rama's brother, Laksmana. Decency triumphs: although a demon tries to capture beautiful Sita, Rama defeats him. In the process, coals become splayed on the theatrical floor, where Rama must kick the ground-covering fireworks into victory.

But I am thinking too deeply here. My fire dance seems far more simple. I stand before a beloved house once torn to its marrow and now muscularly sound. In the evenings, I light a fire pit that used to be an industry-saving device—a kiln aflame in the middle of the ocean—and that now brings my family, and my extended family, together on our lawn, inhaling a mixture of summer smoke and the wind's curative salt.

Selected Sources

Argüelles, José. *The Transformative Vision: Reflections on the Nature and History of Human Expression*. Boulder, CO: Shambhala, 1975.

Bachelard, Gaston. *The Poetics of Space*. Translated by Maria Jolas. New York: Orion Press, 1964.

Baldwin, James. "Sonny's Blues." *Going to Meet the Man*. New York: The Dial Press, 1965.

Ball, Philip. *Bright Earth: Art and the Invention of Color*. New York: Farrar, Straus and Giroux, 2001.

Balliett, Whitney. *American Musicians: 56 Portraits in Jazz*. New York: Oxford University Press, 1986.

Bellosi, Luciano. *Cimabue*. New York: Abbeville, 1998.

Berryman, John. *The Dream Songs*. New York: Farrar, Straus and Giroux, 1969.

Bishop, Elizabeth. "The Armadillo" and "The Fish." In *Poems*. New York: Farrar, Straus and Giroux, 2011.

Blair, Lawrence. *Rhythms of Vision: The Changing Patterns of Myth and Consciousness*. New York: Schocken Books, 1975.

Blair, Lawrence, with Lorne Blair. *Ring of Fire*. London: Bantam, 1988.

Bonsanti, Giorgio. *The Basilica of St. Francis of Assisi: Glory and Destruction*. Translated by Stephen Sartarelli. New York: Abrams, 1998.

Canby, Vincent. "The Savage Is Loose." *New York Times*, 16 November 1974.

Cooper, Bernard. "Just What Is It That Makes Today's Homes So Different, So Appealing?" In *Open House: Writers Redefine Home*, edited by Mark Doty. Saint Paul, MN: Graywolf, 2003.

Crawford, Barbara. "Day of the Circus: A Short Novel." *New Ventures* 1 (1954): 1–62, 83–84.

Creeley, Robert. "The Window." In *The Collected Poems of Robert Creeley, 1945–1975*. Berkeley: University of California Press, 1982.

Crow, Bill. *Jazz Anecdotes*. New York: Oxford University Press, 1990.

Davis, Keith F. *Clarence John Laughlin: Visionary Photographer*. Kansas City, MO: Hallmark Cards, Inc., 1990.

Dickey, James. "Kudzu." In *Poems 1957–1967*. Middletown, CT: Wesleyan University Press, 1967.

Dixhoorn, Frank van. "Wisteria." Liner notes. *Wisteria*. Jimmy Raney. Criss Cross, 1019, 1991, CD.

Doctorow, E. L. *Homer & Langley*. New York: Random House, 2009.

Doty, Mark. "A Green Crab's Shell." In *Atlantis*. New York: HarperCollins, 1995.

Feinstein, Sam. "How Does Cézanne Do It?" *Drawing* 18, no. 3 (Winter 1996–97): 75–78.

———. "Philadelphia." *Arts Digest* (December 15, 1954): 12–13.

Feinstein, Sascha. *Ajanta's Ledge*. Rhinebeck, NY: Sheep Meadow Press, 2012.

———. *Black Pearls: Improvisations on a Lost Year*. Spokane: Eastern Washington University Press, 2008.

Frost, Randy O., and Gail Steketee. *Stuff: Compulsive Hoarding and the Meaning of Things*. Boston: Houghton Mifflin Harcourt, 2010.

Hamill, Sam, ed. *Poets Against the War*. New York: Thunder's Mouth Press/Nation Books, 2003.

Hayden, Robert. "Those Winter Sundays." In *Collected Poems*. Edited by Frederick Glaysher. New York: Liveright, 1985.

Hofmann, Hans. "The Resurrection of the Plastic Arts" and "The Mystery of Creative Relations." *New Ventures* 1 (1954): 21–23.

Homer, William Innes, and Lloyd Goodrich. *Albert Pinkham Ryder: Painter of Dreams*. New York: Abrams, 1989.

Hornby, Nick. *High Fidelity*. New York: Riverhead Books, 1995.

Howes, Joshua Crowell. *Genealogy of the Howes Family in America. Descendants of Thomas Howes, Yarmouth, Mass., 1637–1892. With Some Account of English Ancestry*. Yarmouthport, MA: Fred. Hallett, 1892. Reproduction.

Kees, Weldon. "A Salvo for Hans Hofmann" and "Five Villanelles." In *The Collected Poems of Weldon Kees*. Lincoln: University of Nebraska Press, 2003.

Kimmel, Roberta. *In Artists' Homes*. New York: Clarkson Potter, 1992.

Komunyakaa, Yusef. "My Father's Love Letters. In *Magic City*. Hanover, CT: Wesleyan University Press, 1993.

———. "Anodyne." In *Thieves of Paradise*. Hanover, CT: Wesleyan University Press, 1998.

Kruglov, Alexander, and Martin Dean. "Voronovitsa." Translated by Steven Seegel and Ksenia Krimer. In *The United States Holocaust Memorial Museum Encyclopedia of Camps and Ghettos, 1933–1945*. Edited by Geoffrey P. Megargee. Bloomington: Indiana University Press, 2009.

Lanza, Marco. *The Living Dead: Inside the Palermo Crypt*. London: Westzone Publishing, 2000.

Larkin, Philip. "The Whitsun Weddings." In *Collected Poems*. New York: Farrar, Straus and Giroux, 2004.

Laughlin, Clarence John. *Clarence John Laughlin: The Personal Eye*. New York: Aperture, 1973.

Lawrence, John H., and Patricia Brady, eds. *Haunter of Ruins: The Photography of Clarence John Laughlin*. Boston: Bulfinch Press, 1997.

Lee, Bill "Spaceman," and Richard Lally. *Have Glove Will Travel: Adventures of a Baseball Vagabond*. New York: Crown Publishers, 2005.

Leggett, John. *A Daring Young Man: A Biography of William Saroyan*. New York: Knopf, 2002.

Levin, Phillis, ed. *The Penguin Book of the Sonnet*. New York: Penguin Books, 2001.

Mailer, Norman. *The Fight*. Boston: Little, Brown and Company, 1975.

Matthews, William. "Blues for John Coltrane, Dead at 41." In *Search Party: Collected Poems*. Boston: Houghton Mifflin, 2004.

McKnight-Trontz, Jennifer. *Exotiquarium: Album Art from the Space Age*. New York: St. Martin's Griffin, 1999.

Meek, A. J. *Clarence John Laughlin: Prophet without Honor*. Jackson: University Press of Mississippi, 2007.

Melville, Herman. *Moby-Dick*. Berkeley: University of California Press, 1979.

Michener, James A. *The Source*. New York: Random House, 1965.

Nemerov, Howard. "The Goose Fish" and "The Icehouse in Summer." In *The Collected Poems of Howard Nemerov*. Chicago: University of Chicago Press, 1981.

Olson, Charles, and Robert Creeley. *Charles Olson and Robert Creeley: The Complete Correspondence*. Volume 1. Edited by George F. Butterick. Santa Barbara, CA: Black Sparrow, 1980.

Orwell, George. "A Hanging." *Why I Write*. New York: Penguin Books, 2005.

Reading Eagle. "Josephine, Pet Pachyderm, Dies in Philadelphia Zoo." 13 March, 1943, 11.

Roethke, Theodore. "Cuttings," "Dolor," and "The Waking." In *The Collected Poems of Theodore Roethke*. New York: Doubleday, 1966.

Schele, Linda, and Mary Ellen Miller. *The Blood of Kings: Dynasty and Ritual in Maya Art*. New York: George Braziller, 1986.

Search for the Real: Drawings by Hans Hofmann and His Students. Museum catalogue. Provincetown, MA: Provincetown Art Association and Museum, 2009.

Sexton, Anne. "All My Pretty Ones." In *The Complete Poems*. New York: Mariner, 1999.

Sims, Gayle Ronan. "Samuel L. Feinstein, Artist, Teacher." *Philadelphia Inquirer*, 19 June 2003.

Stevens, Wallace. "Anecdote of the Jar." In *The Collected Poems of Wallace Stevens*. New York: Alfred A. Knopf, 1987.

Stuart, David. *Palenque: Eternal City of the Maya*. New York: Thames & Hudson, 2008.

Tiesler, Vera, and Andrea Cucina, eds. *Janaab Pakal of Palenque: Reconstructing the Life and Death of a Maya Ruler*. Tucson: University of Arizona Press, 2006.

Tyng, Anne Griswold, ed. *Louis Kahn to Anne Tyng: The Rome Letters, 1953–1954*. New York: Rizzoli, 1997.

Veidlinger, Jeffrey. *In the Shadow of the Shtetl: Small-Town Jewish Life in Soviet Ukraine*. Bloomington: Indiana University Press, 2013.

Winchester, Simon. *Skulls: An Exploration of Alan Dudley's Curious Collection*. New York: Black Dog and Leventhal, 2012.

Yeats, W. B. "The Lake Isle of Innisfree," "Lapis Lazuli," and "A Prayer for My Daughter." In *The Poems of W. B. Yeats*. New York: Macmillan, 1993.

Zukav, Gary. *The Dancing Wu Li Masters: An Overview of the New Physics*. New York: William Morrow, 1979.

Discography

Armstrong, Louis. "Potato Head Blues." OKey 8503, 78 rpm.

Azama, Ethel. *Exotic Dreams*. So Far Out OUT5003, LP.

Basie, Count. *Basie Land*. Verve V-8597, LP.

Colon, Augie. *Sophisticated Savage*. Liberty LRP-3101, LP.

Country Joe and the Fish. *I-Feel-Like-I'm-Fixin'-to-Die*. Vanguard VRS-9266, LP.

Denny, Martin. *Exotica*. Liberty LRP-3034, LP.

Ferguson, Maynard. *Primal Scream*. Columbia PC33953, LP.

Gleason, Jackie. *Music for Lovers Only*. Capitol SM352, LP.

The Golden Gate Singers. *Dip Your Fingers in the Water/Stalin Wasn't Stallin'*. OKey 6712, 78 rpm.

Hackett, Bobby. *The Bobby Hackett Quartet*. Capitol ST1235, LP.

———. *Hawaii Swings*. Capitol ST1316, LP.

The Hanna/Fontana Band. *Live at Concord*. Concord Jazz CJ11, LP.

London, Julie. *Make Love to Me*. Liberty LRP-3060, LP.

Lyman, Arthur. *Taboo: The Exotic Sounds of Arthur Lyman*. HiFi R-806, LP.

Mrs. Mills. *My Mother the Ragtime Piano Player*. Liberty LRP-3359, LP.

Monk, Thelonious. *Brilliant Corners*. Riverside RLP 12-226, LP.

———. *Criss-Cross*. Columbia CL2038, LP.

David Peel and the Lower East Side. *Have a Marijauana*. Elektra EKS-74032, LP.

Phantom Foley. *Phantom Foley Plays Piano Rolls*. Pickwick PC-3014, LP.

The Polynesians and Buddy Collette. *Aloha to Jazz*. Bel Canto SR-1002, LP.

Raney, Jimmy. *Wisteria*. Criss Cross 1019, CD.

The Surfmen. *The Sounds of Exotic Island*. Somerset SF-10500, LP.

Filmography

30 for 30: Muhammad and Larry. Team Marketing, B0039YAL6M, DVD.
Aliens. 20th Century Fox, 11, DVD.
Children of Paradise. Criterion, 141, DVD.
The Gleaners and I. Zeitgeist, Z1015, DVD.
Hans Hofmann. Sam Feinstein, VHS.
Muhammad Ali: The Greatest Collection. HBO, 91867, DVD.
My Architect: A Son's Journey. New Yorker Video, 90105, DVD.
Ring of Fire: An Indonesian Odyssey. Mystic Fire, MYS76496, DVD.
Sam Feinstein: Scargo Pottery 1986. Route 6a Productions, DVD.
The Savage Is Loose. VCII, B0001E86R4, VHS.
The Seduction of Mimi. Kino Lorber: K948, DVD.
When We Were Kings. Polygram, 440 045 847-2/, DVD.

~

Acknowledgments

For a variety of reasons, I would like to thank Joyce Barrow, Melissa Correll, Thorpe Feidt, Paul Fitzgerald, Tanzina Fazal, Pam Gaber, Sally Kuhn, Carol Martin, Lynne Miller, Jessica L. Munson, Bob Reid, Lilli Sentz, Jeffrey Veidlinger, Patricia Walker, and Bonnie Warwick. In the final stages, I received invaluable guidance from G. W. Hawkes, David Jauss, and my wife, Marleni.

Some or parts of these chapters first appeared in the following publications: "Eternal Machinery" in *Callaloo* ("Portrait of Gratitude" from *Callaloo* 8, no. 3: 488–90. Copyright © 2005, Charles H. Rowell. Reprinted with permission by Johns Hopkins University Press); "Children of Paradise" in *Hunger Mountain*; "Exotic Dennis" in *Jazziz*; and "Unrecognized Prophets" in *Soundings East*. I am grateful to Lycoming College for a Professional Development Grant that allowed me to complete this book, and to the various houses that granted permission for reprinting material:

Berryman, John. Dream Song #1 "Huffy Henry" from *The Dream Songs* by John Berryman. Published by Farrar, Straus & Giroux, LLC, and Faber & Faber Ltd.

Blair, Lawrence. *Rhythms of Vision* published by Inner Traditions International and Bear & Company, © 1991. All rights reserved.

Creeley, Robert. "The Window" from *The Collected Poems of Robert Creeley, 1945–1975*, © 2006 by the Regents of the University of California. Published by the University of California Press.

Dickey, James. "Kudzu" from *The Whole Motion: Collected Poems, 1945–1992*, © 1992 by the estate of James Dickey. Reprinted with permission of Wesleyan University Press.

Doty, Mark. "A Green Crab's Shell" from *Atlantis* by Mark Doty. Copyright © 1995 by Mark Doty. Reprinted by permission of HarperCollins Publishers.

Frost, Randy O., and Gail Steketee. Excerpt from *Stuff: Compulsive Hoarding and the Meaning of Things*. Copyright © 2010 by Randy O. Frost and Gail Steketee. Reprinted by permission of the authors, Houghton Mifflin Harcourt Publishing Company, and the Sandra Dijkstra Literary Agency. All rights reserved.

Keys, Weldon. "A Salvo for Hans Hofmann" and "Five Villanelles." Reprinted from *The Collected Poems of Weldon Kees*, edited by Donald Justice, by permission of the University of Nebraska Press. Copyright 1962, 1975, by the University of Nebraska Press. © renewed 2003 by the University of Nebraska Press.

Komunyakaa, Yusef. "My Father's Love Letters" and "Anodyne" from *Pleasure Dome*, © 2001 by Yusef Komunyakaa. Reprinted with permission of Wesleyan University Press.

Larkin, Philip. "The Whitsun Weddings" from *The Complete Poems* by Philip Larkin. Published by Farrar, Straus & Giroux, LLC, and Faber & Faber Ltd.

Roethke, Theodore. "The Waking," copyright © 1945 by Theodore Roethke; and "Dolor," copyright © 1943 by Modern Poetry Association, Inc; from *Collected Poems* by Theodore Roethke. Used by permission of Doubleday, an imprint of the Knopf Doubleday Publishing Group, a division of Penguin Random House LLC; and Faber & Faber Ltd. All rights reserved.

~

About the Author

Sascha Feinstein's previous books include another memoir (*Black Pearls: Improvisations on a Lost Year*), two collections of poetry, and *Ask Me Now: Conversations on Jazz & Literature*. His awards include the Hayden Carruth Award for *Misterioso* (poems) and the Pennsylvania Governor's Award for Artist of the Year. In 1996, he founded *Brilliant Corners: A Journal of Jazz & Literature*, which he still edits; he also hosts *Jazz Standards* for WVIA, the NPR station for central Pennsylvania. Professor of English at Lycoming College, he lives in Williamsport, Pennsylvania, and Dennis, Massachusetts. www.SaschaFeinstein.com